A REGULAR AMERICAN GUY

SMALL TOWN KID, WASHINGTON STATE UNIVERSITY COUGAR, VIETNAM VET., ALASKA BUSINESSMAN, BUSH PILOT, POLITICIAN, AUTHOR AND FAMILY MAN.

Bob Bell

PUBLICATION CONSULTANTS
We Believe In The Power Of Authors

PO Box 221974 Anchorage, Alaska 99522-1974
books@publicationconsultants.com—www.publicationconsultants.com

ISBN Number Soft Cover: 978-1-63747-106-7
ISBN Number Hard Cover: 978-1-63747-222-4
eBook ISBN Number: 978-1-63747-107-4

Library of Congress Number: 2023911329

Sketches by Tanya Ramsey. tjramsey@joycreating.com

Manufactured in the United States of America

DEDICATION

This book is dedicated to all the regular American veterans who stepped up when their country called. Over one million Americans gave their lives to form and then defend our country. Their sacrifice will never be forgotten.

ACKNOWLEDGMENTS

Once again, I have to thank my family and friends for supporting my writing by editing the text and advising on the content.

FORWARD

There are many different types of books: fiction, non-fiction, how-to, adventure, and many more. *A Regular American Guy* is a memoir, but I don't think it fits well in that category. This is a story about me, but with a few minor changes, it could be the story of tens of thousands of regular American guys. So many of us served our country in the military or in other ways, raised families, served on community boards, been little league coaches, and even fell into the black hole of politics.

So, is this a memoir or a story about one person who reflects the lives of so many Americans?

Looking at all the genuinely dumb and dangerous things we did growing up, particularly in high school, it is a wonder we survived. Then on to college for more IQ-challenged misadventures. Surviving Vietnam was a close call, but not self-inflected like high school and college. Finally, in my case, Alaska has many ways to kill you, including weather, swift rivers, steep mountains, and, of course, sic'ing her critters on you, all of which I have experienced.

Looking back on all of this, it is a wonder I am still alive. Mom made us go to church every Sunday, so I guess that paid off. How many American guys have had similar experiences and survived? I am sure folks in other countries make questionable decisions in the course of their lives, but I think we American dudes have perfected the art of dubious decisions.

I kept the humor of my first books in this *A Regular American Guy*, except for the Vietnam fighting, to make it a fun read. Chronicling my life from a kid in a small Eastern Washington town, through college and Vietnam, to becoming a bush pilot, business executive, family man, and politician in Alaska was an enjoyable process. I hope you enjoy the read and can identify with the journey through your own experiences or those of someone you know.

PROLOGUE

Reaching back 75 years to recall people and incidents is difficult. Memory fades with age and time. I did my best to remember the details, but probably got some things wrong. Therefore, I may have mixed up some of the people in some of the stories. If I did, I am sure they will let me know. They are all equally culpable in my misadventures, so it doesn't matter.

Regarding Vietnam, I chose to place the combat in a different location and not use the real names of those involved. These fights did happen, but not necessarily in the place or with the people depicted. I did this to avoid opening old wounds for the families of the guys' who didn't come home. Unfortunately, I had no way to contact them to get permission.

This book could have been written about a multitude of regular American guys; I think of it that way. Technically it is about me, but philosophically it is about all of us, past, present, and future. I hope you enjoy the read

William Bell family traveling to Missouri in 1786

CHAPTER ONE

FAMILY HISTORY

I was fighting like crazy to keep the panic from surging from my gut up into my throat, as I lay there in the tall grass. Bullets were slicing through the vegetation and slamming into the dirt all around me. It was absolutely terrifying. Looking back on this extremely stressful situation I cannot think of a single place in the whole world that would be less attractive to me than where I was.

I was somewhere in the Iron Triangle of Vietnam and in a lot of trouble. We were on a "Bird dog" patrol. This is where the powers on high send a lieutenant and two squads of troops into the jungle to sniff out NVA (North Vietnamese Army) units and then call in artillery, gunships or both to blow them up. A simple plan with a whole lot of unattractive scenarios, one of which is sometimes they sniff you out first. This is never a good deal, but it was the situation on this day. I was the lieutenant leading 23 guys into this mess. I remember thinking "I am 24 years old and about to get killed and so are my guys, that is not fair." Trouble is, in war, fair is not a valid concept.

So, how does a "run of the mill" kid from the small town of Ephrata Washington end up in this predicament? It's a long American story that began in 1750 in Dauphin County Pennsylvania when my great, great, great, great, great grandfather, William Mordecai Bell, was born. Boy I am glad the Mordecai moniker didn't hang on until my generation.

The records in the 1750s were somewhat sketchy. In those days the internet was the gill net between the shore and the outer net. We are not sure who his parents were, but suspect they were William Mordecai Bell

Jr. born 1720 in Ulster Ireland and died in 1785 in Agusta, Colorado and Mary McGowan. Don't know anything about her. Therefore, our family are not immigrants as we were here before the United States got here. I guess that makes us "Non-ethnic native Americans".

Our family history parallels the history of the American expansion westward. Willian Bell was raised in Pennsylvania on a dirt farm. He received no formal education, so his resume was somewhat lacking, academically speaking. When he left home, he took any job he could and scraped by. I guess he was a migrant worker prior to the term being in vogue. He met Barbra Clingensmith along the way, and they married in 1773. He acquired some land and they settled down to farming. The Couple had eight kids between 1774 and 1788. That was a lot of mouths to feed on a small farm. This created some significant cash flow problems for the family. Problem with kids in those days is you couldn't really work them much until they got to be nine or ten years old. That was a long lead time for a dirt farming enterprise.

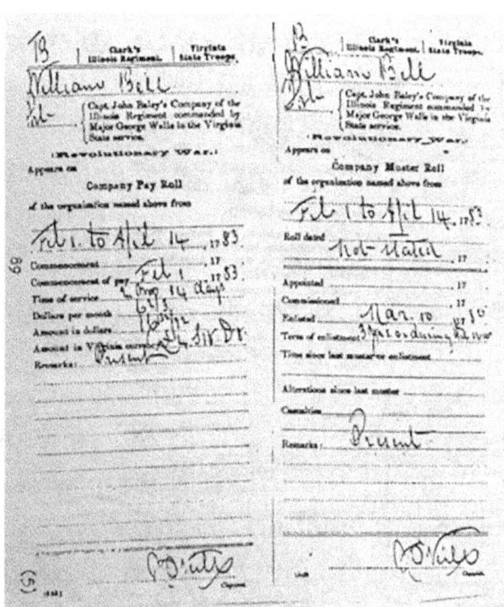

When the Revolutionary war rolled around William signed up as a private in George Washington's army. That was when he hit the big bucks. His pay was $6 2/3 a month, an astronomically high rate of pay for an illiterate dirt farmer. (pay stub above) The being shot at was a drawback, the food was terrible, the accommodations were dreadful, and leadership was questionable. I ran into the same conditions in Vietnam, but the pay was a little better. At least the Army is consistent.

I researched the 2/3-dollar thing. Was it 66 cents or 67 cents as a penny was worth a lot in those days? If the troops were paid in Continental dollars, which were somewhat worthless as there was no country to back them up, there were problems. Kind of like trying to buy something with an IOU from your unemployed deadbeat cousin, not many takers of that deal. It turns out $6 2/3 was equal to two pounds. Did George pay his troops in English pounds? Awkward!

After William finished shooting Red Coats, he gathered up his brood and set out for Spain. Well, actually Missouri, but it was governed by Spain, so they said they were going to "Spain." We tracked their progress on this journey by the birth records of the kids they had in route. They stopped in Kentucky for two years and had one more kid and then moved on. They also survived a few less than pleasant encounters with Native Americans who objected to their travels as they considered them illegal immigrants. Travel in those days had some serious drawbacks that were much more significant than being in the middle seat on an airplane.

They arrived in "Spain" sometime around 1789 with one more kid. A Spanish land grant on the Missouri River was acquired just north of present-day St. Louis. William Bell and his family traveled in a small group during their trek to Missouri. He addressed everyone with a reflection on their adventures in getting to their destination. Using the dialect of 18th century America, it probably went something like this.

"Family and friends when we set out on this journey, I had many doubts and reservations. You, by your Indefatigable exertions, toils and privations have allowed us to persevere over the obstacles of our route. Having procured farmland and with our livestock, with ordinary prudence in the management of which, should afford us a comfortable abode and an adequate livelihood. For this I feel myself under great obligation to you. I shall always be proud to testify to the fidelity with which you have stood by me through all danger and the loyalty which you have ever, one and all, evinced toward me. For these faithful and devoted efforts, I wish you to accept my thanks. The gratitude I express to you springs from my heart and will retain a lively hold on my feelings.

To my fellow travelers who continue on, whenever any of you return thither, your first duty must be to call on me at my house, to talk over the scenes of peril we have encountered and partake of the best cheer my table can afford you.

To my family, we can now wash our hands of the perils of the journey and embark on a new life in a new land.

We are truly blessed,"

Daniel Boone, who was relatively well known at the time, had a land grant just across the river. Willian Bell ended up buying Boone's property a few years later. Don't know if they were friends or not. Probably not, as William didn't end up fighting indian wars or, worse yet, in congress as Boone did.

America cut a real estate deal with the French called the Louisiana Purchase, so William was now back in the United States without changing his address. At this point he had lived under four flags, English, Spanish, French and American. You would think he would have developed an identity crisis. He may have, but shrinks were in short supply in those days so we will never know.

The legal system was somewhat more casual in the rural USA. Case in point, there was a dispute about some pigs. People let their stock run loose back then, there were no fences, so they wandered freely across everyone's properties. One day three of William's pigs were found in a neighbor's barn. The charge was made that the neighbor intended to steal the pigs. The neighbor called him a liar. They were no longer in Spain so the traveling magistrate of the "New United States" would hold a trial when he got there. The trial took place a month later. The miscreant was found not guilty of intending to steal the pigs but was found guilty of calling William Bell a liar without proof thereof. The sentence was to be "hated out of the community". I suspect this guy had some social problems prior to the trial. It was a different world than today.

A small town grew up on an island in the Missouri river named Andre' Del Misuri. Everything was going well, and the Bells settled into farming and trading. Unfortunately, there was a flood that washed the town away and most of the Bell farm. In today's world there would have been a FEMA response, all kinds of aid and government grants to help rebuild. Not so much in the 1700s. They got squat or maybe a little less. They just decided to move away from the river and start over. The attitude was that you had a good year if you didn't get killed or hurt. So, if your land washes away, but not your kids and livestock, you just move. If you are hand to mouth on a piece of land you can be the same on another piece of land. The only fixed assets in your portfolio were your wife and kids.

One of William's sons, John Bell, managed to acquire some land when they moved and began farming next to his father. Land was cheap in those days because they kept finding more of it as America moved West. He married Barbra Crow in 1800. They also had eight kids. Those Bells could really turn out offspring. John Bell died in 1844. His estate was comprised of the following:

1. Deeds for land of 600 acres and 120 acres.
2. 19 overdue notes payable for amounts ranging from 50 cents due from James C. Worth to $ 189.87 from A.W. Reader.
3. Cash $21 dollars.
4. An inventory of personal items to include:
    a. One looking glass
    b. A wooden block
    c. 3 bottles
    d. A flat iron
    e. 2 buckets
    f. Many other similar items
    g. 5 horses
    h. A yoke of muly oxen
    i. A yoke of horned oxen
    j. 11 head of cattle
    k. 22 hogs
    l. 2 sheep

John Bell 1779-1844 Traveled from Pennsylvania to Missouri with parents

looking at his estate it is obvious that the Bell clan wasn't in the upper 1% net worth crowd. Barbra Bell cleared almost $300 when they liquidated the estate. It is also interesting to note that six of his brothers signed the estate inventory and they all have the exact same handwriting as James Barnes one of the Franklin county clerks. I suspect the education level of the family had not progressed much. I find this surprising as they were an international family being English, Spanish, French and American.

One of John's sons, William L. Bell, one upped his dad and grandad and turned out 10 kids. The countryside was overrun by Bells. One of his sons, John A Bell was a captain in the Confederate Army (they lost). He was a total slacker and only had two offspring, Nancy Bell and William Lafayette Bell. Are you beginning to see a John Bell and William Bell pattern here?

William Layfette Bell, he was called "Layf," got back on track kid wise and produced a brood of 11 Bells, enough for a football team, one of whom was my grandfather Arthur L. Bell who married Effy Wade. They had two sons Harvey and Frank Arthur Bell, my dad. The John/William chain was broken.

William "Layf" and Emma Bell In 1900

Dad and Uncle Vic with panicked horses

CHAPTER TWO
EARLY DAYS 1900-1945

In 1916 dad's family was traveling to Lakemp, Oklahoma, in a covered wagon to visit family. They stopped to freshen up at the edge of town. When they lit the stove, the wagon caught fire. My dad was the only survivor. His parents and brother all died. He was 4 years old. His face and arms were badly burned, and he wore those physical and emotional scars the rest of his life.

Arthur and Effy Bell Died In wagon fire 1916

The family fortunes had not improved much. They were all still scratching a living from the soil with few assets. No one was prepared to take on another kid. After the funerals, Dad was taken in by a bachelor uncle who lived in a sod hut. That didn't work out. He then went to live with his aunt Molly and Uncle Marion in Texas. They had seven kids and one more soon proved to be too much, so they put him on a train to travel, by himself, from Texas to Ephrata, Washington. He was six years old.

Frank T. and Bertha Bell with their children Victor and Mable met him at the train station. Dad had never met these folks, so he was apprehensive when he got off the train. He had already been dumped by two relatives therefore he wasn't anticipating a good experience. When they introduced themselves Dad promptly knocked Vic off his tricycle and took off down the street, pedaling like crazy, with grandpa in hot pursuit. A less than auspicious beginning to a new life. Frank and Bertha managed to raise him to be a good man. We always called them grandpa and grandma. I didn't even know they were actually my dad's aunt and uncle until I was in college. Dad never spoke of his mom, dad or brother. I am sure it was a painful memory for him.

For many years they lived in a ranch house on a bluff overlooking Moses Lake. Grandpa was well educated, with high school and college diplomas, and therefore a bit more prosperous than Layf Bell. He raised some livestock and crops and was employed as a bookkeeper by the county. Later grandpa became chief of staff to US Representative Dill and then Senator Dill. He put together a run for the US senate in 1938 but was unsuccessful. President Roosevelt appointed him US commissioner of fisheries and he served in that capacity from 1933 to 1939. Another accomplishment was being instrumental in getting Grand Coulee Dam built and his name is on a plaque displayed on the dam. I remember looking at mementoes of his time as commissioner. One was two telegrams. The first was from the foreman on a fisheries department construction job.

It read. "I have the men on site, but we don't have any shovels. Can you get us some shovels?"

Grandpa's reply was "The shovels will be there in two days. In the meantime, you can lean on each other."

Frank T. Bell United States commissioner of Fisheries 1933 - 1939

His humor was as dry as the land around Ephrata. In 1935 he built the Bell Hotel in Ephrata and it is still there. The hotel was one of the first handicapped facilities in the State of Washington. It had ramps between the floors instead of stairs. This was to accommodate President Roosevelt's wheelchair. He visited the hotel once, so it was a typical government project. Lots of effort and cost, but of very little use.

Life was good, but hard, for the kids on the ranch. It was several miles to school on horseback and then working on the ranch feeding livestock etc. They made a few bucks picking fruit for neighbors in the summer, but that was about it as far as supplemental income. Grandpa said he paid them well. They got food, clothes and a roof over their heads for their labor. Frank T. and Bertha Bell were good down to earth people. He was a very in-charge kind of man. Grandma was small in stature but was someone you were well advised to agree with. Small, but fearsome. Mable was the older sister and watched with interest as Dad and Uncle Vic got themselves into one pickle after another.

One dramatic incident involved the boys driving a wagon pulled by two horses. One of the horses was notorious for not pulling his load. Dad figured a good solution was to load the shotgun up with rock salt and give the laggard horse a shot in the butt. The initiation of this plan resulted in both horses stampeding with Dad and Vic hanging on to the wagon seat for dear life. The situation deteriorated further when the horses and wagon went over the bluff and 100 feet down the very steep slope into the lake.

Once the animals were up to their necks in water, they quit running. It was a major chore to get the wagon back up the bank as only one horse was operational. It seems a rock salt blast at five feet inflects considerable damage on horse flesh. Dad hadn't sufficiently done his due diligence in researching the ballistics of rock salt shotgun shells. Grandpa wasn't pleased when he got home and doled out punishment liberally. It took the horse several weeks to heal. It took a little less time for dad.

Aunt Mable went to college and became a teacher. She taught English in the Ephrata school district for over 40 years. When she turned 65, they told her she had to retire per district policy. She sued them, won, and taught until she was 70. She stated she would not recognize legislated senility. She lived to be 102 years old.

Uncle Vic never really had a steady job. He was always promoting something for a living. He was a very personable guy and always had some kind of scheme in the works. When World War Two broke out, he enlisted in the Army.

Grandpa took him down to the train station to send him off and said, "The war will be over in six months."

Vic replied, "How do you know that?"

Grandpa replied, "Because you have never held a job for more than six months."

Uncle Vic got on the train. He was at Dutch Harbor when the Japanese bombed the place. He survived unscathed and spent the rest of his enlistment in the occupational army in Japan. His most dramatic war story was when he crashed his jeep into a honey bucket truck hauling raw sewage in Tokyo. It wasn't a pleasant experience for him or anyone else within a block of the incident.

Dad never completed high school. He worked on a Washington State DOT crew surveying the North Cross State Highway in north central Washington in 1931. He was a rear chainman and brush cutter. Thirty years later while in college I worked summers on a Washington State DOT crew surveying the same road. I was a rear chainman and brush cutter. I got paid more than he did, my pay was $15/day.

Mom and Dad married in 1932 and they shipped out for Alaska. Grandpa had just been appointed US commissioner of Fisheries and nepotism was OK in those days, so Dad oversaw the fisheries department docks in Naknek. Uncle Vic also worked for the fisheries department as the supervisor of the fish trap guards. Their job was to guard the salmon traps to keep people from stealing the fish. Fact was, they would sell salmon to people. Uncle Vic got a cut of the profits. Always working a deal. He and Aunt Lil lived in Anchorage, Aunt Mable and Uncle Ben were in the Pribilof Islands working for, you guessed it, the fisheries department. I am quite sure grandpa had some influence on them getting those jobs.

Mom was born in Minot, North Dakota to Ed and Mirtle Neville. This was a quintessential Irish family. Hard working, hard drinking and very rough and tumble. She had two sisters and three brothers. Only Mom and Uncle Louie lived past 50. They moved to Seattle when she was just a toddler, so she was really a city girl. How she got hooked up with an eastern Washington rube was never explained to me. When Dad got the fisheries job, going to Alaska was an adventure, until she got to Naknek. This is a small fishing village hundreds of miles from the nearest road. It was crowded with people from Seattle in the fishing season, but when the season ended, they all left. In the winter they were the only non-native people in town.

There was another couple who lived on Lake Iliamna so they mushed their dog team the 90 miles to their place for Christmas. The picture of mom in her imitation mink coat and high heeled shoes standing in the snow, is a study in conflicting cultures. The Alaskan adventure turned into an Alaskan nightmare for her as time went by. With the hunting and fishing Dad loved the place. He often talked about shooting a brown bear with his 30-30 saddle rifle and the guys going out on the tundra and shooting 20 or 30 caribou to supply meat for the town. This caused some marital tension between the newlyweds, but apparently not too much tension as my older sister, Sali, was conceived in Naknek.

In addition to the government docks job Dad purchased the trading post. He had some really unusual transactions with this business. There was a trapper who came into town in the spring. He would trade what he had trapped that winter for whatever he needed for the next year. It was usually a fairly even trade. One year he had an exceptional year and his furs were worth much more than the needed supplies. The old boy didn't care, it was still an even trade. Dad asked him if there was something special, he could get for him next time to make up for the inequality of the trade.

He said, "Yes, I would like some fresh eggs. All the eggs you have here are very old."

The next spring Dad had eggs flown from Palmer, Alaska to Naknek by Noel Wein a famous Alaskan pilot. When the trapper came in Dad presented him with the eggs. He was very

Mom and dad in Naknek in 1933

grateful. The next spring when asked how he liked the eggs, he said he was disappointed, he didn't know where dad got them, but said they were so old the yellow part stayed in a clump when you broke them open. Dad didn't try to explain what fresh eggs looked like. He just apologized and blamed Noel Wein.

The other transaction involved watermelons. The ships coming up to Naknek to get the fish usually picked up any cargo they could get, along the West Coast, and then tried to peddle it on the way up so they could make money going both ways. Well, one captain made the mistake of buying a load of watermelons in California. Nobody along the coast wanted the fruit so he ended up in Naknek with several thousand watermelons. It was the end of the season and most of the Seattle fishermen had returned to the lower 48. The local people had never seen a watermelon, let alone tasted one. Dad bought the whole load for $200. He stacked them on the tundra behind the trading post and proceed to give away 50 or 60 melons. Soon the village was crazy about watermelons. Then he started selling them. Everyone was flush with fish money, so he cleared over $2,000 in profit. In 1933 that was serious money. He would have made much more except that a brown bear developed a taste for watermelon and reduced his inventory significantly one night. This is called "inventory shrinkage" in the financial world.

In the spring they traveled to Dillingham to see the doctor. It turned out mom was expecting my older sister Sali. When they got back to Naknek mom advised dad that she was going to be on the next boat to Seattle. She wasn't going to have a baby in the wilderness. Dad was confused by her attitude but agreed to go along with the plan, as if he had any other choice. He would try to get to Seattle for the birth if he could catch a boat. It was a two-week trip, depending on weather, so planning an arrival time was difficult. Mom solved the problem. Six months before Sali was born she sent a letter to Dad saying she wasn't coming back up there, so he needed to figure out what he wanted to do. That left him with limited options. He sold the trading post to Nick Beze, gave up his job with the fisheries department and got on a boat. He had $10,000 in his bank account.

That was big money in 1935. The Alaskan adventure was over, at least, until I got there 35 years later.

They moved to Ephrata, Washington, and Dad went to work on the construction of Grand Coulee Dam. While working there he won two residential lots in a poker game. He managed to sell them quickly with a big profit. This was much easier money than construction work. He decided to go into the real estate business and did that for the rest of his life. Dad was an outgoing and friendly guy. He had no tolerance for dishonesty or unfairness which were admirable qualities, but often got him into disputes.

After Sali was born they had another girl, Frankie Jean, and then they really lucked out and got me, Frank Robert. Later my brothers came along John and Victor Edward. We all lived in the small town of Ephrata so you had Frank senior (Grandpa), young Frank (Dad), my older sister Frankie Jean and me Frank, AKA Bobby.

Grandpa used to say, "If you came to Ephrata and asked for Frank Bell, half the town showed up."

We had Uncle Vic so my brother, Victor Edward was Eddie. John was three years younger than me. When I was three, I had an imaginary friend named John. This led me to constantly bug my parents to get me a baby brother named John. So, when he was born the die was cast regarding his name. He was christened Johnny Neville Bell. I determined the first name and mom the middle name. It was noted in the book on the Bell family history in America there was a John Bell in all nine generations. How odd is it that a three-year-old would pick John for his imaginary friend, thereby assuring a John Bell for that generation? John has a son named Johnny Clyde Bell.

When World War Two was heating up Dad decided to enlist in the Merchant Marines. He ended up on an ammo ship in the north Atlantic carrying raw nitroglycerin in gallon jugs. The experts would draw out a few drops of the fluid or add a few drops every day to prevent any ripples in the stuff. It was very sensitive. These guys were floating across rough seas sitting on a powder keg with a hair trigger. If there was a life insurance salesman on board, he was maintaining a very low profile.

They were over 2,000 miles north of New York when they were attacked by enemy aircraft. Dad was an ack ack gunner. While he was blasting away at the airplanes an enemy round went right through his bunk. I also took a round through my bunk in Vietnam. Our family bunk casualty rate is much higher than most.

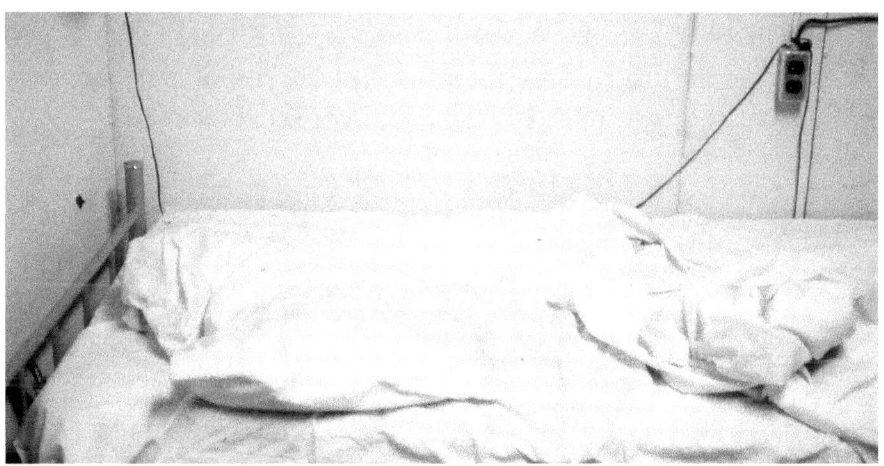

My shot-up bunk and hole in the wall

The other ammo ship with them blew up, with no survivors. The destroyer escort was badly damaged, and Dad's ship took some direct hits but didn't explode. I am sure there was not an alimentary canal on the ship that was not slammed shut about that time. The ship was severely shot up. The engine room had been hit causing considerable damage to the engines. The destroyer limped off for port leaving Dad's ship to fend for itself. To add to the problem the radios had also been destroyed so they had no communications. They got one engine running, but just barely and intermittently. The best they could do was about one knot and they had 2,000 miles to go. It took 80 days to get to New York. When they got there the war was over. Not sure what they did with all that nitro.

The ship had provisions for a four-week trip, so food became a major issue. When they finally got to New York all they had been eating for three weeks was sauerkraut and crackers. Sauerkraut wasn't a menu selection in our house after the war. Dad was six foot three inches tall. When he got home, he weighed 115 pounds. Uncle Vic said you could feed him a bottle of strawberry pop and he would look just like a thermometer. Due to his emaciated condition he had a massive heart attack and came very close to dying. He recovered and went back to selling insurance and real estate. The new business was Nixon and Bell Real Estate and insurance. Business was good so he bought a brand new 1947 Kaiser, the luxury car of the time. We were part of the upper crust of Ephrata. It wasn't much crustwise, but we were part of it.

Dad with his 1947 Kaiser, his first new car

He was a good businessman and a community leader. He served as exalted ruler of the Elks Club, president of the Moose Club and participated in many other civic organizations. Not bad for a high school dropout with a tragic beginning to his life.

I was born in Seattle in 1943. Mom didn't trust the hospital in Ephrata as it was old and poorly equipped, therefore she went to Seattle to have her babies. Also, her family was in Seattle. I have a note from Dad to her after I was born. He had to leave for Ephrata shortly after my birth. The note says that there is $100 enclosed. He instructed her to use that money to pay the doctor, the hospital and buy the girls new dresses. You would need a few more zeros to cover those costs today.

When I was born the nurse told Dad I was a girl. He called Grandma, Vic and Mable to tell them the news. Later the doctor came out and Dad said it was his third daughter.

The doctor said, "What are you talking about? I only delivered two boys today."

Grandma said it was a totally different guy who called the second time. It seemed this would have been a precursor of high status in the family for me, first born son and all. Didn't work out that way. Sali was on the top of the heap. A status she maintained with the liberal use of a wooden spoon. I was relegated to just the third born kid.

The local paper in Ephrata is the Grant County Journal. It used to have a column that listed events from past editions. The one I have is, "50 years ago today Mrs. Frank A. Bell returned to Ephrata with her infant son Frank Robert." The Bobby Bell era had begun in Eastern Washington.

There was a poultry farm outside of town where Dad would buy turkeys and chickens for Sunday dinner and holidays. The way it worked is you pick out the bird you want and then they lop off the head on a chopping block, put it through the feather picking machine, take out in innards and wrap it for you. A somewhat grisly process which can go horribly wrong for a little kid.

My earliest memory was when they chopped the head off a chicken, and it chased me all over the yard with blood squirting out of its severed neck. I think I was three. Still remember it clearly. I also remember everyone laughing like crazy, except Mom and, of course, me.

There was another incident when I was four. We were at Deep Lake and I was in the back seat of the Kaiser. It was a hot summer day so both back doors were open. All of a sudden, a young deer jumped into the back seat with me. It was totally panicked and starts kicking like crazy. I am getting pummeled big time. Dad is trying to grab the critter with limited success. I finally managed to exit the vehicle with the deer in close proximity. We both hit the ground and took off in opposite directions. Neither of us were seriously injured, but it was an unnerving experience for me, I suppose for the deer also. Seems all my earliest Memories are traumatic events with critters.

Having survived to the ripe old age of five I was off to kindergarten. Unfortunately, I had to drop out after a week. Rich Emery my friend who lived across the alley from us broke his leg and couldn't go to school, so I stayed home with him. When you are five you look out for your people. We did manage to graduate with only a half year of kindergarten, probably because we were so much smarter than the other kids. Who needs a whole year? That is our story and we both stick to it to this day. It was then off to a grueling year of first grade.

During this time, the Bureau of Reclamation was building the Columbia Basin project, a huge irrigation network with many miles of concrete canals. One of the canals ran through Ephrata next to the school. The first thing they did was to excavate a large trench. One of the consequences of this was they displaced a lot of rattle snakes who found their way onto our school grounds. Our teacher advised us that they were very dangerous, and we should report any sighting. I have participated in raising five kids. I know for a fact you can't explain anything to a six- year- old and have it stick for more than two minutes. Two or three times a week we would find snakes. When we did a big rock would be used to terminate the serpent. We were a gang of macho first graders. The kindergarteners were in awe of us. This all came to light when Mrs. Erickson found our stash of snake rattles. We then had an adult playground monitor. The snakes were safe and so were we.

First graders terminating rattlesnakes

CHAPTER THREE

THE EARLY YEARS 1945 TO 1956

Dad truly enjoyed hunting and fishing and passed it on to us boys. Our sisters didn't get the bug. He would take us fishing several times each summer and we usually made one trip to the west coast to fish for salmon. The fish in the lakes around Ephrata were six to 10 inches so to hook into a 25-pound salmon was a major thrill. I recall one year when John was about 10 or 11 years old. We were fishing for salmon at a place called Lapush. Dad, John and I were in a small skiff when John hooked his first Chinook salmon and he just went nuts. The kid was screaming at the top of his lungs and holding onto that fishing pole like his life depended on it. Dad was trying to calm him down with little success.

I was yelling instructions to him, "Hold your pole up, reel faster" and so on.

It was total chaos in that little boat. I suddenly got the feeling there was something behind us and turned to see a big Coast Guard ship with 30 or 40 Coastguardsmen at the rail cheering for John. They were about 100 feet from us. John got the fish and the guys on the ship yelled congratulations and steamed off. I have often wondered if they heard the screaming and came to see if we were in trouble.

Another adventure involving John was my first deer. I was 14 so he was 11. The whole family had traveled to northeastern Washington to hunt whitetail deer. We set up our tents on the edge of a large clearing. In the morning John and I set out to find a deer. Dad and Mom were not morning people. I had a lever action 30-30 rifle, John was carrying the knife. It was like the Lone Ranger and Tonto except younger and dumber.

After hunting through a lot of timber and brush for a couple of hours with no sign of a deer we decided to go back to the camp. Just as we walked into the big clearing a spike buck burst out of the brush and ran right in front of us. I brought the gun to my shoulder and fired without even looking at the sights. The deer dropped in his tracks.

John said, "What was that, a coyote?"

I said, "No it's a deer."

He asked, "Where did it go?"

I said, "It's down right in front of us."

As usual, he went nuts and ran over to the deer and, for some reason, grabbed both of its back feet. About that time the deer came back to life and started kicking like crazy. John continued to hold on and scream at the same time per his M.O. It was like a scene out of a horror movie with a comedic theme. John was finally shaken free and the deer stood up. I shot it again finishing him off.

It got quiet and then we could hear Dad shouting at us from across the clearing, "What are you guys doing over there?" We yelled back that we had a deer. He came running across the clearing and was more excited than John.

He kept saying, "That is a great first deer."

We dressed it out and dragged him to camp to a hero's welcome. When we got back to Ephrata Dad drove all over town to show all his buddies his kid's first deer. In his excitement he forgot to take me with him. It was a milestone in my life. I was overdue for one.

The next year Dad took me, for the first time, on the annual elk hunt in the Blue Mountains. We took a pack string of horses and rode several miles into the wilderness. It was a super adventure for me. We set up the tents and got organized. The first order of business was to check the guns. A bottle was put out in the clearing. They selected me to shoot first. My gun was a 300 Savage with open sights. I laid down on the ground and rested the gun on a log. It was a gimmie shot.

Dad whispered to me "Miss the first shot." Per instructions I missed it by two feet.

He then turned to the other men and said, "I will bet each of you $5 he hits it next time." They took the bet and, of course, I broke the bottle. He didn't give me any of the money. Seems to me I should have got a cut, at least, for not ratting him out. These guys gooned each other like this all the time. It was all in good fun.

The next morning everybody went in different directions. Dad and I ended up on a small hill where four different gullies ended. It was an ideal location because any elk coming up those gullies would walk right into us. I was about 50 feet lower on the hill than Dad when I saw an elk coming through the brush. I had been given strict instructions to not shoot anything unless told. I looked back and could see he saw it too. The elk stopped about 100 feet from me sporting a set of horns. I kept looking back to get the OK, but he just stared. It turned out Dad couldn't see the elk's head, so he didn't know if it was a bull or not.

He finally whispered, "Can you see horns?"

I nodded "yes" and he said, "Then shoot it!"

I put the first round into the ground between my feet and the second round straight up into the sky. There may have been some buck fever involved. Dad quickly determined the possibility of me being a positive contributor to the procurement of elk meat was doubtful. He shot the elk in the eye and that was the end of Mr. Elk. I was convinced that my shot had killed the elk.

We had two tags so while Dad was dressing out the bull, I wandered off to look around. After crossing one of the gullies, suddenly, a whole herd of elk were coming right at me. I hid behind a log. They were moving across in front of me and heading toward Dad who didn't see them as he was busy dressing out the elk. A lot of cows went by, but finally a two- point bull came out. The buck fever had not completely dissipated so I jumped up and shot the bull right in the butt. He took off running and I shot him in the other side of his butt. Shooting elk, or for that matter any big game animal, in the butt is not recommended in most hunting circles. It ruins a lot of meat and is unpleasant for the critter. As the herd ran past Dad, he shot the bull through both shoulders. It staggered over the hill and then we heard two more shots. Someone else had shot him.

We walked over the hill to find another hunter with the elk. He had shot it in the gut and in the shoulders. His first comment was, "This is my elk I shot it last." Dad said no problem you can have it and we went back to our first elk. I asked him why he gave our elk away. He noted that the elk was so shot up that there was hardly any salvageable meat left on it. He also gave me a lesson in hunting ethics. The man should not have shot an elk that was mortally wounded and about to go down. Also, the elk belongs to the person who shoots it first. It didn't really matter because the five of us ended up with four elk which was plenty of meat, so no harm, no foul.

all of us with elk from Blue Mountains 1955

When Grand Coulee Dam was finished, part of its function was to pump water up into a big coulee to form Banks Lake which is the water source for the Columbia Basin Project. This was a great fishing venue. There were largemouth bass, yellow belly perch, freshwater ling cod, blue back salmon, rainbow trout and many other fish. It was several miles long and two or three miles wide.

Dad took John and me there the first time we fished the lake. I was about 12 years old. Up to that point John and I had only caught the small rainbows at Sun Lakes and some salmon on the coast. Neither of us had ever seen a bass or a perch. Top water plugs that were three or four inches long were the lures of preference. We had no idea how this worked.

The technique is to wade out in the shallow flats and cast the plugs as far as you can and then reel them in as they splash along on the surface. On my second cast a four- pound bass came up under that plug and smashed into it flying a foot in the air. I was dumbstruck. I didn't set the hook, so the bass threw the plug five feet across the water and disappeared. I just stood there slack jawed.

Dad said, "That is not the way you do it. You have to set the hook when they strike." John, of course, went nuts.

He kept screaming "Did you see that fish???"

It took a few more strikes until I finally figured out how to hook them, the problem was landing such a big fish. We went home with several bass collected by Dad and two that I caught. John had several strikes and hooked one fish which he lost. He used up a lot of adrenalin on that trip, but then he always did. It would be some time before he made a dent in the bass population.

We made many trips to Banks Lake with Dad and later on our own as we got older. Another memorial trip was when we were about 12 and 9 years old. There is a little cove along the highway called the Devil's teacup. It is only about an acre or so in size. There were lots of bass in there, but the weeds were so thick you couldn't fish it without getting your lure wrapped up in the weeds. Dad came up with a plan. His plans usually worked out. I didn't inherent that ability from him. He got two 20- foot long bamboo poles and tied 20 feet of 15- pound test line on each one. He then tied on a hook and a waterdog. John and I would wade out up to our armpits and dip the waterdogs in small holes in the weeds. The bass would grab them as soon as they got down below the weed line. We were killing the bass big time.

The shore of the Devil's Teacup has steep banks of large boulders the size of a beach ball to a small car. While we were fishing I spotted a rattlesnake on one of the rocks. John and I took off after that snake, as we were prone to do. When we got to the rock, it tried to escape by crawling into a crevice. He was about halfway into the opening when I grabbed him by the tail. I held him while John stuck a hook into his hide and then we stood back and worked him out of the rocks with the cane pole. We now had a very angry rattle snake hanging from the line at the end of the pole. In some circles this would be considered a bad idea and somewhat inadvisable for a 12 and 9-year old, but not in our family. We started back towards the car so we could put our catch in the metal fishing box. Dad looked on with mild interest. The sporting goods store paid $2 for live rattle snakes. We didn't consider any of this to be unusual activity. Just collecting a snake, and consequently, two bucks.

There was an woman sitting on the bank with two little kids. She appeared to have a different perspective on our activities.

She just lit into Dad, "What is the matter with you? Those babies of yours are going to get killed. What will you tell their mama?" Dad reassured her it was OK we had dealt with snakes on many occasions. It didn't mollify her she continued to berate him for another 10 minutes. Then she gathered up her kids and exited the area. I suspect she was concerned about the snake population in the vicinity. We went back to catching bass, didn't see any more snakes.

The demise of Tommy's 1953 Mercury

CHAPTER FOUR

TEENAGE YEARS 1956 TO 1962

A couple of other Banks Lake stories involved me being the guide for adults. My high school wrestling coach , Mr. James, loved to fish. I was telling (bragging) about my fishing success at the lake. It was suggested we go fishing there. The coach would provide the transportation, to include the boat, and the lunch. He asked what kind of sandwich I liked.

Being a wise guy, I said, "I will eat whatever you make." To goon me, sardine, peanut butter and tomato sandwiches were provided. They have a somewhat unique taste. I think he was surprised when I ate two. Don't remember if he ate one or not.

On one particular trip we had figured out how to catch some really big rainbows. The limit at the time for rainbows was ten fish a day or seven and a half pounds and one fish. A 5-pound rainbow was a real trophy. It would get you written up in the local newspaper.

Well we were trolling large flies where there was a sudden drop off. The rainbows were laying below the edge of the drop off. When we trolled by, they would dart up and grab our fly. I had a five pound and a three-pound fish and Mr. James had a six- and one-half pound and a four-pound rainbow. This was a front page of the newspaper catch of fish. We would be local celebrities. Being limited on rainbows we decided to catch some bass. Catch and release was a foreign concept in those days I suppose some of the urban fishermen in Seattle practiced this depraved concept while their children starved.

The fish were on a stringer attached to the stern of the boat.

I fired up the engine and Mr. James said, "Before you put it in gear pull the fish into the boat."

I replied they were fine in the water. If we put them in the boat, they will die. Fish will keep better if we leave them in the water where they will stay alive. He reluctantly agreed and off we went to the bass area. He knew better that to take my advice, but he dropped the ball this time. Over the years since he never made that mistake again.

When we arrived, I turned to shut off the motor and to my horror noted that the stringer was gone as well as the fish attached to it. I didn't say anything as my mind whirled trying to think of what to say.

Mr. James said, "Are the fish OK?"

My short life flashed before my eyes. In a shaky voice I advised him of the situation. Now this guy was the wrestling coach and a former NCAA national champion, so he could inflict a lot of pain. He sat there for what seemed like an hour and then said, "Well there is nothing we can do about it now." I suggested we go back and see if we could catch some more big rainbows. He noted we had caught our limits and because we had lost them didn't change that fact. We went home with a couple of small bass, didn't get written up in the local paper. I did have a few really tough wrestling practices that week.

Banks Lake was a great place to fish and all of us fished there the rest of the time we lived in the Columbia Basin. There were lots of other places to fish in the area. We fished the Sun Lakes, Moses Lake, Potholes Reservoir, Blue Lake and many others. We spent 80% of our time hunting and fishing. The other 20% was wasted on school and other non-productive activities.

Moses Lake was our crappie hole. In the evening, a couple of hours before dark the crappies would come in close to shore to feed. The technique was to put a piece of pork rind on a fly and catch a crappie on almost every cast. We would fill up a gunny sack and head for home. They are really good eating, but a lot of work to clean and fillet. There was a downside to this as we were casting quickly and in the dark. One night my good buddy Ed managed to sink a rather large fly into the back of my neck right between those big tendons at the base of your skull. We couldn't get it out so we continued fishing until it was time to go home. We had priorities.

I went to the doctor who said he thought he could get it out without any pain killing shots. I was assured it wouldn't hurt much. Well, he was wrong. After a rather stressful session for both of us, he managed to remove the fly. I was several blocks down the street heading home when I realized he hadn't given me my fly. I ran back to the office where he was waiting for me with the fly in a little plastic bag. In a small rural community, everyone knew what was important. A hot crappie fly was in that category.

Upon arriving home, we noticed that the fish were still alive and flopping around. We put some in the bathtub and they started swimming. We came up with a grand plan. Most of the farms around Ephrata have ponds to water the livestock. Some of them are over ten feet deep. Therefore, they don't freeze to the bottom in the winter. We decided to stock crappies in the ponds. The one on Grandpa's farm was the first to benefit from our stocking program. The next spring, we went fishing there and were delighted to find the fish had survived just fine. We referred to them as "pre-caughts." It wasn't long before most of the farms around town had crappies.

We would get out of school and someone would say, "Let's go get some pre-caughts" and away we would go to the ponds. It was later discovered that the fish reproduced so there were fish for future generations of local kids. I suppose this made us the first conservationists in Grant County.

As noted before, the irrigation canal ran through Ephrata. It was made of concrete and was about 50 feet wide and I would guess 15 feet deep. The sides sloped down from the road at about 40 or 50 degrees. As kids we were warned to stay away from the canal because it was dangerous due to the currents and the difficulty of climbing up the slope if you fell into the water. This was particularly dangerous where the canal went under one of the main roads in town. It flowed through a reverse siphon. If you fell in upstream of the siphon you would be sucked under water and through the siphon. You would be one dead kid when you came out the other side.

Due to this hazard a chain link fence was placed on either side of the canal for 100 feet upstream of the siphon. There was also a cable running across the water surface 50 feet upstream so if you did fall in you could grab the cable and then hang there like a piece of flotsam until somebody fished you out. It would seem these safeguards would be sufficient for normal people, but not for a bunch of I.Q. challenged kids with a lot of desire to fish and not so much in the common sense department. Also, we never did achieve the "normal" level on anything.

We would routinely walk around the end of the fence and then go along the one- foot wide trail between the fence and the edge of the canal. The cable collected a lot of water weeds and other debris, which would attract the yellow- bellied perch. So, we put our lives at risk to catch some 6 to 10- inch fish. Fishing between the cable and the siphon by holding onto the fence and leaning out over the slope of the canal to drop our bait next to the perch was the technique we used. This was a level of stupid way beyond normal kids. We excelled in this department.

The cops would come by and run us out of there explaining that what we were doing was not only dangerous, but quite stupid. We didn't comprehend the danger and were used to being called stupid, with ample justification. Therefore, the siphon fishing expeditions continued until we got older and found other, more exciting, ways to put ourselves at risk. I don't know how our moms survived our antics.

In the state of Washington, you had to be 14 years old in order to hunt without an adult. By the time we reached that age we all had .22 rifles and single shot shotguns. We weren't old enough to drive so we would hike out of town and hunt the nearby hills for jack rabbits, game birds and ground hogs. We all had dogs that were mostly curbstone sitters. One dog, named Rusty, was a real good rabbit dog. He would jump a rabbit and stay right on his tail for a quarter mile or more. When a rabbit is being chased by a dog they tend to run in a big circle. Therefore, when Rusty would jump a rabbit, we would just wait until they came back. The trick was to hit a running rabbit with the .22 and to not hit Rusty. Calculating the lead at various distances and speeds was tricky. Rusty lived to a ripe old age, so did most of the rabbits, but it was pure luck on their part. We did have a market for the few jack rabbits that were bagged. You couldn't eat them due to various diseases. So we sold them to old lady Georgy for 25 cents apiece. She boiled the critters and fed them to her chickens. They laid eggs with funny colored yolks. That didn't stop anybody from eating the unusual eggs.

In terms of game birds, we had water fowl, quail, chuckers, huns, doves and pheasants. The pheasants were the prize bird. My first pheasant was on a trip with Dad. We were driving out to Grandpa's farm to do some hunting. It was about a mile from the farm when a rooster pheasant ran across the road in front of us. Dad slammed on the breaks and said, "He has a broken wing." I jumped out of the car and took off after him. Pheasants can run really fast, but not as fast as an eleven-year-old with the adrenalin pumping full blast. I jumped on him after about a 100-yard dash. The walk back to the car with the sound of everyone's shouts of encouragement ringing in my ears was a winner's lap for me. I was the man! It wasn't nearly as good of a moment for the bird.

There are many milestones in our lives. One of the first is turning 16 and getting that driver's license. With that little document in your pocket there is a whole new world of ways to injure or kill yourself, particularly for boys. To begin with the hunting and fishing areas expanded dramatically. Ed, one of my best friends, and I bought a 1943 Ford Super Deluxe Coupe for $50. It had some minor defects. No taillights, one headlight, no brakes and it wouldn't turn to the left, you had to make three rights to go left. Other than that, it was a fine hunting and fishing car. Looking back on the deal I think we got ripped off on the price. We did sell it two years later for $25 so I guess we got our money's worth.

With our newfound mobility we ranged far out from Ephrata. We added whitetail deer and elk to our hunting adventures and discovered new places to hunt and fish. Life was good. Well, maybe not all good, but most of it was.

Banks Lake noted above wasn't only a good fishing spot it also was a major resting place for the Canadian geese. They would sit out in the middle of the lake where they were safe. Every evening they would fly off the lake and up over the rim rock bluffs to the wheat fields to feed. Then fly back to the lake for the night, returning to the wheat fields the next morning. They usually went back to the same field. We would watch them in the evening and see where they were feeding and be waiting for them in the morning. On a good day we would get our limit of geese, but most of the time just one or two. Typically, the geese coming into the field would fly close enough that a few of them could be picked off as they went by, sometimes not.

On one of these hunts we found ourselves in the middle of a 1,000-acre wheat field lying face down in the 10- inch high wheat stubble waiting for the geese to show up. We were all armed with semi-automatic shotguns with the plugs taken out, so we had five shells each in the guns instead of the legally mandated three. Totally illegal, but quite effective which is probably why it was illegal. We often had trouble distinguishing between legal and illegal which caused us a lot of problems over the years. The team included me and lifelong friends Doug and Bob. Doug was the strong silent type and Bob was a farm kid. We did a lot of outdoor activities together.

The first flock of about 50 Canadian honkers came in with first light. They landed about 50 yards from where we were and started feeding. Every 15 minutes or so another flock would arrive until there were several hundred geese in one big bunch. They were still too far away but feeding in our direction. What happened is the geese in front of the flock would eat all the wheat so the ones behind them would jump up, and fly over the leading birds land, and start feeding. When the geese caught up to them then they would do the same thing. We had several hundred geese leap frogging right at us.

Geese have excellent eyesight so we knew we couldn't move a finger, or they would be gone. I was lying, face down, with my forehead resting on my forearm therefore it wasn't possible to see the geese but could hear them when they were getting close. I expected Doug or Bob to give a signal when the geese were close enough. Problem was they were doing the same thing as me so none of us knew where the geese were. I remember dirt being blown in my face when what seemed like about a million geese landed right on top of us. Upon looking up there was nothing but goose heads as far as you could see. I came up shooting as did the other two guys. There were geese as close as five feet. I let all five rounds go as fast as I could pull the trigger as did my companions. It was raining geese. We found ourselves surrounded by a multitude of dead or dying geese. We quickly reloaded and picked off the cripples. There was a sea of dead geese all around us. We had mixed emotions, elation for getting so many birds and fear that we would get caught. Then there was the "Now what?" question. Teenaged boys are not known for their critical thinking abilities. We tended to consider the consequences of our actions after the fact rather than before.

We had always felt the game laws could be interpreted in many ways. The bag limit on geese was three per day. If you got four that was close enough. It turned out we had 47 geese. No way to interpret that any way but big trouble trying to explain what happened. We were out in the middle of nowhere so there were no witnesses. We gathered up all the geese and hid them in a ditch. Doug's brother- in- law, who was an avid goose hunter and unfortunately a stickler for game laws, had a place nearby with a barn. We came up with a plan to haul the geese nine at a time (legal limit for three guys) to his barn. This was accomplished without detection. The process of picking and cleaning the birds was commenced. We were about half done when the brother- in- law walked in.

He stood there for a long time and then said, "I see you got some geese." We explained what happened. It was noted that it could have happened to anyone, at least anyone with less than half a brain. He just said to make sure all the birds were picked and cleaned before we left. He gave us freezer bags and we were told to put the geese in the chest freezer when they were done. It was midnight when the job was finished. The geese went in the freezer and then the long drive back to town. The next day we promised all our friends a goose. This made us the big men around town, at least among the small minority of people who still believed anything we said.

It was two days later when we drove out to the barn to recover our booty. The freezer was empty! We were shocked and dismayed. Who would steal geese? We went to the house where we found the brother in law and inquired about our geese.

He looked surprised and said, "Did you guys want those geese? I thought you gave them to me, so I gave them to the old folk's home in Soap Lake." We stood there in stunned silence. All we had gone through to get those geese and then 12 hours of picking and cleaning and they were gone! We would also have to explain to all our friends why they were not going to get a goose. How embarrassing is that. On the drive back to town Bob and I berated Doug as to what an idiot his brother in law was. It was not until much later we realized we had been taught a lesson on violating the game laws. It didn't really take until a few years later. Fact is, I don't think 90% of our brainpower kicked in until we were 25.

The most embarrassing episode was the time Doug and I decided to skip school and go up to Sun Lakes and do some fishing. We were hitch hiking at the edge of town when the local cops drove by. We already had a history with these guys, so they turned around and asked why we weren't in school. They were informed we were going fishing instead. They seemed to have a problem buying into that plan.

We were put in the back of the police car and drove to the high school. Now when a cop car pulls into the school parking lot everybody is watching. Every eye in the school was on Doug and me as we were escorted to the principal's office with our tackle boxes and fishing poles. I can't imagine a more humiliating perp walk. Everybody was pointing and laughing, except us. Never did that again.

Ephrata was a typical small town. It had about 7,500 people when I lived there. I like to say it has since grown to 5,000. We had a movie theatre and the Ephrata Recreation center and that was about it. So, the main entertainment for us guys was hunting, fishing, drinking beer and chasing girls. We were marginally competent at hunting and fishing. The girl thing just never seemed to work out even when we turned on the charm, such as offering them a beer. It was assumed all of us would die virgin bachelors. We excelled at the beer drinking.

My first girlfriend was Judy when we were in fourth grade. She didn't know she was my girlfriend. Not sure if she even knew who I was, but in my mind, she was my girlfriend. I gave up on her when she didn't acknowledge my existence for a couple of years. My next girlfriend was

Deloris. It was my junior year in high school when I met her. She lived in Soap Lake, a nearby town. I was very debonair and couth, Eastern Washington style, which means I could get beer on weekends. Delores took my virginity in the back seat of my brother-in-laws Ford Edsel parked at the Soap Lake city dump. How romantic was that! My love life stayed at that level for several years.

1961 Ephrata High Prom with Deloris

My best buddy, Tommy, took up with her little sister so we double dated a lot. Being the father of three daughters I can imagine the agony their dad must have been going through with his daughters hanging out with the two of us. He lucked out and neither of us became a son-in-law. Tommy was an unusual guy. He was up for any adventure. Loved to drink beer and tell jokes. He could listen to a song one time and be able to sing that song from then on. He was very likeable. All my other buddies dated mostly girls in our class or the one behind us, they didn't have to date "out-of-town girls." Several of them married and lived happily ever after.

Tommy had a 1953 Mercury convertible. We drove that thing all over the county hunting, fishing and whatever. One of the "whatevers" was a football game in Quincy, a nearby town. I was on the team, but I weighed 112 pounds, so I didn't get much playing time, like none. Quincy was a big football power at the time, Ephrata wasn't. Somehow, we won 16 to 7. Everyone was really hyped up about that victory.

Tommy and I were driving back from the game in the Mercury convertible, cruising along at about 100 MPH with the top down. We still had hair for the wind to blow through. Some of our pals were behind us going about the same speed when we noticed some other guys from our school hitch hiking. Tommy slammed on the breaks so we could give them a ride. The guys behind us didn't see us stopping, they slammed into the left rear side of the Mercury going about 100 MPH. It didn't work out well for either car and the potential for serious injury to the occupants was significant.

The Mercury rolled violently down the shoulder of the road. When it came out of the first roll it flipped me out and I went sailing up into the air. Seat belts were a vague concept in those days. I recall being above the telephone wires and looking down and thinking, "Don't want to fall down there I will get all dirty." Well, I did and, I did. Landed flat on my back in a small irrigation ditch with about six inches of water and 12 inches of mud which made for a soft, but quite messy, landing.

I looked over and saw the mercury was standing on its front bumper and slowly turning while falling over. Tommy was laying on the ground right where the car was going to land. To my horror the car landed right on top of him and then bounced away. He lay there for a second or two and then kind of flopped once. I thought it was a dead cat bounce and that he was dead as a doornail. You can imagine my surprise when he sat up and then walked up to the road and sat down on the edge of the pavement. I pulled myself out of the mud and walked over and sat down beside him. There were car parts, traumatized teenagers, State Troopers and general chaos all around us. We were silent for some time and then he said, "Guess I will be needing a new car," I concurred. The cops took us home. Not the first time they performed that service.

The other car with four kids in it spun down the road shedding fenders and other parts while flattening all four tires, but it stayed upright. None of those guys were hurt either. The only injury was that Tommy had a hairline fracture in his scapula. Our moms had made us go to church every Sunday since we were toddlers. I guess it payed off. The combined value of both cars was reduced to about $9.50. Car insurance was another vague concept for us.

Tommy's, extremely tolerant, dad got him a new used car, which was a dramatic downgrade from the Mercury. It was some obscure brand of car with a really weird transmission. The shift lever was a little handle to the left of the steering wheel. There were four horizontal notches and you moved the lever to the various notches to shift gears. It was a very small station wagon and did not qualify as a chick magnet like the Mercury. The engine was about two- and one-half horsepower, maybe less.

His dad figured if he couldn't go fast, he wouldn't have wrecks, flawed thinking on his part. Seems like all the plans our parents came up with to keep us out of trouble were defective. Obviously, they passed that bad planning gene on to us. So, it was all their fault when things went wrong.

The demise of the weird little car came about on a duck hunting trip. All excess water from the Columbia Basin irrigation project would flow into a large dirt ditch that carried the water to a lake which was called the Winchester Waste Way. The ditch was about 25 feet wide and 10 to 15 feet deep with a gravel road on one side. There were lots of sharp curves and ninety-degree bends. A prudent person would therefore drive very slowly and carefully on this road. Problem was we didn't know any prudent persons or even the meaning of the word.

Our duck hunting technique was to drive at a high rate of speed along the road with one guy driving and the other guy sitting in the passenger seat with a loaded shotgun. So, it was literally riding shotgun. We would come around a corner, slam on the brakes and the shotgun guy would jump out of the car and blast away at any ducks we surprised. It worked like a charm and lots of ducks met their demise.

This technique was so successful we seldom went more than a couple of miles down the road until a limit of birds was acquired. Then we would turn around and drive back to the highway and home. On one trip the hunting was not good, causing us to venture further down the road than before. This was new territory. Five or six ducks were on the floorboards, but the limit was eight apiece therefore the hunt continued.

We came careening around a ninety degree turn and immediately noticed another canal intersecting with our canal. It was also noted that the road ended abruptly at the edge of this canal. Needless to say, in the next split second we were airborne. This was not something we had anticipated. Tommy was hitting the brakes for all he was worth, but the traction you get with pure air is marginal at best. A primeval scream emanated from the car. Not sure which of us it came from, maybe both of us. We landed in the water with a magnificent splash.

The car floated for a few seconds, so we did manage to get out and to grab our shotguns, shotgun shells and the ducks. All the valuable stuff. Everything else went down with the ship in 15 feet of muddy water. We took a short swim to shore on the other side of the new canal.

It was only a mile to the lake and we saw smoke from a fire so we decided to hike in that direction. We ran into three guys sitting around a fire drinking beer and picking ducks. By now it was late in the day, so they offered us a ride to town. They seemed perplexed as to our wet clothes but didn't ask. We were a sorry looking pair of duck hunters. They required us to ride in the back of the pick-up as they didn't want to get their vinyl seat covers wet. The next morning Tommy reported the car stolen. One question the local cops had was who would steal that car? Our relationship with these guys was somewhat shaky so I suspect they were skeptical in regard to our story. No new news there.

Tommy's dad owned 6,000 acres of dryland wheat and at that time the price of wheat was up, so he had lots of money. One of the few people in the county who did. Still he declined to buy Tommy another car, a prudent decision on his part. We were relegated to being pedestrians. It was imprudent to drive my 1943 Ford in town. It was our senior year, so we survived until I went off to college and Tommy joined the navy, but our level of excitement dropped off considerably. Mom had a lot fewer dead birds to cook. Not sure she was overly upset by that.

It seems like High School was a series of close calls for us. Car wrecks, hunting accidents, over imbibing on beer, and various other IQ challenged activities. It is astounding that we survived. Another example of this was a duck hunting trip to Lenore Lake. We would go out on a point of land and put out our decoys. The ducks would usually drop right into our spread and we would let them have it with our various single shot guns. A lot of ammo was used at $5 a box which was unbelievably expensive in our financial bracket.

On this trip we had brought along a classmate named Ryan. He was not one of our group but wanted to be part of the gang. Ammo was running low, so we turned to Ryan and told him to hitch hike back to Ephrata and get us more shells. Probably should have given him more instructions on the procurement process. He took off and was back in a couple of hours with five boxes. It was a pleasant surprise. We gave one to him and took the rest. What was not known was he didn't have any money, so he went to the hardware store and shop lifted the shells. We all had a sordid record with the local police. Mostly illegal consumption of beer (under 21) and assorted traffic issues, but nothing as serious as stealing shotgun shells. Ryan wasn't invited on any more hunting trips or anything else. We lived in fear of the long arm of the law for several months. Upside was a limit of ducks.

Next to the point of land was a 200-foot-high cliff. It was a blue bird day, so the ducks were flying high. I made a questionable decision to climb to the top of the cliff so I could shoot the ducks from this high perch as they flew over. There was a 12-inch-wide trail going up the face. I started up by hugging the rocks and shuffling my feet along the path. Problem was the higher up I got the thinner the path. By the time it occurred to me that the situation had deteriorated significantly I was 100 feet above the foot of the cliff and standing on a six inch ledge. The trail got much steeper and considerably thinner so continuing was not an option. To turn and start back down was a tricky maneuver. My friends were shouting advice such as "Throw down your gun so we can catch it." I suspect they had kissed me off but didn't see any reason why the gun should get busted up too. They were my best friends, but a bit too pragmatic at times.

After a reasonable amount of reflection, I deduced that the only chance I had was to turn and go back down the ledge. I pulled my right cheek off the face of the cliff and put my left cheek on the rock. I then moved my gun from my right hand to my left hand, took a deep breath and moved my right foot six inches down the trail. Going up was like doing something right-handed and going down was like doing it left-handed. None of this was good.

If you think about this at all it made very little sense. I had put myself, and my 20 gauge, in extreme danger in order to shoot a couple of spoon billed ducks, which are held in low esteem in the duck hunting fraternity. In my teenage mind this made perfect sense, as did driving too fast, drinking too much beer and fishing above the siphon. It is unbelievable any of us made it to 20, yet we did. Anyhow back to the ledge. My life kept flashing before my eyes, but it didn't take long as I was only 16. Needless to say, my single- shot 20 gauge and I made it to the bottom. I got the definite impression my "friends" were somewhat disappointed that they didn't get to be heroes dragging my broken body up to the highway and flagging down a car to take me to the hospital. A few years later I made it possible for them to have that experience.

We were on our senior sneak to Sun Lakes. It was an all-day party with swimming, playing ball and drinking beer. Towards evening we decided to head for home as the beer had run out so there was no reason to stay. I was riding in Tommy's convertible with the top down. As we were heading down the road Doug passed us in this car named "tragedy" and for some reason I opted to change cars and go with him. Problem was we were going 40 MPH and Doug was 20 feet away when I exited Tommy's car. Not a well thought out plan that I am sure was influenced by the beer. I vividly remember sliding down the road on my back thinking, "So this is what it feels like to get killed." Not a happy thought. Well, all my buddies got to rush to my aid and call the ambulance and then load my severely scraped body into the vehicle. I am sure they were all very proud of themselves.

On the ride to the Soap Lake Hospital, I was in intense negotiations with the paramedics to just stop and let me out as I had only scratched up my back a bit and my dad would kill me over this. My pleas were for naught. We arrived at the hospital, and they lifted me out of the ambulance on the stretcher. As soon as I cleared the door I jumped off and high tailed it across a vacant lot. My ripped-up shirt and pants flapping in the wind. One guy ran me down and held me there until the other guy could bring the stretcher so they could carry me back to the hospital strapped very firmly in place.

The doctor bandaged me up from the back of my head to my butt and then called my dad. I had an unpleasant ride home. It is reasonable to think he would have been used to this sort of thing by then. I was put in my bed and then we had a short but intense talk and he went back to the social event they were attending. Which I am sure was considerably different than the one I had been attending. Mom checked in on me when they got home. She suggested that I should think things through before acting. I was puzzled as to what she meant.

I had friend who was a Colville Indian. Craig was a typical Native American. Dark black hair and eyes, seldom spoke and always looked solemn. He could hunt on the reservation and would take me with him. The hunting was much better there than anywhere else in the state. I couldn't hunt there because I was as Irish as he was Indian and there was not an Irish reservation in the area. Looking back on it I think he just took me to do most of the work like packing out the deer and elk he shot. He did give me a few pounds of the meat, but not much. I was happy to just be in on the hunt.

One day we were duck hunting near Quincy. The ducks were few and far between, therefore, it was getting boring. There were lots of coots on the pond. They are not good to eat and are considered scrap birds. In fact, people called them mud hens as that is what they tasted like. It was determined that some practice was in order and knocking the coots out of the air when they flew into the pond would serve that purpose.

We had busted five or six of them when the game warden's car was observed coming down the road, at a high rate of speed, right at us. Our MO is if you don't know why the game warden is coming, run. Craig had a 1958 Pontiac Bonneville muscle car. We jumped into it and took off for Ephrata at 100 MPH. Craig said, "He will never catch us with that puny car of his." He was right, but the warden's radio was much faster than we were, so we were pulled over within a couple of miles by a state trooper. So much for our evasion plan. It didn't look good for us. Not recovering shot waterfowl, flight to avoid arrest and speeding were just a few of the violations being discussed.

The trooper escorted us to the justice of the peace in Quincy, who worked out of his garage. The Grant County justice system was kind of rudimentary in those days. We were fined $150 which we had to pay right then and there or go to jail until we did pay the money. We had about $5 between us. It seemed there were no good options.

The justice of the peace asked me if I was any relation to Frank T. Bell and I said, "Yes he is my grandpa." He turned to the trooper and said, "Frank Bell is a personal friend of mine. I would prefer this boy not go to jail if you could stop at his father's office on the way so he could get the money, I would appreciate it." I wasn't sure I appreciated it. The wrath that was going to fall on my head when I was escorted into dad's office by a state trooper and needing $150 for shooting coots was probably much worse than any jail time. My opinion wasn't solicited so off we went to the office.

The 30-minute drive from Quincy to Ephrata was the longest 30 minutes of my life. Sitting in the back seat of the trooper car with Craig following in his muscle car, thinking of some way to blame me for all of this, was not an ideal situation.

We arrived at the office and I said to the trooper, "You don't need to come in. I will get the money and bring it out to you."

He laughed and said, "I have known your dad for 20 years and I want to see this first-hand." I was out of ideas and options, so I just accepted my fate.

We walked into the office and Dad said, "Hey, Jerry what's up?" Then he saw me, and his happy face went away. As it was wont to do when I showed up with law enforcement personnel. I explained what had happened. He turned to the trooper and said he thought coots were scrap birds and you didn't have to keep them. The trooper filled him in on the law which says they are waterfowl and you have to keep them. I figured things were going well as Dad agreed with me on the coots.

Problem was the unlawful flight to avoid arrest and speeding issues were brought up which didn't go well for me. After he was finished berating me at great length for that, "Jerry" brought up the $150 and things deteriorated even further. Did I mention that Craig was still out in his car and missing out on all of this excitement?

The fine was $75 each, but the justice of the peace had not instructed the trooper to allow Craig a stop before the jail, so I had to ask for a lone for him, then he would go to his place and get money to repay Dad. After more beratement he agreed to pay my fine and loan Craig his money. We paid the trooper and as it was quitting time he and Dad went out for a beer. I went to Craig's house so he could give me the $75 dollars as I didn't trust him to show up with it at dad's office the next day. I have never shot another coot in my life. They are way too expensive and taste like mud.

Tommy and I thought we had a knack for business. Now most people define the word "knack" as being good at something. In our case it had the opposite meaning. Our financial adventures usually resulted in losing money, which is not the outcome desired, unless you're Uber or the government.

One of Tommy and my major business ventures had to do with domestic geese. Back in the 1950 and 1960s the mint farmers around Moses Lake and Quincy would use geese to eat the weeds in their mint fields. The geese didn't eat mint, so they would deploy thousands of geese in their fields every year. The birds would snarf up the weeds and leave the mint to prosper from the goose droppings. A win-win deal.

The weeds were not good feed for the geese, so they were very skinny therefore not part of the win-win, and of little commercial value. When it was time to harvest the mint, they had to do something with all those geese. Some were kept to make more geese in the spring, but they had to dispose of a lot of excess geese. Most were killed and taken to the dump. Tommy and I were at the dump shooting rats, another of our intellectual activities, when a dump truck showed up and dumped a load of dead geese. This caused us to immediately begin pondering as how to take advantage of the situation. We had come up with a few business ideas, but none of them ever panned out.

After considerable thought we developed a business plan. Our plan was somewhat less detailed than say General Motor's business plan, but it was a business plan. The main elements were that we could buy geese from the farmers for 25 cents apiece. We would then get one of Tommy's dad's wheat trucks and transport the geese to his 6,000 acres of harvested wheat land. When they harvest quite a bit of wheat is knocked to the ground and goes to waste. We bought 2,000 geese for $500, borrowed from his dad, and turned them loose on the 6,000 acres of unfenced wheat stubble. They quickly began eating that wheat like crazy. Our business plan was implemented. A fortune was about to be made. We had visions of being the goose suppliers of America, or at least Eastern Washington.

These were domestic geese so they couldn't fly, therefore, we did have some shrinkage due to coyotes, badgers and hawks, but by late fall we had about 1,700 nice fat geese. Next problem, where do you sell 1,700 geese? The Ephrata market for geese was limited. Through a friend of my dad we found a company that would buy the geese for $6.25 each. Problem was they were in Chicago and the $6.25 price was delivered. This issue put us in the railroad's business office in Seattle. They agreed to ship the geese to Chicago for $3.75 each. We would make $2.50 per goose or $3,750 net profit. That was more money than either of us had ever earned. We were financial geniuses. Move over Warren Buffet, the new kids are in town.

The plan was the railroad would drop off a box car with several levels in it on a siding near Ephrata. We would then load the geese in the box car just prior to the next train picking it up. It worked like a charm. We had sold 125 geese around town for a nice $875 profit used to pay Tommy's dad back with $375 in our pockets. We loaded up about 1,500 geese and watched them disappear down the track on their way to Chicago. Visions of great wealth dancing in our heads.

Now when you embark on a business venture like this it is advisable to do a little research, but it was not in our business plan, so we didn't. It turns out when you ship livestock it is your responsibility to arrange for that livestock to be fed and watered while it is in route. There are businesses along the tracks that do that for a small fee, but they are of limited value if you don't contact them to make the arrangements to provide said services.

Bottom line, a week later when they arrived many of our geese were dead. The ones that were not dead were of limited value due to their poor condition. We sold the survivors and pooled that money with the money we earned selling the 125 geese in Ephrata and only lost $350 on the deal. We covered that cost by bucking hay on grandpa's farm, at $1.50 an hour, for a week. We got out of the goose business.

Undeterred we went into the railroad tie business. The railroad was replacing the ties for several miles of track around Ephrata. They would take up the tracks and throw the old ties to one side and put in new ones then replace the rails, so there were all these old ties laying alongside the tracks, seemly there for the taking. They were putting up new barbed wire fences on grandpa's farm. The corner posts must be very sturdy to carry the stress from the wire. A railroad tie would be ideal for this purpose.

Seizing on this requirement Tommy and I took one of his dad's trucks and picked up a few railroad ties and sold them to the guys putting up the fence for $5 apiece. It was easy money. Well, not all that easy as we had to carry the heavy ties from the railroad track to the road, sometimes up to a quarter mile. Regardless we persisted and started to build up a good client base. We were selling 15 to 20 used ties a month. It was plenty of money to keep us in beer, shotgun shells and junk food. All of our basic needs were covered. Once again, we were business tycoons.

We probably would have been OK if greed hadn't kicked in. One day we drove by the railroad yard and there was a huge stack of new railroad ties. There had to be several of thousand of them. This was just too tempting for two IQ challenged teenagers. We figured we could drive the truck right up to the pile and load a few hundred ties in a couple of hours rather than packing used ties to the road. They wouldn't miss a few hundred ties from such a big pile so we would be home free. Some would call this logical thinking others would call it just plain stupid. You have to go with the latter.

This was our first venture into crime, other than Ryan and the shotgun shells. We were to find out we were not good at it. We loaded up the ties late one night and took them to a remote piece of scrub land near grandpa's farm. They were dumped in a pile out of sight from the road. We then put into action our marketing plan of selling new ties for $6. It didn't go well. Our clients were concerned as to the legality of our supply chain regarding the new ties. Sales were down considerably, didn't sell any of them. We contemplated what to do with our inventory but didn't come up with any viable plans.

The problem was solved for us a few weeks later when Dad showed up at the farm with Tommy and a very ominous looking stranger. I was in the field bucking hay in order to keep up appearances for being rather wealthy for no apparent reason. Dad yelled at me come to the car. I was then introduced to the railroad detective who had a few questions for me. It turned out Tommy had already answered all his questions. He just wanted me to confirm we were a couple of incompetent thieves. I promptly did just that. We were busted. Dad wasn't pleased.

The next day we were told to report to the sheriff's office at 8:00 AM. When the two of us arrived, our dads were not there, just the railroad dick and the sheriff. This wasn't a good sign. The sheriff escorted us up to his office and told us to sit in some chairs next to the wall then he and the railroad detective went into his office. Tommy and I sat there for an hour wondering what was going to happen to us. We were not enjoying the experience.

The next thing we knew they brought two guys out from the jail covered in chains. They had their hands handcuffed to a chain that went around their waist and through their crotch. Another chain went around their neck and was attached to the chain on their waist. One guy wanted a drink of water and a deputy had to hold the drinking fountain button for him because he was so chained up. It was obvious that these guys were in deep kim chee. They both had a resigned look on their face.

The sheriff came out and told us to follow him. It was into the elevator with the criminals, the sheriff and two deputies. We got off on the first floor. Then out to the parking lot where these two guys were put in the back seat of the sheriff's car. A steel bar was lowered across their laps and the chains locked to the bar. Those guys couldn't move a finger. They drove away. We stood there and watched as the car disappeared down the road. It wasn't the happiest moment of my life. If those guys were an example, being a criminal really sucked.

The sheriff took us back up to his office where the railroad dick was waiting. He sat us down and explained that the two guys we just saw being hauled off to prison had stolen some merchandise worth about half as much as the railroad ties. I got kind of dizzy at that point. Tommy was white as a sheet. The sheriff and the railroad guy went back into his office and we sat there for another hour scared to death. I thought about making a break for it and starting a new life in neighboring Douglas County under a new name, but I had no money and no car. Besides Mom would have tracked me down anyway.

I found out later that the railroad guy was an old friend of my dad, but I didn't know it at the time. Therefore, the long ride in chains was never an issue. He had agreed to no jail time with Dad, but I didn't know that either. Tommy and I were sure we were going to jail for the rest of our teenage years, maybe more.

It turns out the railroad did inventory the used ties. They said there were 175 of them missing. We were sure we didn't take anywhere near that many, but we were the only ones who got caught. He insisted we pay for the ties. They were valued at $7.50 each. That amounted to about $1,300. The money we had collected on sales had long since been spent on beer, junk food and shotgun shells. Our total net worth was about $2.25. We were $1297.75 short.

We were in the Future Farmers of America and were both raising two steers to be sold at the Grant County Fair the next month. The detective suggested the revenue from the steers might just cover the bill. It did, but just barely. I don't know how many hours we bucked hay at $1.50/hour to feed those animals, but it was in the hundreds. One good thing from all of this was that our crime career was over for the rest of our lives. They say, "Crime doesn't pay." Well in our case we lost money on it, with a lot more trauma than the goose deal.

This venture convinced Tommy to forego any further business adventures. He was content to just drive a wheat truck for his dad during the harvest and then odd jobs around town for wages. I, on the other hand, determined earning money bucking hay for $1.50 an hour wasn't where I wanted to be in the world of commerce.

I worked weekends on grandpa's farm for $5 a day. Every now and then we would butcher an animal. Usually a sheep or steer. I got to where I was pretty good at this task, so I decided to branch out and started my next business which I named "Bell's Killing Service." The name would be politically incorrect today, but in the late 50's and early 1960s it was just fine. Short and to the point. I suppose some disillusioned spouse might have misinterpreted the business services, but none contacted me.

I made arrangements with the local butcher/cold storage company to deliver all the animals to them for cutting and wrapping. In return I could use their truck with a cherry picker on the back plus they would supply me with all the tools I needed such as knives. It was a joint venture between me and Polar Lockers.

The services provided involved coming to your farm and killing your steer or sheep, gutting and skinning it and then delivering it to the butcher. I charged $12.50 and the head, heart and hide for a steer. I could get another $ 3 for the tongue and brains from the head and $5 for the hide. I love heart so I kept them for personal consumption. My total costs were the gas to drive to the farm. I would clear 20 bucks per steer. Sheep were bumped off for $5 each. The business continued all the way through college. I would come home for various vacations and pick up my hit list and go on a financially rewarding killing spree. My room and board bill at the fraternity was $85 a month, so this was good money. Four steers and a sheep cover a month of living expenses.

My technique for doing a hit was to walk up to the steer and mentally draw a cross between the base of the horns and his eyes. Then I would put the .22 rifle about six inches from the middle of the cross and pull the trigger. The steer was dead before he hit the ground. I would pick him up by the hind legs with the cherry picker, then I skinned him and finally laid the soon to be steaks, roasts, and hamburger down in the bed of the truck and wrapped it in a tarp. It was then just a matter of driving to the butcher and offloading him. Usually took about four hours depending on how far out of town the farm was. This was way better than bucking hay for $1.50/hour. A lot less physical effort, but quite a bit bloodier.

Most of the hits went smoothly, but there were a couple of exceptions. The most exciting was a sheep project. The farmer had 20 sheep in a pen with a less than sturdy wire fence. The method I used was to herd the sheep into a corner and then jump on one of them and grab his front legs, which would bring him to the ground. He would then begin his journey to becoming lamb chops.

I was a little concerned about taking on 20 sheep by myself. I cut a deal with Dennis who lived across the alley from me. Told him he would earn $1 a sheep to help me so he could make $20 in one day. He had no idea what was involved, but signed on in a heartbeat. We retrieved the truck from the butcher and were on our way. Dennis was about to have one of those experiences you remember the rest of your life or more likely one you try to forget for the rest of your life. Dennis was a good-hearted kid. He got along with everybody and was well liked. He also liked animals. This deal had the potential to be traumatic for him.

We got to the farm and set up. I jumped on the first sheep and promptly terminated him. Dennis went quite pale at that point. The next pen over had about 40 feeder hogs. They were in a sturdy wooden fence as hogs tend to be quite adept at escaping. Per the farmers instructions I threw the entrails over the fence and the hogs tore into them, they were totally consumed in a couple of minutes. This wasn't a pleasant activity to watch. At this point Dennis was having second thoughts about the deal he had made. I think he went into shock for a short time. Anyhow it was time for the second sheep. The sequence was repeated. By the fourth sheep Dennis was warming to the process. He finally asked if he could do one. I said sure so he jumped on a sheep and followed my instructions on dispatching him. Afterward he staggered around for a moment but recovered just fine. It was not long before he seemed to enjoy killing the sheep. That did concern me a little. Sometimes when you bring out someone's basic instincts it can get ugly. You just never know what lurks under that nice guy persona.

The nice thing about sheep is they will bunch up with each other and stay in one place, therefore it is easy to catch them. The problem arises when you get down to the last sheep. There are no other sheep to bunch up with, so they just run like crazy when you try to grab them. We found ourselves chasing that last sheep around the pen with little success. I suspect his observing the fate of his companions added to his desire to avoid being caught. As noted above the fence was a marginal wire fence. The sheep managed to get through the fence and took off across a grain field. I took off after him. Dennis thought he could cut him off by jumping over the wooden fence into the hog pen. Big mistake! The hogs were in a feeding frenzy from the sheep entrails so anything that came over that fence was fair game and at this moment that was Dennis. I remember hearing him yell and I turned to see him clearing that six-foot fence standing straight up. He hyperventilated for an hour. With the sheep dispatching issues and now the pig attack his emotional turmoil continued to escalate. The $20 pay probably seemed less and less adequate.

In the meantime, our quarry had traversed the grain field and ran across the bridge over the canal into several thousand acres of unfenced sagebrush. There was no way we could catch him there. The only thing we could think to do was to go to the farmer's house and explain what had happened. He expressed some concerns about our competence which was OK because we had heard that many times before. We were then given a .22 rifle and told to shoot the sheep, but don't ruin any meat, so shoot him in the head. Easier said than done.

We trooped back to the bridge. The sheep was next to the canal, but every time we tried to cross the bridge he would spook. If he took off into that open range, we would need a lot more people to hunt him down. In order to minimize that risk, I decided to pick it off from across the canal. The plan was to shoot him through the lungs and not ruin any meat. It was only a 25- yard shot. I got a good rest and fired the first shot. He jumped but didn't seem hurt, so I shot again. Still no significant reaction. It was determined that shooting him in the body wasn't productive, so I went for a head shot. Missed a couple of times, but finally scored a hit and he went down. We ran across the bridge and just as we got close, he jumped up, so I shot him in the back with no results. He then turned so another head shot was possible which put the escapee down for the count. That drama was behind us, at least we thought it was.

We dragged him back to the pen and hung his carcass up. Once we got the skin off, we saw that we had a problem. Those .22 rounds were hitting all that wool and then just gathering wool as they went. So, they were hitting the sheep real hard, but not penetrating the hide due to the wool cap the bullet was wearing. This resulted in bruising the whole side of the sheep. This wasn't good regarding the instructions to not ruin any meat. We determined we didn't need to enter into that conversation with the farmer as it would have a negative impact on our net profit. We put the bruised sheep on the bottom of the pile picked up our pay and headed for Polar Lockers. We all know that if you just ignore a problem, it will just go away. Well, it didn't.

The butcher expressed some concerns about the bruised sheep. He was assured that I would deal with it, told him to go ahead and cut and wrap him along with the others. It was assumed he would mark the bruised sheep, but he didn't, so I had 20 boxes with a cut and wrapped sheep in each one, but no clue as to which one was damaged goods. As noted above if you ignore a problem..........

There was a side deal with the farmer that he would give me $5 for every sheep I could sell around town, which doubled my revenue on this job. I was going door to door selling sheep for $115 apiece. The result was most of the sheep were peddled. It was not long before I found out who got the bruised sheep. It was my high school English teacher. She drew me aside after class and inquired as to the odd color of the sheep meat. I explained that it was the feed they were given. It had a purple color to it and so the meat was purple. She seemed to accept that explanation with some skepticism as she had known me for most of my life and had reason to be wary. I never heard any more about it. The next year when I was selling sheep, she didn't buy one, can't imagine why.

Another less than normal hit job had to do with a five-year-old steer located on a 2,000-acre ranch between Ephrata and Moses Lake on Rocky Ford Creek. Most steers do not see their second birthday before they are converted to hamburger. This guy was five, so he was huge. Another problem was the critter had been running loose on the ranch all of his life and was as wild as a deer, but much bigger. None of these facts were relayed to me. I assumed I would go to a corral and do the .22 thing. Well, that didn't work out.

I arrived at the ranch and was brought up to speed on the conditions of the project. With this new data it was necessary to reorganize, so it was back to town to get my dad's 30-06 rifle. I then went steer hunting. This was mostly open sagebrush country except along the creek. For 20 to 50 feet either side of the water were cattails, brush, small trees and swampy areas. Not an ideal environment for steer shooting or recovery. The steer seemed to prefer this area. It took me a couple of hours to just find him. Next problem was to get him out of the brush which was dicey as he tended to charge me when I got too close which had several potential downsides. For me, not so much the steer. This thing probably weighed close to a ton. I finally decided to just piss him off enough that he would chase me out into the open. It worked great except that once we were in the open, he just kept after me. This wasn't in my plan, so I had to do some adjusting. We played tag around the truck for a while being tagged having significant consequences, but eventually he gave me a shot that put him down.

It seems like when something is finally going well, it doesn't. This critter was so big and heavy the cherry picker couldn't lift him. I had cut him in half to get him in the truck. It was totally dark by the time the job was finished. When I returned to the farmhouse everyone was gone so I couldn't get paid and, of course, the butcher was closed for the night. I wasn't a contented businessman. The steer spent the night in the truck in my parent's back yard. A neighborhood dog got the heart, other than that it was OK the next morning. There was a rather intense negotiation with the farmer the next day regarding the extra work. All I got was sympathy and the agreed upon $12.50. I determined I needed to review my business plan, but I never got around to it. The killing service served me well through high school and college

Mr. Atkinson advising a clueless Bob on college admissions

CHAPTER FIVE

COLLEGE 1961 TO 1966

The college deal was uncertain. I had no intention of going to college. I saw my future as graduating high school and then getting a good paying job so I could finance the necessities of life such as beer, junk food, shotgun shells and chasing girls. Any other expenses would be minimal.

One day Dad took me aside and suggested that I should consider going to Washington State University when I graduated. I rejected that out of hand. High School was a pain in the butt, college had to be even worse. The next day the local Army recruiter looked me up. He explained the draft situation, which was that my chances of avoiding the draft were slim and none and Slim had left town. So, he suggested that I should join the Army. He said they were bussing a bunch of my fellow Ephrata tigers up to Spokane to be tested. Hey, a free trip to Spokane, why not? A few weeks later I was on a bus with a couple dozen of my classmates in route to the big city. We did all the physicals and mental tests and then went to see "Thunder Road." We were put up at the YMCA, they probably never agreed to do that again, then back on the bus to Ephrata. For Eastern Washington guys this was a major adventure in the big town. The Army was looking good to me at that time. Dad still argued that I should at least try college. He had the son of a friend of his who was home on leave come talk to me. He painted a very different picture of the Army than the recruiter had described. Suddenly college looked pretty good.

The next day I went in to see Mr. Atkinson, the boy's counselor, and informed him I wanted to sign up to go WSU. I was under the impression it was like signing up for the wrestling team. You tell them you want to do it and then show up at the next meeting. He looked at me with a quizzical expression for several minutes, then said, "This is a complete surprise. What caused you to make this choice?" I relayed the information I had got from the Army guy who was on leave and noted that I didn't think that was for me. He nodded and told me to wait while he got my file. This was the first time I knew the school kept files on us. Could not imagine why they would do that or what was in it.

When he got back, he looked at my file for some time and then did some calculations. He finally said "Bell, you have to have a grade point average of 2.0, a "C" average, in order to get into WSU. You have a 1.8. You are starting the second semester of your senior year which most colleges don't count regarding admissions. So, it doesn't look good for you."

Unfazed, I said, "So, what do we do about that?" He laughed and noted that he had always liked me for my cheekiness. He then noted that the admissions guy at WSU was a friend of his and he would see what he could do for me. I thanked him and went to wrestling practice. Problem solved.

About a week later Mr. Atkinson called me back to his office. He had talked with the admissions guy and had cut a deal with him. He would admit me to WSU contingent on my getting a high enough GPA in the second semester to bring my total GPA up to a 2.0. I am sure he didn't think there was much of a risk that he would have to let me in. I agreed to the deal and then asked what GPA I would need to get to the required 2.0. He replied 3.6!!! I sat back in my chair in shock. Maybe the problem was not solved. That Army recruiter's face flashed across my mind, as beads of sweat formed on my forehead.

We sat in silence for a while and then I said, "How am I going to do that?" He pointed out to me that at the beginning of each semester the teacher would give us a book on the subject of the class. I noted that I was vaguely aware of that fact. He then asked if I had ever read any of those books. I hadn't. He then suggested that if I did read the books I might do better on the tests. I figured, what the heck, I might as well give it a try, but I was skeptical. Then he did something that I have been thankful to him for all my life. He instructed me to report to his office at the end of every school day for a one-hour study period with him as my tutor. I became a student, at the ripe old age of 17. Responsibility was a new word in my vocabulary, and I embraced it with enthusiasm. Well, Mr. Atkinson embraced it and then passed it on to me, somewhat vehemently. He was one of those rare people who really cared about the people he knew. I was just one of the 109 seniors in the school, but one who needed help. He didn't hesitate to provide that help. He was truly a good man.

Mr. Atkinson

The new name of the outhouse at survey summer camp

CHAPTER SIX

SUMMER WORK AND CAMPS

It worked. I got a 3.8 that semester. Several of my teachers were either in shock or very suspicious, as were my classmates, many of whom had known me since birth. Either Bell had suddenly transformed into a smart guy or he had figured out how to cheat. Probably the latter. Anyhow I was going to Washington State University. All was good with the world. Well maybe not so much for the admissions guy who probably had to explain to his boss why I was there.

That summer I worked on a survey crew for the Washington State Highway Dept. We were surveying the North Cross State Highway in North Central Washington. The road went through the Cascade Mountains from Twisp on the East side to Bellingham on the West side. I was a rear chainman/bush whacker working for $15/day. It was the same job, surveying the same road, as my dad had done 33 years earlier. We found their old survey markers and it was amazing how accurate they were after all those years. The big difference was that they built the road this time.

On the first day I was dropped off at the end of the road and told to go find the crew who were between 15 and 20 miles up the trail. When I asked as to how to find them, I was informed they were the only humans in there so it should be easy. With this limited information I started up the trail with some apprehension. I had lots of experience hunting deer and rabbits, but none hunting surveyors.

It turned out it was easy. When within a half mile you could hear the chainsaws. I got off the trail trooped through the brush and found the crew. There were three guys all in their late 30s or early 40s. I reported to the party chief, named Clyde, and asked him what my job was. He replied, "Your job is to do what I tell you to do and to do it quick and well." He handed me the dumb end of the chain and a machete and pointed up the hill. To explain chain nomenclature, on one end of the 100-foot chain the last foot is broken down into tenths, the dumb end of the chain is just a foot. Welcome to the wonderful world of surveying. Clyde was from Boston, so he didn't have the letter R in his vocabulary. He told me one day he had just bought a Dodge Dot. Clyde was a good boss, but he always expected you to do your best. If you didn't he was quick to point out your shortcomings and the consequences of not correcting those faults. He was a very competent surveyor.

We were living in tents about 20 miles from the end of the road. It was hard work. Nine-hour days climbing up mountain sides and cutting brush so the instrument man could see through to lay out the center line and then 300-foot cross sections every 100 feet. The party chief (the boss) would give everyone directions. The instrument man would run the transit and take notes. The rear and head chainmen would measure all the distances with the chain. The head chainman would hold the smart end of the chain while the rear chainman, me, would pull the dumb end of the chain up the mountainside while hacking the brush out of the way. In regard to physical labor I was the only one involved, but hey, $15 a day and all you can eat at every meal. There was not an 18-year-old in the state who wouldn't take that deal.

At the end of the day we packed up our stuff, stashed the survey gear in some brush and hiked a couple of miles to the camp. It was less than luxury accommodations. There was a cooking tent, a dining tent, two sleeping tents and an outhouse constructed of two by fours and tarp suspended over the creek. We got our water out of the creek, upstream of the outhouse. The pack train would come in one time in our nine-day shift with supplies. It was like being on a hunting trip, but with no hunting or beer.

I was assigned to a tent with Big Bob, he weighted over 250 pounds (I was Little Bob), and Orville, a regular small-town guy, high school graduate, lower middleclass and family man. He had no ambition to do any more than earn a decent paycheck to support his family. He was very content with his life. Kenny was the instrument man. He was always studying something. Loved to learn new things. We soon bonded. The standard saying on survey crews was to be nice to the rear chainman as he is most likely a civil engineering student and could be your boss in a few years. So that helped with the bonding thing. They didn't know I had not picked a major yet. Fact is I didn't even know what a major was, probably the guy between a captain and a lieutenant colonel. We were all small-town guys so that entered into the equation.

It was a rather routine existence. We got up at 5:00 AM, had breakfast, packed a lunch and went off to work. Got back at night had dinner, played penny poker for a few hours and went to bed. Did it again the next day. As a teenager I did appreciate the menu. We had pancakes, waffles, bacon, eggs and ham for breakfast. Our lunch was steak sandwiches, fruit, candy and fruit juice. I recall that I had a standard paper lunch sack that was so full you couldn't close the top. Dinner was usually steak, chicken or ham with potatoes, beans, corn bread and pie. I am sure I was consuming at least 6,000 calories a day and not gaining an ounce of weight. You can do that when you are 18 and working hard. For a young guy getting to eat all you want, go fishing every evening and play poker at night, it just don't get any better than that. Nowadays if I walk past a piece of pie, I gain two pounds.

We had a few "incidents" during the three summers I worked on state survey crews. One impacted me for the rest of my life. We got into camp one day after work and were informed the "Engineer" was coming in the next day to see how things were going. He would come out to where we were working so be prepared to answer his questions. Clyde seemed concerned by this information. He didn't play poker that night. He was too busy studying his notes and checking all the calculations. This caused me to have visions of Braveheart riding in on a white steed to inspire the troops. Unlike Clyde, I was looking forward to meeting the main man. Wasn't sure exactly what an engineer did, but it must have been important.

The next day I was halfway up a hillside when the engineer rode up on his rather ordinary gray horse. His name was Al and he seemed like an OK guy. He talked with Clyde for a while, said hello to each of us and then asked me where I was going to school. I told him WSU and he said they had an excellent engineering college and I should do well with a civil engineering degree from there. Up to that point I had not even thought about a major. He rode off into the sunset and we went back to work. I had expected him to be more regal but got over it.

That night I lay in my sleeping bag and thought about what he had said. I considered the fact that all of us walked the 20 miles into camp, he rode a horse. I was told he made considerably more money than anyone on the crew, including Clyde. He also worked in an office in Wenatchee. Finally, he was the boss of all of us. Maybe this engineer thing is not a bad idea. I had taken trigonometry in my junior year and got a "C", so I was all set math wise. I had no idea what a civil engineer did, but I was sure I could figure that out when I got to WSU. That one meeting set the course for my professional and business career. I did end up with a civil engineering degree and practiced professional engineering and land surveying for over 50 years. Al gets credit for planting the seed in my teenage brain, which was fertile ground for seeds of any kind.

The next incident was a little more exciting. I was just dropping off to sleep one night when I noticed someone coming into the tent. I started to ask who it was when Orville came up out of his sleeping bag blasting away with his .357 magnum revolver. I was somewhat taken aback by this and promptly fell off my cot onto the floor of the tent. Then it got really quiet.

Kenny said, "Did you get him?"

Orville said "Yep".

I then inquired as to what the heck was going on and why he shot that guy?

Big Bob said, "It was not a guy it was a bear and it was about to bite your ass off." This information didn't make me feel any better.

About that time Clyde yelled, "There is a bear running around the camp."

Orville reloaded and rushed out of the tent, in his long johns, and started blasting away again. I was totally tangled in my sleeping bag, so it took me a minute or two to get out of the damn thing. When I exited the tent, I had to step over the dead bear I noted another dead bear by the cook tent and Orville standing there with his smoking revolver. It was quite a scene. I had done a lot of hunting in my life, but never for bears inside a tent at night. I was a bit stressed by this situation. Orville was the man, standing over the vanquished intruders, in his long johns with a smoking pistol in his hand.

The whole event took place about 10:00 PM. Clyde told us to skin the bears and throw the carcasses into the creek so they would float away. He then went back to bed perturbed by all the commotion. We were finished about midnight and were up at 5:00AM for breakfast. There was no extra time off for bear shootings. I kept one of those hides and tanned it myself. During the fraternity hell week, the bear hide was the good god Odin and the pledges had to pay homage to it twice a day. The moths got to it 40 years later and I threw it away. The survey bear incident was complete.

Bear rug with Lady

We were running line along the Methow River near Washington Pass. I was chopping brush and giving shots to Kenny on the transit. The routine was to clear a hundred feet or so and then get out my plumb bob, he would get me on line and I would drive a hub (wooden peg) put in a survey tack and then move on while he moved forward to the tack. On one set I came out on a cliff that dropped about 20 feet into a large pool at the bottom of a waterfall. Over thousands of years the water had created this pool in solid rock that was several feet deep. I looked down into the water and could see several fish one of which was HUGE!! I was sure it was a salmon. When the rest of the crew caught up to me, he had dropped down into the deep water so you couldn't see him. My description of the fish and my estimation of its size met with considerable skepticism. We moved on.

We were camped at a place called Lone Fir and it was only about a mile above the falls. That night after dinner I decided to forego poker, took the fishing pole, the only lure we had, a four-inch Daredevil, and headed for the pool. After climbing down to the water level, I flipped the lure out into the middle of the pool. It was instantly hammered by that huge fish. The pole was outfitted with six-pound test line so it took me 30 minutes to subdue that monster. Once he was out of the water, I put him on a stick and headed back to camp.

It was a Dolly Varden and we weighted it at 16 pounds. This made me the local hero for a day. Everybody in camp were singing my praises, well maybe not singing, but I did hear someone say, "That is a big fish." We cut him up and had it for dinner the next night. A few years later I found out that it would have been the state record if we could have got it to an official scale in Wenatchee. It was a chance for fame and glory totally squandered. Sort of like the big rainbows and Mr. James. The endorsements for the pole, line and lure would have been worth more than I made in all three summers working on that crew. Oh well, it was sort of good eating.

In this day and age safety has a high priority on job sites and survey crews, as well it should. In the early 60s, not so much. We were swinging axes, machetes and running chainsaws all day long. No safety glasses, shin guards or anything else to protect our bodies. I recall one time when I was cutting off a limb. I had a double-bladed ax. I raised the ax over my head and then brought it down with considerable force. Well, that ax went through the limb like a hot knife through warm butter and continued right down to the front of my boot. The boot had leather laces that were tied in a knot in the front. The ax cut through the knot, the boot, my heavy wool sock, my skin and stopped before it hit the shin bone. If it hadn't hit the knot it probably would have split the shin bone like a piece of kindling. We put a couple of Band-Aids on the cut and went back to work. I had to buy a new lace for my boot. Other than that, no harm no foul. If this happened on one of our job sites today there would be several safety "professionals" involved, an incident report, a root cause analysis and a lessons-learned discussion. Clyde did note that it was good I didn't break the axe as they do not heal like a leg does. There was no reimbursement for the boot lace and sock. I was out 50 cents on the deal.

George, one of the other college hires, wasn't so lucky the next summer. We were about 17 miles from the end of the road cutting centerline. George was using a machete to cut off a bunch of small trees with about one-inch trunks. He would hit the trunk two or three times to get them cut. The little tree would snap back and forth as he hacked away, fir needles and wood chips were flying all over the place and George was sweating like a democrat at an NRA meeting.

After observing this process for some time Clyde went over and showed him how to bend the tree, putting stress on the trunk, and then it would only take one hack to cut it off. George thanked him for the instruction, problem was Clyde neglected to include in the instructions the fact that because the tree was bent it took much less force to cut it. Therefore, he should swing the machete with considerably less enthusiasm. George grabbed a tree and swung the giant knife as hard as he could. It went through that tree like it was not even there and then continued on to George's right knee and sliced off his kneecap, and the front of his pants, as clean as a whistle. Blood shot out of him like a fire hose and the kneecap went flying into the brush.

We all stared in disbelief for a few seconds but snapped back to reality when George started yelling and jumping around on one leg. Clyde grabbed him, sat him down and started yelling for the first-aid kit. I was told to retrieve the kneecap, which I did with some reluctance. Clyde then put the kneecap back on and wrapped the leg in some bandages. He turned to me and said, "Go get help I am not sure I can stop this bleeding." I took off down that trail like a cat with its tail on fire. This was my sophomore year at WSU, so I was in good shape from being on the wrestling team. I ran that whole 17 miles at full speed, a rooster tail of pine needles and dirt flying out behind me. I am sure it was some kind of mountain trail distance speed record. I was convinced George was going to bleed to death, which kept the adrenalin pumping.

The packers corral was two miles from the end of the road. When I got to the road there was a truck parked with two guys getting out their fishing gear to hike up the trail to fish the creek. I told them what had happened and asked for a ride to the coral. They seemed reluctant to help. They talked it over and finally decided to give me a ride. Damn nice of them to suffer the inconvenience. I neglected to thank them when I got out of their truck.

I got to the packer's place and told them the story. They saddled three horses and we started back up the trail at a full gallop. I hadn't ridden a horse since my junior year in high school and never charging up a rough mountain trail. After a couple of miles my posterior was not doing well, but I hung in there. The adrenaline was still pumping like crazy. We were in about 14 miles when we came upon the crew carrying George down the trail. They had got the bleeding under control by wrapping all their t-shirts around the wound. Not sure what sanitation issues this created. Thankfully, nobody was going to die. I am sure he survived but suspect his desire to work on a survey crew was diminished. He was also not going to ever be a long-distance runner or professional dancer.

The packers put George on my horse and headed back. We never saw him again. Probably found less dangerous summer employment. We went back to work. I was feeling considerable discomfort due to the ride, but kept it to myself until Kenny said, "Hey, Little Bob, you seem to be bleeding out of your butt." This wasn't good news no matter how I looked at it. First of all, I was not going to drop trow with these guys pointing and laughing. Second, it is difficult to do an inspection of your own butt without a mirror and lastly the blood, most likely, indicated a significant loss of hide in a place difficult to bandage. By the time we got back to camp I was in some pain and in a quandary as to what to do. The sympathy from the sensitive crew members was non-existent.

I got some clean underwear and the first-aid kit and adjourned to the river. I stripped down and sat in the cold water for several minutes and then gently felt around to assess the damage. It appeared I had a half dollar size piece of skin missing from the inside of both cheeks. To my humiliation, not only was this a physical injury it was a prime subject for the crew to discuss at length. I managed to get some disinfectant on the wounds and to cover them with gaze pads and medical tape. It was a lesson in body contortion I never want to do again. The crew could be heard laughing away about my predicament so asking one them to help was out of the question. This was a daily ritual for the rest of the tour. When I got home my brother John would change the bandages for me, but physical abuse had to be threatened to get him to do it. He would complain tempestuously the whole time. I was sufficiently healed by the next tour, but the story continued to be told until the summer was over and I went back to WSU. The packers seemed particularly entertained by the story. I have always wondered what became of George. Probably ended up being an accountant.

Another incident was when we lost our substitute head chainman. Big Bob was on vacation, so Fred was taking his place. He seemed like a nice guy, except he didn't play poker, so he was out of the social scene at the camp. He was only in for one tour therefore no one really got to be friends with him. He just did his job and kept to himself.

We were running centerline up in Washington Pass. It was thick forest so both of us were cutting brush with Fred giving Kenny the shot with his plumb bob, as he had the smart end of the chain. We had just cut through some fir trees and Fred was holding his plumb bob in front of him and backing up as Kenny was telling him to go back another 10 feet. Kenny was shooting through a tunnel we had cut in the trees so all he could see was the plumb bob string and Fred's hand. He yelled "Go back another 10 feet" then said, "Where the heck did he go?" I was halfway between them, so I yelled, but no answer. Clyde told me to go find him. I walked out of the trees and noticed there was a cliff about 15 feet from the trees and a plumb bob was laying on the ground at the edge. It didn't take a genius to realize we had a serious problem. I started yelling "Fred fell off the cliff." Clyde came running as did Kenny. We all went and looked over the edge and there was Fred piled up on a bunch of broken rocks the size of suitcases 20 feet below. He didn't look good.

We had to go a mile to get around the cliff and back to Fred. He was really broken up. Once again, I was dispatched to the packers. This time the injuries were too great to use a horse, so a helicopter was sent to take me back in to show them where he was and bring Fred out. It was a much less physically demanding return trip. My butt wasn't negatively impacted this time. Fred had a broken hip, several broken ribs and a cracked collar bone. We never saw him again either. Maybe Fred and George hang out together now. It was my first helicopter ride and I really enjoyed it. I had several helicopters rides, in Vietnam, a years later that were no fun at all.

The last drama had to do with Al, the engineer. Over the course of two summers Al had lost some of his hero status with me. He was the boss of everything, and I was impressed with that, but he also seemed somewhat lazy and aloof. He always rode a horse to camp, he never stayed and had lunch with us and he had little to say except work related stuff. I was still determined to be a civil engineer, but maybe a more personable one than Al, which wouldn't be much of a challenge.

It was the start of our typical nine-day tour. We had been instructed to go up through Washington Pass and then five miles down the other side to pick up some data the design engineers wanted. This was a 30-mile slog, so they provided horses for us to make the trip. I am sure coming up with justification for $20 apiece for horses for surveyors to ride was an issue. I suspect they didn't want us to get used to riding instead of walking. The plan was to ride to the site, gather the data, ride back to camp and send the horses back to the road with the packer. Al was coming with us to make sure we got everything the engineers wanted. This survey data was no different than what we collected all the time without his personal supervision. I suspect the fact it was a nice summer day had something to do with his participation.

When we were leaving the office in Wenatchee, we got a note from Al telling us to saddle a horse for him and to lead it the two miles to the end of the road. He would meet us there in his truck and then ride in with the crew. It seemed to us he should have driven to the coral and saddled his own horse, but we were just surveyors and he was the engineer, so we followed orders.

When we got to the coral there were seven horses. Two for the packers, four for us and one for Al. The packers had already picked their horses, so we had a choice of the remaining five. Two were gentle animals so Clyde took one and Kenny took the other. Seniority rules in these cases. Big Bob took a more spirited horse as did I. That left the last horse which was a semi-broke mustang that nobody wanted to ride, for Al. It took three of us to get him saddled which required half an hour of hard work, as this was one spooky animal. The packer kept hitting him between the ears with a stick to get him to stop bucking, which had limited effect. It was quite the scene. We were assured he would settle down once we got going, although none of us believed it. Our little posse then set out with this less than desirable mount trailing behind. Upon arriving at end of the road, Al was nowhere to be seen. We waited a while and then Clyde told Orville and me to go ahead and they would catch up when he got there.

I was not present when Al arrived, but got the story from Clyde. It seems the horse didn't want Al on his back and kept jumping away when he tried mount up. So he led this less than happy critter over to a large rock and got up on the rock and jumped toward the saddle. Not a good plan. The horse spooked and took off at full speed. Al had his right knee around the saddle horn, his left leg under the horse and both arms around his neck. This is not considered a good riding configuration, particularly with a spooked horse.

In the meantime, Orville and I were crossing a rockslide where the trail was only about a foot wide when there was a commotion behind us. We turned to see Al hanging on the side of a horse in full stampede mode blasting through the forest. It was obvious that if he continued on in that condition, he would hit the slide at a considerable rate of speed. This would most likely result in him and the horse going off the trail and then taking a very long and uncomfortable roll to the bottom of the slide. This also occurred to Al, so he just let go. He hit the ground and the horse's rear legs ran over him. Once relieved of his burden the horse stopped. Which was a good thing because if he had run into us it would have probably resulted in a big ball of horses, gear, and people rolling down the rockslide. It's doubtful that would have turned out well.

Once the situation stabilized Orville and I started laughing. We had never seen anything like that. Orville dismounted and walked back to Al. He was propped up against a log and not looking all that comfortable. When he got to him Al could barely speak. He did manage to say, "I can't breathe." I took off back down the trail to get help, except this time the horse did the running. An ambulance from Twisp was dispatched and hauled him away. He had several broken ribs and a punctured lung. The uninjured horse was returned to the coral, we went on our way, just another day at the office.

The location was named Al point and Kenny made a sign that showed a cowboy on his horse falling through the air with the cowboy pulling back on the reins and shouting, "Whoa, you SOB whoa." The sign was put up the next tour. Don't know if it is still there or not. Al never took another ride with us.

We named a lot of features as we worked along the route. For instance, creeks were named after us. There was a Big Bob Creek and a Little Bob creek. Named another creek after Kenny and a large ravine after Clyde. These were all duly recorded in the field books. Don't know if they made it into actual place name status or not. I need to go drive that road someday just to see how it all turned out and what the creeks are named.

The two summers I didn't work on the Cross-State Highway survey crew was due to summer camps. WSU had a requirement of civil engineering majors to attend a six-week survey summer camp. It was composed of log cabins sleeping six guys each, individual cabins for the professors, a main building containing the mess hall, kitchen and classroom and then there was the outhouse.

The outhouse was a typical engineering inspired building. The term "Engineering inspired" usually involves a lot of math and very little artistic input. There were six toilet seats positioned over holes in a wooden bench. Underneath was a trough leading out to an underground perforated pipe system. At the high end of the trough was a large 75-gallon metal tank with no top. It tapered from a wide top to a narrow bottom that was mounted on a round pipe. A hose fed water into the top of the tank. The tank was designed to be slightly off center so that when it was almost full it would tip over and the water would splash into the trough and wash all the material into the perforated pipe, then a spring would pull it back up into place. This could be a mildly traumatic event if you were seated and not aware of the process. A loud crash and then a tidal wave rushing under your exposed butt is something you have to experience in order to appreciate the drama involved. We learned to always check the tank level before sitting down.

There were 30 of us at the camp and all but one was between our junior and senior years. I had five roommates. One named Scott had a car which was a big deal because we could go into town once a week to hit the bars or go up to Rainier Lodge and hit on the co-eds working there. We were much more successful with the former than the latter. Engineers have a reputation of not being very adept socially. Well, it is true, but we are really good with math. Not sure if socially inept people are drawn to engineering or if engineering classes make you a nerd. Somebody should do a Ph.D. thesis on this.

Scott was up at the lake fishing one day after class and came across a porcupine. He managed to capture it without getting any quills in his hide. I gave this considerable thought and couldn't come up with one good reason to capture a porcupine. Fact was, Scott was not known for his good reasoning ability, even in this crowd. He took the critter back to the cabin and put a leash on it, named him Ralph and tied him to a tree behind the cabin. We were in deep discussions as to what we could do with Ralph. We contemplated turning him loose in Rainier Lodge in revenge for the poor receptions to our overtures to the co-eds. We thought about turning him loose in one of the professor's cabins and many other nefarious ideas. It was all for naught as he was discovered by one of the professors and we were ordered to set him free back at the lake. Said professor escorted us to the lake to assure compliance. I recall all six of us standing by the lake sadly waving goodbye to Ralph as he trundled back into the forest.

This professor wasn't held in high esteem by most of us. The subject he covered at WSU was a requirement for graduation. Problem was his class was awful. He talked about his boat, his garden and a bunch of other stuff we had no interest in whatsoever. Then he would hit us with tests covering the subject we had received little or no instruction on, and now he made us turn Ralph loose. His positive rating among us was in the toilet.

Speaking of toilets, most of the building on college campuses have names and are usually called Halls. Slone Hall is the engineering building at WSU. We decided to name the outhouse after this guy. In the interest of fairness, I will call him Professor Smith to hide his real identity.

We cut a 10-foot-long 18-inch diameter log down the middle with a chainsaw. We then used a chisel to carve out Smith Hall in 12-inch letters on the flat side of the log. The inside of the letters was painted black so they would stand out. Two legs were attached to the log and it was installed in front of the toilet. The outhouse was now Smith Hall, a lot of work, but we figured it was worth it to goon him. The next day at breakfast we were informed as to how proud he was that we named a building after him. His wife took pictures of him with the sign and everything. We were devastated. This guy was too dense to know when he was being gooned or maybe, it was a counter goon. We will never know. We heard from the guys who went the next year that the sign was still there.

We were doing sun shots along the road when a department of fish and game truck full of rainbow trout went by on its way to stock the lake. I didn't have a fishing pole, but I knew Professor Smith had one. That afternoon when we were done surveying, I asked to borrow his pole. He was gracious and let me have it. This was one of those telescoping rods with the closed face spinning reel that you pay $5 for to include line and a lure. I figured the fish in the truck were less than 10 inches long so this less-than-optimal fishing gear would work just fine. Turned out not so much.

Scott and I drove up to the lake got in the boat and started catching fish. Those hatchery fish are pretty dumb, so we were staying busy. I noticed the drag on the reel didn't work. If you pulled any line out against the drag it would go to no drag and then you just had loose line. These were little fish, so they didn't pull out any line therefore it was no problem.

It became a problem when I hooked a five-pound rainbow. This giant fish would take off and the drag would go slack, so I had to pinch the line between my thumb and finger with one hand and hold the pole with the other. This was pushing the envelope in regard to the strength of the pole as well as my dexterity in pinching line and fighting the fish. Scott was rowing the boat as best he could to help in pursuing our quarry. Every time he would stop running, I would click the drag back on and reel like crazy, but he would take off again and then the whole process would be repeated. It was a frenzy of frantic rowing, pinching the line and holding the pole. Obviously, it took a considerable amount of time and profanity to get this fish. He finally gave up and was towed to shore where Scott flipped him up on the bank. We had a trophy.

We drove back to camp to show off our prize. Upon arrival I went to Professor Smith's cabin to return the pole and show him the fish. The fish was behind my back when he came to the door. He asked how we did. I said, "We just got one" and showed him the fish. He got very excited and yelled for his wife to bring the camera. She then took a picture of him with the fish and the pole. I stood to one side wondering what stories he would be telling the next class in his lecture. Probably wouldn't involve me catching the fish. I thanked him for the use of the pole. We then took the fish up to the mess hall and the cook prepared him for Scott and I the next night. Never did get a picture of that fish. The other guys were impressed by Professor Smith's fish.

At the time of the summer camp surveyors were still using transits. One of the classes was how to prepare a new transit for use. It just so happened the department had just received a new instrument. They showed us how to take out the packing tabs and calibrate all the dials as well as many other procedures. This was a morning class. That afternoon we were going out to run a traverse through the woods. It just so happened my crew got the brand-new transit. We had a guy named Cap on the crew. He was about a half bubble out of level and definably not the sharpest knife in the drawer. Don't know how he got through three years of engineering classes, but he was there.

Cap was carrying the transit, attached to the tripod, over his shoulder. We had to cross a creek and there was a big log lying across the water so we could just walk across the log 10 feet above the stream. The creek was just some water running through a lot of rocks. Cap should have gone down the bank and crossed. Instead he took the log route and, of course, lost his balance and dropped the brand-new transit and tripod the 10 feet onto the rocks below.

This was a $750 instrument. My budget for room and board, tuition, books etc. was $950 a semester. The economic ramifications of this situation could be catastrophic. After we were finished yelling at Cap we trudged back to camp with a totally destroyed transit that had never turned a single angle. Our reception was less than cordial. I remember all the professors being quite vehement while screaming at us in unison. Thank goodness we didn't have to pay for it, but I do think it did have a negative impact on our grade for the course.

The camp was an excellent experience for us. Most engineers don't have any practical experience with surveying. That isn't a good thing as they need to know what it takes to survey something so they can compile a good estimate of the cost and time involved. Unfortunately, the university cancelled the program many years ago. I suspect they are now graduating survey challenged engineers.

At the end of survey camp there were six weeks left in the summer break. My grandpa gave me a job, as a bar tender, in the Ring Room Bar at the Bell Hotel. I had no idea of how to tend bar, but hey, nepotism works on occasion. He got all his kid's jobs with the fisheries department in the 1930s and that worked out fine. He assigned me the day shift, 8:00 AM to 4:00 PM. Sometimes it was necessary to work the night shift when Uncle Vic was not available. I was 21 years old, just barely old enough to be in the place. The state liquor inspector came in one night and checked my I.D. A somewhat embarrassing thing to happen to a bar tender.

In the morning I would have to unlock the front door of the hotel restaurant, then the door to the Ring Room, then the cash register and finally the liquor cabinet. There was an old retired navy chief who spent 20 years in the navy as a lock pick. Three or four days a week I would find him and one of his cohorts sitting at the bar with drinks in front of them and everything locked up. The money for the drinks was in the cash register. He had unlocked all four locks, poured the drinks, put the money in the till and then locked it all back up. I assumed they brought their own ice.

Most of the patrons were friends of my folks and had known me since birth. This made it difficult to pick up their drinks at closing time. They would use the old "I used to change your diapers; you are not going to take my drink" line. I would then explain that they didn't change Grandpa's diapers. This was his business that the liquor board would shut down if we got caught with drinks on the table after closing hours. Grandpa was a person who was a great friend to have and a horrible enemy to deal with. I never had a problem picking up drinks after playing the grandpa card. Still got the stink eye.

A little old nurse would come in twice a week around 3:30 PM in her white nurse's uniform and have two straight shots of Jim Beam. I assumed she was done with her shift at the hospital. Drinks were 50 cents apiece so she put out a dollar and I would bring her the first drink and change for the dollar. She would drink it and then order another. Then she would leave. I don't recall her saying much, and she kept to herself.

One day when I brought her the second drink, she looked at me and said, "You are Bobby Bell, aren't you?" I replied that indeed I was. She then said, "I was walking across the street near The Rock Tavern 15 years ago and you were coming the other way. I said, "Hi" and you spit on me." My checkered past had resurfaced.

I didn't remember the incident, but I was only six at the time. I frantically searched for a reply and only came up with my usual dodge and said, "I am sure I wouldn't have done that, I bet it was my brother John." I had great success in blaming John for my indiscretions. She didn't buy it. She informed me she chased me home and reported me to Mom. I am thinking this has been festering in her mind for 15 years, what is she going to do now? I figured I could mollify her with the second drink, so I told her it was on me. That didn't work either. She informed me that the price of the drink would come out of grandpa's pocket not mine. This was one tough old lady who was cutting me no slack.

I didn't know what to do as all the other patrons in the place were focused on us by now. I left the 50 cents on the table and retreated behind the bar. The next time I looked she was gone, and the money was still on the table. One of the guys sitting at the bar looked at me and said, "You spit on her?" Then the whole place broke into laughter. It was a very embarrassing incident for me. She continued to come in, but the subject was never brought up again. I filled her glass to the top every time.

Another interesting lady was Mrs. Blair. The juke box played three songs for a quarter. She would show up and put in three quarters and play the song "Chug a Lug" nine times. She would sit there and nurse her beer through the songs and then leave. Everyone hated it when she came in and some would just head out the door. This wasn't good for business or mental health. What was going on with this lady?

I finally had to ask her what the deal was with that goofy song. She explained that she was at the Town Tavern two years prior with her husband of 40 years. He was sitting on a bar stool and had a heart attack, fell off the stool and died. "Chug a Lug" was playing on the juke box. The song brought up memories of him. After that whenever she came in, I would announce the purpose of the song to everyone. They were all more tolerant of the situation. It was still difficult to sit through nine "Chug a Lugs."

The Washington State Blue laws were in effect in those days. One of the laws was that women couldn't sit at the bar. They had to sit at a table. Never did figure out what was the purpose of that law.

One night I was covering for Uncle Vic because he was not feeling well. His apartment was next door to the hotel. At one end of the Ring Room was the bar with six stools and the juke box. In the middle of the joint was an archway. There were four tables on one side of the arch and two on the other. The place was full that night, so every seat was taken. I wasn't an experienced bar tender, so it took me longer to mix drinks because I had to look some of them up in the book. This caused some problems with tempers, including mine. I wasn't having a good night. Unfortunately, it got worse.

I had six guys sitting at the bar two of whom had graduated from Ephrata High School three or four years ahead of me, so I knew them. It was obvious that they had not parlayed their high school diplomas into significant financial success. They were having a verbal dispute that was threatening to escalate into a physical confrontation which was a rather common occurrence in Ephrata. I was trying to negotiate a truce with marginal success. In the meantime, everyone was calling for drinks, so my control of the room was tenuous at best. This required delivering drinks on the run and then back to the bar to referee the dispute. About this time one of the women sitting at a table, as required by the blue law, next to the archway threw up on the floor right where I needed to get through to serve the other four tables. Her husband started yelling at her and the other guy at the table told him to shut up. He didn't respond well to that instruction. That was when my two friends at the bar escalated the dispute to the physical level. There is now a full-blown fight going on at the bar, another fight about to start at the table and a puddle of puke in the middle of the whole thing. The situation was deteriorating at an accelerating rate.

I picked up the phone and called Uncle Vic and said if he wasn't in the bar in five minutes, I was shutting it down and hung up. Next call was to the cops. The police station was a block away, so they got there about the same time as Uncle Vic. The cops hauled the two pugilists off to jail, a place they were quite familiar with. They then escorted the puker and her friends out of the bar and informed Uncle Vic he needed to maintain better control in the bar, which got me an intense stare.

I determined at that point that my decision to be an engineer, rather than a bar tender, was quite sound.

The other summer camp was Army ROTC (Reserve Officers Training Corps) camp at Fort Lewis Washington. This was also a six-week commitment. We were all officially privates in the U.S. Army and they treated us accordingly. It was a boot camp for all practical purposes. We were living in army barracks, wearing army uniforms, eating army food and being terrorized by real army sergeants. Fort Lewis is in Western Washington. The joke was if you can see Mount Rainier it is going to rain, if you can't see it then it's raining. Growing up in arid Eastern Washington I wasn't used to this much water in the air.

We had been on a maneuver for about four days, living in pup tents and eating out of mess kits. There were no shower facilities. It was a miserable existence. Trying to eat while sitting in the mud, wearing your poncho with the rain falling into your food isn't a pleasant culinary experience. We had just got back to camp after being run ragged for 12 hours when the rain turned into a torrent. I had never seen rain like that in my life. We had a guy in the platoon from the University of Washington who was an odd duck, but aren't they all? He grabbed a bar of soap, stripped off his clothes and started taking a shower. Soon all of us were naked as jay birds soaping up in the good Lord's shower stall. Our hard-hearted sergeants stood by and laughed their heads off. It was one of the few times we saw them smile. There was no need to towel off as our uniforms were already soaking wet. We just put them back on and sat back down in the mud. It was nice to be clean, if only for a minute or two. It was an introduction to the life of a solder. You make do with what you have.

The Army threw everything they could at us, but we hung in there. Only one guy in our platoon quit. The food was terrible, the accommodations were sparse, the management was surly, the pay was miniscule, we were run into the ground every day and the entertainment was nonexistent. Other than that, it was enjoyable.

The one fun thing we had was an event the military called a mad minute. It is quite a show. One morning they took us to some temporary grandstands on the edge of a huge field. There were some old cars and trucks and sandbag bunkers in the middle of the field. Once we were all situated in the bleachers two companies of infantry took up a position in front of us facing the objects. We sat there wondering what they were going to do. After a few minutes they opened up with M14 rifles, M30 machine guns and M79 grenade launchers. We all thought that was cool. They were shooting up those cars big time. What happened next set us all back on our heels.

Several batteries of artillery opened up from somewhere a long way from us because we didn't hear the guns going off. The result was the whole field blew up in a spectacular bombardment of 155 howitzer rounds. Not one square inch of that field was spared. Just as we were recovering from that jolt to the ear drums and eyeballs several F-4 jets steaked in and dropped napalm. Then more artillery and infantry fire. It seemed the whole world was blowing up right in front of us. This went on for one minute, but it seemed like much more. When the smoke cleared there was nothing left of the bunkers and vehicles, but a few spare parts laying around the field. The whole place was pock marked with artillery craters. We were all impressed regarding the fire power of the U.S. military. I saw it put to use for real a couple of years later.

The whole experience of the six- week course was kind of a blur. We were gently woken up at five o'clock in the morning by the sergeant screaming at us while beating on the lid of a garbage can with a stick. I guess the Army couldn't afford alarm clocks. Then it was into the latrine to shave etc. and finally get dressed and form up in front of the barrack. They then double timed us to the mess hall where there was a chinning bar in front of the door. You had to do 10 chin ups prior to going in. I guess this was to stimulate our appetites. We then dined on the gourmet menu. The term "gourmet" is definitely subject to interpretation in this case. We did 10 pull ups on the way out and double timed it back to the barrack. We were allotted 15 minutes to make our beds (the blankets had to be so tight you could bounce a quarter off them), put our stuff away and clean up our area. We formed up outside and were taken off to whatever torture they had planned for us. At the end of the day we did the same routine for dinner and spent the next two hours scrubbing down everything in the building. We then went to bed. The next day was a repeat performance. If you treated civilian employees like this, they would put you in jail.

I have always wondered why the Army wanted those barracks so clean. In the two years I spent on active duty I never saw an Army facility that clean. In fact, in Vietnam I never saw anything that could be described as "clean" by any standard. I can't imagine that it was just to harass us. In retrospect, it was good training to be treated like enlisted people, it made us better officers.

After Fort Lewis I had six weeks left in the summer break. I lucked out and got on a survey crew for the state. It wasn't the North Cross State Highway, but it was with a crew working out of Okanogan Washington. I was allowed to live in the highway facility. It was a dorm for four people, a small office, a ten vehicle garage and a toilet. I was the only one living there. The term "extremely spartan" springs to mind. The crew would all meet there in the morning and we would be off to work. This was a five day a week gig.

I was getting a free room, so food was my only expense. I determined that I would exist on $1 a day. My pay was $23/day so I would net $22. As noted above my room and board at the fraternity was $85/month so every four days I would cover a month. Eating on a dollar a day even in 1965 was a challenge. Particularly for a 22-year-old who is working hard every day. The meals at Lone Fir Camp were a vague memory.

Okanogan is a small town of about 2,500 people in Northeastern Washington and it had a few restaurants, but the best buy for me was the Caribou Hotel Café. They would sell me a plate of French fries with beef gravy for a buck. The waitress soon figured out this was my only meal of the day, so the plate of French fries kept getting bigger. She would usually throw in a beef patty or some other extra. I also started getting invitations to have dinner with various families around town. I am sure as a result of said waitress spreading the word about the one meal a day kid. At one of these dinners I met Gary who was going to WSU that fall. He was encouraged by me to pledge the fraternity. He ended up being my little brother. The survey crew brought me donuts in the morning. I was doing great at meeting my goal. I also picked a few apples in the local orchards to tide me over. I was quite successful in my $1/day quest. The town had adopted me. Small town America was really special in those days. Still is most places.

I had one big exception to the dollar a day goal. A few miles from Okanogan is Omak Washington. Every summer they have a big celebration and rodeo called the Omak Stampede. I budgeted $5 for this event. In those days it was a real blow-out. I suspect it still is.

They have a race where a bunch of drunk cowboys and a few Colville Native Americans (equally impaired) saddle up on their ponies and race several hundred feet down a 45-degree dirt bank into the Okanogan River and then swim across the river. The first one, still on his horse, to the finish line on the rodeo grounds won. Several of the contestants didn't make it to the river as they ended up rolling down the bank with their horses. A few ended up downstream various distances, depending on how quick the rescue guys could get to them and some made it to the finish line. Never found out what they won, but doubt if it was much. I think this race is why they call the event the Omak Stampede. I don't recall anyone, or any horses being injured. I always figured that in order to participate in this fine athletic event you needed to find a horse with a very low IQ. The IQ of the guy on his back had to be quite a bit lower. A few of the horses and most of the guys in Eastern Washington qualified.

In addition to the rodeo there are several other events, carnival rides, lots of food, a parade and a big dance on Saturday night. People came from all over the state to participate. Two of my high school buddies Rick and Ernie showed up on Saturday from Ephrata and we made plans to attend the dance. I had a 1950 Nash sedan. Not really a chick mobile, but semi-adequate transportation. The battery didn't work so it was parked on a steep road near the dance venue so I could pop the clutch to get it started. We then embarked on a quest to secure some beer which involved bribing a local ne'er- do- well to buy it for us as we were not 21. We drank some of the beer, put the rest in the car and went to the dance. The Ephrata guys were in courting mode and we had beer.

It was a huge dance. There must have been a couple thousand people there. Two bands and lots of girls. We split up and turned on the small-town charm. Over the next couple of hours all three of us had picked up a girl. This was a rare occurrence for us. Usually only one or none of us would find a companion and that was when we were courting girls we grew up with. Of course, there was the factor that these girls didn't know us where the Ephrata girls did and were forewarned.

All three of the women were big city girls from Seattle but didn't know each other. We advised them that we had some beer. With this revelation our attractiveness went up four-fold. We all adjourned to the car. Six people in a 1950 Nash is somewhat crowded. We drank beer for a while and then decided to go up to a nearby lake. Things were looking good for the three amigos. I let off the brake and popped the clutch and the Nash roared to life. I then promptly drove off the road and rolled three times to the bottom of the bank. We landed right side up. The inside of the car was full of some really upset girls, a lot of spilled beer and considerable debris from the bank and car contents. We all piled out of the car and our dates immediately disappeared into the darkness on a dead run back to town. We never saw them again. Rick remarked, "Well, that didn't go well."

It is hard to pop the clutch on flat ground when the car has just rolled down a hill so we didn't try. The only option was to limp back to the dance, get cleaned up and try again with the girl thing. The word was out on us, so we failed miserably.

When the dance was over, we walked to the D.O.T. facility and planned our next move.

We agreed to find somebody to jump start the car and then drive it back behind the dorm where it could be repaired and cleaned up. A good plan. We were out of beer, so it was into the bunks for a good night's sleep.

The next morning, we got up bright and early around 11:00 AM and went to find a jump. Arriving at the scene of the accident we noted that during the night the car had disappeared. Who would steal a beat up 1950 Nash? It was a short walk to the state trooper's office to report it stolen. Upon approaching their building, we noted the Nash in their fenced yard. It was agreed that this was a bad sign. The car was registered to me, so I had no choice but to go in and see what was up. Our record of dealing with law enforcement was spotty, therefore the chances of this going well were not great

The first question was if we were 21 or not. The answer was no. Then the trooper inquired as to the beer in and throughout the area near the car. We had no idea how that got there must have been some people who came by after we left. It was obvious he was not buying our story. We then gave him a line about rolling down the bank and leaving the car to find help just to come back and find it gone. That didn't seem to sell either. It wasn't looking good for us. He then turned to Rick and asked if he was any relation to a trooper sergeant by the same name. You could see Rick's mind racing, but coming up with nothing, he said "Yes." The whole dynamic of the investigation changed dramatically. It went from you guys are going to get busted for illegal consumption and possession to we are calling your dad and advising him to come and get you. I think Rick would have preferred to go to jail. One thing was sure, the party was over.

Rick's dad showed up in uniform, in a very bad mood, and driving a state trooper car. After berating us for an extended period of time he took Rick and Ernie back to Ephrata leaving me to negotiate the release of my car. They took pity on me after the ordeal I had just gone through with the sergeant and gave me a jump start. I drove my very crumpled car back to the dorm. It never moved again. Sold it at the end of the summer for $45 and went back to school as a pedestrian. The killing service was doing well so used some of that money to buy a 1955 Chevy for $200. I was back in the saddle.

Delta Tau Delta fraternity slingshot

CHAPTER SEVEN

COLLEGE YEARS

I began my college career by driving that Nash from Ephrata to Pullman with two of my buddies, Tank and Lloyd. They drove it back to Ephrata for me as there was no place to keep it at WSU. I opted to go through fraternity rush, can't recall why. It was a very new experience for me. Some fraternities seemed to be interested in me, others not so much. I didn't feel comfortable with any of them with one exception, Delta Tau Delta. This house was full of a bunch of small- town hicks just like me. I pledged to the house and to my surprise, they accepted me. If you have seen the movie, "Animal House," that was us. A bunch of ding bats doing crazy things. Even our house looked similar. I was assigned a big brother named Orlin, a math major, and put in a study room with two sophomores. Study hours were 6:00 PM to 9:30 PM Sunday to Thursday. I enrolled in the civil engineering program, to the surprise of everyone who knew me, except Mr. Atkinson. I was now a college man.

I recall in the first week the College of Engineering had a freshman orientation lecture for all engineering students. The professor giving the talk, Emmett Moore, told us all about the various programs and facilities etc. then at the end of the lecture he asked each of us to look at the person on either side and the person behind and in front. He then said, "They won't be here when you graduate." I noticed that four guys were looking at me. Not a good feeling. He was right. Out of 600 freshman engineering students 112 of us got our engineering degrees. When classes started, I was somewhat distressed that the fraternity had study hours. Sitting at a desk for three and a half hours every night wasn't in my college social plan. Drinking, chasing co-eds and junk food was. Turns out this policy saved my bacon.

My decision to go into engineering was impulsive and based on my experience on the survey crew. The only math I had taken in high school was trigonometry. No algebra, calculus or anything else. I was hanging 10 regarding the other engineering students. It was necessary to take remedial algebra just to enroll in the calculus course. Another piece of luck, my big brother was a math major and he helped me a lot. I signed up for the beginning calculus course the second semester. It was all Greek to me. I had no idea what an integral or a derivative was, and it didn't look good in regard to me ever figuring it out. Orlin did his best to clue me in with limited success.

I went home for Thanksgiving break and walked into my dad's office to announce I was going to change my major to economics. He said, "If you get a degree in economics you will end up working for the government all your life, not good. Bell men are businesspeople not government employees." About that time Uncle Vic walked in and immediately backed Dad up. He always did. Those two were thick as thieves, regardless of the tricycle incident. We argued for over an hour, but I stuck to my guns. Dad then said, "Lets continue this talk at dad's house." Told him it wouldn't change anything, but OK. We adjourned to Grandpa's. I should have known better. They were bringing in the big gun.

We had continued the debate for a few minutes when grandpa showed up. He was the kind of guy you felt like you should stand up when he walked in the room. He had a well-deserved air of authority. He sat down and asked what was going on. Dad quickly briefed him on the situation. Dad, Uncle Vic and I then resumed our debate. After a few minutes, Grandpa interrupted us and turned to me and said, "Son, how are you paying for college?" I told him that I worked for the highway department in the summers, had my killing service and Mom and Dad filled in when I came up short.

He then locked eyes with me, and I felt a chill go down my spine. In a very calm voice, he informed me that I had the job with the state because the district engineer was a friend of his and he asked him to hire me. He then advised me that Dad sold real estate and insurance in town because he backed him up financially when needed and referred a lot of business to him. If he told the district engineer to dump me and Dad to not back me up financially, they would have no choice but to do just that. He then inquired how I planned to stay in college with no money. I was also advised if my butt were not in college I would be drafted within a month. Next statement was, "You have two choices, stay in college and study engineering or be a private in the Army, in Vietnam." He then got up and left.

I sat there stunned for some time. I turned to Dad and said, "Can he do that?"

Dad said, "Yep. So, I guess that is it. I am going back to work" and he and Uncle Vic walked out. I figured out calculus with considerable help from Orlin. Grandpa was at my graduation, all smiles and very proud of his grandson, the engineer

Most of us in the house were technical majors like engineering, math, pre-med, biology etc. None of us were that smart so we had to study a lot. The few times a year we did cut loose were usually dramatic. A bunch of geeks from small towns with few social skills unleashed on a college campus had a myriad of ways for things to go bad. I will relate a few of the more noteworthy.

One of the guys came up with 40 feet of surgical tubing. We pondered how we could use this material to its best advantage. After several failed attempts to put it to a practical use. Huey came up with a brilliant idea, that had a few drawbacks as we were to discover. He suggested we make a huge slingshot out of the tubing. He was a pre-law major so being as I was an engineering major it was my responsibility to cover the construction phase. We took the leg from a pair of jeans and attached it to the middle of the tubing. We then got up on the roof of our three-story fraternity house. We had two pledges hold the ends of the tubing at one end of the roof while we pulled the middle of the tubing with the jean leg back to the other end of the roof thereby stretching the tubing. We then put a water balloon in the pant leg and let it fly. The first time we tried this the acceleration was too much and the balloon burst before it got to the edge of the roof. After several tries, we figured the balloons should only be three quarters full when launched. This allowed the material to stretch without breaking. We now had an operational slingshot and a couple of very wet and traumatized pledges.

Once we had the engineering figured out, we moved to target selection. The Pi Phi sorority was a block away. They had a sun deck on the back of their house, an ideal target. It took a while, but we finally got to where we could launch a water balloon over the Quad (a three-story women's dorm), located between us and the sorority, and onto their sun deck two out of three times. They had no idea where those water balloons were coming from. There was no line of sight between them and us. This was a perfect prank. I was dating a Pi Phi so discretion was required on my part, but did allow us to get feedback due to her complaining about the barrage.

Just getting them wet was not enough for us. It was taken up a step. We put a balloon full of Old Spice inside a water balloon and sent it over to the Pi Phi's. It then became an obsession for us to find interesting, but not dangerous fluids to put in the water balloons. We were really enjoying our new toy. Then we made the big mistake that resulted in its demise.

We came up with the great plan of tying a rope to the pant leg and then pulling it down from the roof to the ground. Now we can launch stuff straight up into the sky. So. what to launch that won't come down and hurt someone? A water balloon was too mundane. Once again Huey stepped up with a great idea. We would tape a firecracker to an egg with a band aid and send it up over the campus. The firecracker would go off and break the egg thereby raining egg down on the student body as they were walking to class. It worked like a charm. Charm is probably not the right word because as we found out nobody, other than us, was charmed by the egg shower.

We had been launching eggs for a couple of days and were in the process of a launch when the Dean of Men walked around the corner of the house and said, "So you are the idiots who have been throwing egg at everybody." Seeing as how we were standing there with the stretched slingshot and holding the pant leg with the egg and firecracker in it, denial wasn't really an option. The situation deteriorated a little more when the firecracker exploded splattering egg on most of us. Being an engineering major, I wasn't much into psychology, but it seemed to me the Dean was putting on a very stern face while trying to not laugh or show admiration for our device. He supervised us as we cut the tubbing into two-inch pieces and then advised us that if we had another incident it wouldn't go well. He then returned to his castle. The slingshot era was over.

In the 1960s there was a tradition on many campuses, including WSU, called the senior ride. The underclassmen would capture the seniors and haul them off to some remote place where they would be dumped. Often with no money and no shoes. They had to figure out how to get home. It was all good clean fun, except for the victims. The seniors in our house cut a deal back in the 1950s. If the underclassmen would forego the senior ride, they would buy the beer for a party at a place called Rattlesnake Springs located north of Moscow, Idaho. This was a seldom used campground with a small pond. The age group of this party went from 18 to 22 years, mostly under 21. We would arrive at the springs unload several kegs of beer, hot dogs and other snacks and then party hardy. It sometimes got quite drunk out. Fact is it always got quite drunk out. In those days, the term "designated driver" was unknown. Once the beer was gone, we would drive back to Pullman somewhat impaired, usually without incident, with one, rather dramatic, exception.

I think it was my junior year, and we were returning to the house. While our caravan was driving down the main drag of Moscow, Idaho we came up with the grand idea of doing a three man moon out of the back window of the car. I think the beer consumption may have influenced this decision. That is only speculation on my part as I was in the front seat and only peripherally involved in the decision tree. I just assumed they had done their due diligence regarding this action. They hadn't

After some fumbling around the plan was put into motion. The moon lasted about two minutes and was observed by several citizens with varying reactions to the spectacle. We then proceeded out of Moscow and to the Washington/Idaho border. It was then five more miles to the fraternity. We were in the back parking lot of the house and in the process of unloading the empty kegs when the campus police pulled up and said they had some questions. All of us who were under 21 adjourned into the house leaving the seven seniors, who were of age, to explain how they had drunk five kegs of beer by themselves. The campus cops explained to them that one of the cars behind us in Moscow was a local preacher, his wife and young children. He wasn't amused by our performance and had reported us to the Idaho State Troopers who, unbeknownst to us, pursued us to the state line. They then called the Washington State Troopers who tried to intercept us but were too late. They turned the chase over to the campus cops who were now discussing the issue with our senior class. It is reassuring to know our law enforcement agencies work together so well.

Our guys started out by denying having ever been to Idaho as we had all the potatoes we needed. They then informed the cops that the underclassmen were just helping them unload the kegs but hadn't been involved with the drinking. For some reason, the police were a little skeptical of their feckless explanation. They informed the seniors that they wanted to talk to the rest of us and stormed into the house. Unfortunately, for them, we had all gone out the front door by that time and were scattered to the winds. After considerable pontification and somewhat bellicose threats they left. Another bullet dodged. One of many.

Seeing as how we were all a bunch of geeks; we had a rather tenuous relationship with the co-eds in the sororities and women's dorms. We compensated for it with humor. Every year there was a grand celebration called "Hurray Hurray for the 8th of May." A huge poster was made for the front of the house that always had pictures of daisies and two pairs of bare feet and "Hurray Hurray for the 8th of May" in two-foot-high letters. Small copies were taped to the doors of all the women's living quarters. They all thought it was cute until they found out the whole poem was "Hurray Hurray for the 8th of May, outdoor intercourse begins today." Things were a little more proper in those days, so the signs were quickly removed from their doors, by scowling house mothers. This celebration spread throughout the region over the years. It was our contribution to the social fabric of the Pacific Northwest. I observed a sign at a local business in Anchorage in 2009. The tradition was still alive.

We had another tradition in the house called the freshman sneak. This involved the freshmen vandalizing the house and then taking off, for the weekend, to someplace neat. The vandalism was mostly super-ficial as the freshmen would have to clean it up when they got back. Not sure of the reasoning here. Why trash it if you must clean it up, but then we were not known for our reasoning abilities. My freshman year we not only messed up the house, but we took all the toilet seats and gave them to the Pi Phi sorority. They were perplexed as to our intent. Most sororities viewed us with suspicion. One non-freshman was in the house when we left so we tied him up, gagged him and put him in a closet. They didn't find him until late that night when they heard him kicking the wall. He forgave us, but we still felt bad. Not really.

When we returned, we cleaned up the house, but the Pi Phis wouldn't give back the toilet seats without a serenade. This problem was solved by our two music majors. They composed a song about the toilet seats. I can't recall the whole song, but I think the chorus went something like this, "Oh toilet seat, oh toilet seat how we miss your comfort sweet. In the morning at the break of dawn we have nothing to sit on." It went on for three or four verses, but my memory fails me as to what they were. The toilet seats were eventually returned, but for some reason they had been painted pink. Even with the new color they worked just fine. I was in the house for three more years and we always had those pink toilet seats. New pledges moved in each year, but seldom inquired as to the color selection.

Every year we would elect a "Sally Sunshine" who would be the social advisor for the house. Several women from various sororities would compete for this high status position. It was a fun event and the successful person would get to know all of us like a whole herd of brothers over the course of the year. We were always trying to do nice things for her. We would send flowers on her birthday, chocolates on Valentine's Day etc.

The university had a huge farm used for research. One day we were at the farm and noticed a couple dozen white rabbits in a pen. Some of them were maybe a year old and were quite cute. We combined our intellect and came up with a great plan. We would return to the farm that night and steal one of the bunnies and then give it to Sally Sunshine. That was the plan, simple and, as it turned out, stupid.

It was around midnight when we sneaked onto the farm and kidnapped a bunny. Fig leaf, the kid from Okanogan, was carrying the critter on his chest with both arms wrapped around it. Part of our escape route was across the football field. It was very dark so you couldn't see anything. We were running across the field, because we were in a hurry to get back to the house. You don't expect to run into anything on a football field. Well Fig Leaf did find something. He ran full bore into a blocking dummy. The bunny didn't survive the collision. Nor did Fig Leaf's shirt. Bunny innards just don't wash out. We picked up Fig Leaf after a suitable pause in respect for the rabbit, retraced our steps to grab one of his siblings. This rabbit made it safely to the house. The next day we went to the Chi Omega house and presented the bunny to Sally Sunshine. She fell in love with the little guy instantly. We walked back to the house feeling really proud of ourselves. The house mother called the next day and informed us, in a very stern fashion that the rabbit wouldn't be taking up residence in the sorority. We were instructed to come and retrieve it within the hour. Sorority house mothers were a frightening group of older women you didn't want to cross. Our sweetheart was devastated that she had to part with her new pet. Being good guys we told her we would care for the critter at our house and she could visit him anytime she wanted.

We built a pen in the laundry room and a couple of pledges were put in charge of his care and feeding. Unfortunately, we picked two pledges who had never been on a farm or had a pet. The rabbit was dead within a week. The bunny survival rate with us wasn't great. We debated going and getting another one from the farm. After considering our rabbit survival record, we rejected the plan. Sally Sunshine was told it had broken out of its pen and escaped into the wilds of Eastern Washington. The rabbit saga was over.

Our propensity for accidently abusing animals had one more, much more dramatic, episode. It was a Saturday night and we were talking about what we could do to get even with the Chi Omega house mother for kicking out Sally Sunshine's rabbit. We considered various plans as a certain amount of beer was consumed. This resulted in some marginal plans, as it always did.

The one we settled on involved another visit to the university farm. This carefully thought out plan was to steal a young pig, transport it to the Chi Omega house, climb up the fire escape to the third-floor dorm, and release the pig into the dorm through the window. We would then disappear into the dark of night. The number of scenarios of this going wrong substantially outnumbered those of it going well. The ladder to the dorm was totally vertical and had a cage around it. So, you climbed up the ladder inside the cage. This, among several other things, turned out to be an issue

The team picked to deliver the pig was composed of Huey (six foot five inches and 285 pounds), and me (five foot nine and 120 pounds) Mutt and Jeff. Huey was my best friend. We went hunting and fishing together. Double dated with our girlfriends and did a lot of bar hopping. He was a good guy but did tend to get in bar fights on occasion. I often ended up as collateral damage. His real name was Steve, but we called him Huey after the cartoon duck that was popular at the time. The rest of the team had fallen prey to the beer to a greater extent than we had, rendering them not sufficiently functional for this task. As we approached the Chi Omega house, we were quite confident. I am sure the beer was some help in this regard. The pig was very calm, he seemed to be OK with the adventure. Huey put the critter under his arm and started up the ladder with me following close behind. We reached the five-foot square landing at the window to the dorm without incident. Huey leaned through the window and placed the pig on the floor then gave him a nudge. It didn't move. He nudged him again with the same result. I think Porky may have realized that he was involved in a nefarious plot and was considering his options.

Old Delta Tau Delta fraternity house

Even though having consumed several beers I had what seemed, at the moment, to be an excellent idea. I pulled out my pocketknife and reached through the window intending to poke the reluctant animal to get him to move. Problems arose when my hand slipped on the window frame and I plunged the knife a couple of inches into the pig's butt. His response was immediate and dramatic. He took off running between the beds of slumbering co-eds, while squealing and spewing blood in significant quantities. Simultaneously Huey and I determined we should exit the scene.

I then made a tactical error and started down the ladder ahead of Huey. Apparently, he was in a bigger hurry than I was so his 285 pounds slammed into my 120 pounds about halfway down thereby dislodging me from the ladder. I managed to slow my fall by grabbing at the cage on the way down. I landed with considerable impact on one foot at the bottom of the ladder which sprained my ankle rendering me unable to stand or run. I conveyed this information to Huey who was in full running mode after clamoring over my prostrate body. He stopped, hesitated a moment as he considered his options. Finally came back, slung me over his shoulder and ran back to the house with the sounds of total chaos coming from the dorm. We were never apprehended, but Sally Sunshine did mention the incident the next time she was visiting us. We concurred with her that it was a terrible thing to do. Our sympathy was contrived, but she didn't notice. All our brothers considered us heroes. The pig survived and was returned to the farm by the authorities.

The pledges had several duties in the house. They did the janitorial work, kept the lawn and parking lot clean and most anything else of a menial nature that needed to be done. One job was wake up duty.

Everyone slept in one dorm room. It had three tiered bunks. We each had a round tag with our name on it. You would put your tag on a nail in the door that had the time you wanted to be woken up. A pledge would then wake you up at the appointed time. I had the wake- up duty one day. It was 6:30 AM and I was walking down the very thin aisle between the bunks. One of our seniors, named Terry, was an applied music major, in other words he was majoring in violin. He was a weird duck. Proceeding down the aisle looking for the 6:30 wake ups I was startled when he vaulted out of his top bunk and landed right in front of me in a crouch, causing me to freeze in mid step. He was obviously still asleep. He then said, "Don't worry mom I'll get him." Resulting in my immediate exit from the dorm room. Several members were late for morning classes that day.

Having been on the wrestling team in high school, upon arriving at WSU it was natural to turn out for the team. Freshmen don't get many matches. This made it rather boring. I wasn't sure I would try out again. The next year my high school coach took over as the WSU coach, so I ended up wrestling for Mr. James for seven years.

Every year we had a match with the University of Washington. The rivalry between these two schools is very intense. There is an old Cougar saying, "I only root for two schools, the WSU Cougars and whoever is playing against the University of Washington dawgs." This was a big match. I think we won, but it didn't go well for me. I was in the third, and final period, and was ahead of the Husky six to nothing. I had complete control of this guy, so I got complacent. With 30 seconds to go he got me in a hold I couldn't get out of and pinned me to win the match. As I walked back to our bench everyone was looking at me with the "What the ……" look. It was the worst day of my life up to then. The coach didn't speak to me for two days. I think he was even more upset with this than with the Bank's Lake fish deal.

I look back on the training we did and wonder how that would go over today. The gym was built in the 1940s. It had granite stairways. The coach would have you put a guy from the next lower weight class on your shoulders and then run up and down three flights of stairs. A fall on those hard steps would have probably resulted in serious injuries. No one ever fell, but it did cross my mind a couple of times, particularly when I was the guy being carried. We would also arch up on our heels and the back of our heads and then roll our neck so that we could touch our nose to the mat. I don't know how someone never broke a neck.

Due to wrestling practice I would get back to the house after the dinner hour. George was on the gymnastics team and got back at the same time. Eva, our cook, would have our dinner waiting in the kitchen when we got there. She would have gone home a half hour earlier. Several times we would find our dinner had been misappropriated by one of our fraternity brothers. We never did catch him, but if we had I would have wrestled him to the ground and George would have done a back flip on his head. In a house full of 18 to 22-year-old men food is a precious commodity and must be closely guarded.

There were lots of hunting opportunities around Pullman. We hunted deer at Steptoe Butte and along the Snake River. We hunted pheasants in the fields around the campus and chuckars in Wawawai Canyon. It was tough hunting in Wawawai Canyon. Chuckars are a partridge that loves to run, particularly uphill. The canyon is very steep and probably 1,000 vertical feet of basalt rock and sagebrush from the bottom to the ridge tops. So, you ended up chasing the birds to the top of the ridge and then they would flush. You might get one of two out of the flock. The survivors would then glide back to the bottom requiring you to hike back down to start the process over. We really earned those birds.

One day we arrived at the canyon and noted hunting parties up on the ridge tops on both sides. They would flush the birds who would then fly down to where we were. We piled out of the Nash and loaded the guns. As the birds flew past us we would knock a few out of the flock. Then the other hunters would flush a flock and we would get a couple more. It was the easiest chuckar hunting we had ever had. It was so good we ended up with our limits of eight birds each plus 10 more. We had never scored this many birds.

There is only one way out of the canyon and there was usually a fish and game check station at the top. So, what do we do with the extra birds? Being intelligent college students and engineering majors at that, we decided to put the excess birds in the hub caps. We drove up the road towards the game check. The good Lord was looking after us and made the radiator run out of water so, it was necessary to stop to refill it. That was when the effect of centrifugal force on the blood of dead chuckars was noted. All four wheels were covered in blood. I am sure the game wardens would have been curious about that at the check point.

We washed off the tires and then put the 10 very nasty looking birds inside the spare tire and continued. Sure enough the check station was open, and we were waved over. The warden had us pull the 32 birds we had in the trunk out and line them up on the ground so they could be counted. We were sure they were going to search the car and bust us big time. They had us kneel behind the birds, took our picture and sent us on our way. We had lucked out. Two days later our picture was in the local paper with the caption "WSU students score on chuckars." Everyone was impressed with our hunting skills. We fed the whole house with those birds. Picking the hub cap birds was not a pleasant experience.

Pheasant hunting was a very different deal. Pullman is surrounded by dry land wheat fields that are covered in stubble during hunting season. There are a few gullies with some cover. We would hunt these gullies with limited success. If we got a bird or two in an afternoon of hunting that was good. Usually we came home empty handed. The University has an experimental farm part of which consists of various kinds of crops and trees. This is about 400 acres of ground that was fenced off with a four-strand barbed wire fence. Signs were posted every 50 feet saying it was USDA land and no trespassing.

Well this was a haven for the pheasants. They got shot at in the wheat stubble and gullies, but not on the government land. It was the DMZ for birds. There was also lots of cover and food. It was a pheasant paradise. We were hunting the stubble when a rooster got up and flew toward the fence. We hit him, but not hard enough to drop him right away. He ended up dropping about 200 hundred feet inside the DMZ. We figured it would be OK to fetch our kill, so we crossed the fence and started walking toward our bird. Suddenly, birds started jumping up all around us. Instinct took over and we dropped four of them. Our first thought was OK now the government guys are going to come and hassle us. Nobody showed up so we continued to shoot birds until we had a limit and went back to the house. That was enough birds for another dinner for the whole house. Once again arriving as heroes and providers of gourmet meals, everyone was pleased. Well, maybe not the pheasants. We continued to hunt the USDA land for the rest of the season, life was good.

The next year we were blasting away at pheasants when a pickup truck came barreling towards us. There was no way to outrun him, so we just stood there. The guy introduced himself as the manager of the property and he was not a happy camper. He was talking about calling the sheriff and having us arrested. We didn't like the way the conversation was going. He asked where we lived, and we told him Delta Tau Delta Fraternity.

He said, "You guys are Delts?"

We said "Yes."

He then said, "So am I, University of Florida". We were fraternity brothers!

The "sheriff" talk disappeared. He explained that he was concerned with us shooting around the experimental trees as the pellets could damage them but shooting in the areas with crops would be OK. He then gave us his schedule as to when he was there so we could hunt on his shift with no problems. We named the USDA property the Delta Tau Delta Memorial Hunting Preserve and hunted there for the next couple of years, until our guy got transferred. We were relegated back to hunting the gullies.

We did go on one elk hunt while at WSU. It worked out we had a three-day weekend right at the beginning of elk season. The plan was to hunt the Blue Mountain region in southeast Washington. Me and two of my fraternity brothers, Kooky Korach and Fig Leaf decided to go elk hunting on Mount Misery. Just the name of the place should have been a red flag, but some of the stupid from my teenage years had stuck with me. Don't know for sure where Kooky and Fig Leaf got theirs. They say you are never too old to learn something stupid. Kooky was an athletic guy and loved to go on adventures. He didn't have much hunting experience but was up for this trip. Fig Leaf was born and raised in a small Eastern Washington town and had been hunting all his life. As noted before, he was also my little brother in the fraternity.

The plan was to load sleeping bags, our guns, including my trusty 300 Savage, and gear into the Chevy, drive up to the top of the mountain and just shoot an elk and come back to campus. Does this sound familiar to you? My planning protocol had not changed much. Two big differences from my high school hunts were that we brought knives, old Army surplus pack boards and game bags. Also, the Chevy had breaks, taillights, headlights and didn't need the radiator filled every hour or so. This was a high- class hunting trip.

In order to access Mount Misery, you drive from Pullman to Lewiston, Idaho, through a part of Idaho and then back into Washington. The return trip through Idaho turned out to have some issues.

My dad took me on a pack-in elk hunting trip in the Blue Mountains when I was in junior high, but, other than that, none of us had ever been there. We just got out a road map and we were off and running. They say, "Ignorance is bliss" and we had plenty of both as we motored off in a generally eastern direction.

After traversing Idaho, we entered back into Washington on a gravel road and immediately began the climb up the mountain. We connected to the Diamond Creek Road which got smaller and less maintained the higher we went. It finally turned into a dirt two track with lots of big rocks and then sort of faded out altogether. We concluded that this would be a good place to camp. So far things had turned out just as we had planned. All we had to do now was shoot an elk and go home. We had a pleasant meal, drank some beer, told each other some lies and went to bed.

We were camped on a ridge with a very steep slope on one side and a gentle slope on the other. The area was heavily forested with some large clearings. It was ideal elk country and we were the only hunters in the vicinity. This hunt was off to a great start. Seems every time one of our hunts gets off to a great start it somehow doesn't end up that way.

Guys with mount Misery elk

The plan was that Fig Leaf and I would walk down on either side of a small basin on the gentle sloping side and Kooky would work down parallel to us on the next ridge over. This put us a couple of hundred yards apart as we stalked down the slope. It was a bright sunny day with a temperature of around 50 degrees. Can't get any better than that.

We hadn't gone far when I found myself walking along the timber on the side of a large clearing. The clearing was about 100 yards across. Fig Leaf was into the trees about 25 yards on the other side and Kooky was in thick timber hunting the ridge on the other side of Fig Leaf. I could see Fig Leaf every now and then but had no idea where Kooky was.

Kooky told me later he was walking along in the thick forest when suddenly elk were running everywhere. The foliage was so thick he couldn't make out if they were bulls or cows, so he didn't shoot. The elk spooked right at Fig Leaf who had no idea they were coming until they were right on top of him. At that point things got very confusing for him. He saw a bull as it was running through the trees, but his shot hit a tree as the bull passed behind it then they were gone. The shot inspired the elk to accelerate considerably, therefore when they broke out into the clearing they were in overdrive. I saw about 50 elk coming right at me, so I jumped behind a four-foot diameter log and clicked the safety off on my trusty, open sighted, 300 Savage.

A huge bull was lined up to end up right in my lap if I didn't do something significant very quickly. My plan was to take a head on shot and if I missed he would turn to give me a broadside shot and if he didn't turn, to lay down behind the log and shoot him when he jumped over. When you come up with a plan in two seconds it is not always well thought out. This plan was a prime example.

Bull elk tend to run with their nose in the air and their horns laid against their back. This guy had not got the memo and had his head down and was coming at me horns first, a rather intimidating sight. He was about 20 yards out when I fired. The 100-grain bullet hit him right between the eyes just below his horns. His head went down, and his horns dug into the ground and he flipped over on his back and that was the last thing he did. The rest of the herd stampeded past me on both sides and disappeared into the trees. It got very quiet except for a squirrel in the tree behind me who, I am sure, was singing my praises for such a fine shot. I sat there for a few minutes taking in what had just happened and then noticed that Fig Leaf had come into the clearing and was yelling with excitement at our good luck. He came over and shook my hand. This was a tremendous bull. He had four points and double eye guards on both sides for a total of six points to the side. We were standing there in shock as we admired this giant bull. A few minutes later Kooky showed up and was also very impressed. The trip was going exactly as planned.

Kooky and I went to work on the elk while Fig Leaf went back to camp to get the pack boards and game bags. He had been gone about 45 minutes when we heard a shot. We figured there were some other hunters in the area and continued with our work. An hour later Fig Leaf showed up with the stuff and announced he had shot a forked horned bull right next to the camp. Now we had two elk, how good is that? In retrospect, it was an overabundance of good luck.

When you are in your early 20s and in good shape you can pack your own body weight on your back, so we loaded all the meat, the cape and the horns on the packs and headed up the slope to camp. It was a major effort, but we got there in about two hours, totally wiped out. We then inquired as to where the other elk was. That is when Fig Leaf confided to us that he had shot the elk right next to camp, but it had run down the steep slope on the other side of the road. He wasn't sure how far it had gone. This was the beginning of a downward spiral for this trip.

We made a meat rack and hung up the elk and then picked up the blood trail. It went straight down the 60-degree slope. Both of us were glaring at Fig Leaf, but he was not inclined to make eye contact.

We found the bull about a half mile down the slope quite dead. We were prepared with pack boards and rope but still looking at a lot of work. We tied the rope to a tree uphill from us and then loaded up a quarter on our packs and pulled ourselves up the slope to the tree and then did it again. It was dark by the time we got the second elk into camp.

The next morning, we began to contemplate the issues involved with loading two elk, camping gear and three guys into a 1955 Chevy sedan. We debated several scenarios, none of which were very good. We ended up putting as much meat in the trunk as we could. It was so full we had to tie the lid to the bumper with the elk legs sticking out. We then filled the back seat with gear and meat with elk legs sticking out both windows. Finally, we tied the rest of the meat, the horns and the cape on top of the car. We stood back, crossed our arms and admired our work. No one noticed that the ground clearance of the car was severely compromised. All three of us got in the front seat and fired up the Chevy.

We had gone about 10 feet when a rock ripped the muffler off. I stopped and went back to get it, but it was destroyed so we left it there and went slowly, but loudly down the road. Various hunters camped along the road observed us with envy (the rack) and mirth (the muffler.) Luckily, there was no more loss of car parts by the time we got back to the highway in Idaho.

We were cruising along thinking things were going OK when an Idaho State Trooper pulled us over. He had a couple of questions for us. First, what were we doing in Idaho with two elk and Washington hunting licenses and second, where was our muffler?

We explained the deal about accessing Mount Misery through Idaho and he gave us the benefit of the doubt on that one. The muffler was a little more cut and dried. We either had one or we didn't. It was obvious we didn't. I could tell he was somewhat amused by the sight of us, with elk legs sticking out of windows etc., and that he was impressed by my bull, but he couldn't just let us go. So, he said he would give me a warning if we got the muffler fixed before we left Idaho. Lewiston was the next town, the trooper said he would follow us there as it was only 15 miles. Our little convoy of two headed on down the road. We got some quizzical glances from people passing by.

We arrived in Lewiston about 5:00 PM on a Sunday. At the time I think Lewiston had three service stations only one of which was open on a Sunday afternoon. We pulled into his lot and inquired as to if he had a muffler for a 1955 Chevy. He didn't, but his brother-in-law owned the parts store which he could open to get a muffler if the price were right. Seeing as how we had $27 between us the price range was somewhat limited. He advised us it would be $75 to buy and install the muffler. We were only $48 short. The trooper declined to loan us the money. We entered into negotiations for the repairs. After several payment plans were discussed we agreed to give him the $27 and one hind quarter of elk. Only in small town America could such a deal be struck. The repairs were completed in short order. We waved to the trooper as we crossed the bridge into Washington.

We dropped the meat off at the butcher and went back to the fraternity house. I called my dad and told him about the huge elk I had. He was the exalted ruler of the Elks club in Ephrata, so he said if I wanted to get a shoulder mount the elks club would pay for it if we hung it in the club house. I readily agreed, and that mount hung there for almost 20 years. They remodeled the club and, somehow, the mount ended up in a local sporting goods store. The store went out of business a few years later and no one knows what became of my elk. I wasn't pleased.

Elk hunting is always an adventure in the Pacific Northwest, but I think elk retrieval can be more of an adventure if you are unlucky or just plain dumb. It is obvious I managed to employ both qualities in my youth.

The social side of college life was somewhat difficult for me. I was a country hick from a small Eastern Washington town with limited social skills even for Ephrata. So, when I was thrown into a student body of 15,000 kids from places like Spokane, Seattle and Los Angeles I was

*Linda and I at
fraternity dance.*

*Me and Cheryl, an
Ephrata girl, fraternity
Dance picture*

really intimidated. My freshman year I dated two girls who graduated from high school with me. It was more platonic than romantic. My sophomore year I branched out a bit. I would go to the big campus dances with my fraternity brothers and even occasionally ask a girl to dance. The social Bob was emerging, albeit very slowly.

It was at one of these dances that I screwed up my courage and began the seemly long walk every shy young man dreads to ask a girl to dance. When I got to within 10 feet of her, I saw another guy zeroing in on my target. I quickened my pace and cut him off very deftly.

Her name was Linda and she accepted my invitation to dance. The twist was the dance craze then so that is what we did. I wasn't good at it, or any other type of dancing, and felt very self-conscious. She was a good sport and offered to give me some instruction which she did for the rest of the event. I walked her back to her dorm and then asked her out for a date. She accepted which left me flabbergasted. It was her freshman year, so she was adjusting to campus life as I had done the year before. Walking back to the house thinking I had this social thing down pat was a somewhat illusory concept. You can take the boy out of the country and maybe you can take the country out of the boy. In my case, nope.

My success with Linda inspired me to ask out a girl from my sociology class who I had wanted to date for a year. She was a sorority girl in one of the higher end houses. Therefore, the presence of any Delta Tau Delta guys was quite rare. Her name was Tina and it turned out she was from a very wealthy family. Her folks owned a large nationwide business. I didn't know this when I suggested we take in a movie. She accepted. Now let's set the scene here. I am a small-town kid who is getting through school killing farm animals and working on a survey crew. $5 is serious money to me. A movie in those days was about $1 and a coke at the Coug was 50 cents. I figured with two movie tickets and two cokes I was in about $3. A big expenditure, but worth it to impress Tina. You got to go big to win big.

After the movie, which included popcorn, another 25 cents, I suggested we go to the Coug for a coke. She suggested we go to a restaurant and have dinner. My financial life flashed before my eyes. Dinner could be $25 or more. That is the fee for killing a steer and a sheep. I had two choices. One was to say no I can't afford it and then kiss Tina off. The other was to suck it up and take her to dinner. I went with the latter.

We had a nice dinner and that was when I learned about her wealth. I had never met a rich person so not sure what was the protocol. She talked of traveling around the world and the Seattle social scene, things completely foreign to me. I just mostly listened to her and didn't speak much. She seemed to enjoy the date. I skipped the coke at the Coug thing, saved me a buck, and walked her back to her sorority. She said I was a good listener and indicated she would like to go out with me again. "Me too" was my reply I then fled back to the house. Several of my fraternity brothers were in the living room upon my arrival. Orlin had seen us at the movie. He asked who my date was. At the mention of Tina, the whole room jumped up and said do you know how rich she is? I replied that I did now. They were astounded, so was I, that a dink from Ephrata had pulled off a date with her.

We had a couple more dates, but it was driving me into bankruptcy, which was a very short drive, so I just quit calling her and called Linda. Thinking back on this a better plan would have been to call my dad and explain the situation and then ask him for a loan to finance the dates. Could have paid him back ten times over when I had a wife worth tens- of- millions of dollars. Oh well, I would have been a kept man for the rest of my life, or at least for a few years before she gave me the boot. Linda and I dated for the rest of our college years and got married when we graduated, in 1966.

our wedding picture 1966 Pullman Wash.

New wife and new car, both broken down

CHAPTER EIGHT

LOS ANGELES

The weekend I graduated was busy. Saturday morning, we went through graduation ceremonies, in the afternoon I was commissioned as a second lieutenant in the U.S. Army and then on Sunday, we got married. The next morning, I took the 8- hour engineer in training exam. The exam didn't go well. The events of the weekend had pretty much used me up. Tuesday afternoon we took our newly purchased 1963 Chevy and headed out for California. I had a job with the City of Los Angeles Bureau of Engineering and Linda had a teaching job with the school district. The Army had given me a year to pay off my student loan before going on active duty.

The 1960s were not a good time to be 18, male and in good physical condition. The draft board was a constant threat and they were a heartless, uncompromising bunch of truly evil people. At least that was my opinion, shared by the vast majority of the men my age. You would get notices from them all the time demanding information about what you were doing accompanied by threats of being drafted if you didn't reply quickly.

Lt. Bell getting his gold bars pinned on by mom and new wife.

It was like dealing with the devil and his staff, except worse. At least with the devil you are dealing with someone when you are already dead, not someone who is conspiring to get you dead.

We had been in Los Angeles for a few months when I received one of their love letters. It noted that I was no longer enrolled at WSU and demanded to know where I was and if my draft status had changed. The same old threats were included. I read the note a couple of times, with the usual stress, and then thought "Hey, they can't hurt me now." So, I wrote back and informed them I was now a Second Lieutenant in the U.S. Army and no longer subject to their jurisdiction so wouldn't be providing any further information about myself. That really felt good, I had slapped Godzilla in the face. Shortly thereafter got back a very unpleasant letter quoting a whole bunch of regulations and laws and detailing all the terrible things they were going to do to me for not complying. Godzilla had slapped back. You just couldn't help but hate those guys, my macho evaporated.

Then I had a stroke of genius and forwarded the letter to the general staff at the Presidio of San Francisco where my records were held until I went on active duty. It is difficult to explain how great it felt to get a copy of the letter a general sent to the draft board telling them to immediately stop harassing one of his officers or face serious consequences. It is always great when you can take down a bully. In those days almost every young man in America fantasized about telling their draft board to go pound sand. I had and got away with it!

Los Angeles was good and bad for us. We had both grown up in relatively small towns and had never been out of the Pacific Northwest. LA was huge, loud, busy and relatively unfriendly compared to home. The smog was hard to get used to, the Charlie Manson murders took place while we were there, and the traffic was terrible. Life didn't revolve around hunting and fishing season, the wheat harvest or drinking beer. These folks were into fashion, movies, expensive cars, wine and power jobs. It was hard to feel warm and fuzzy about these things. The cultural clash was extreme for us, not so much for LA. I always had the feeling they were just tolerating us hicks.

The good side was that there was so much to do. One of Linda's sorority sisters lived in LA, so she and her husband helped us to adapt to the big city. We went to plays and movie premiers. We even took a shot at being on television. There was a show called the "Newlywed Game." The studio was a block from my office so one day at lunch I walked down there and asked how to try out for the show, they gave me an application said to fill it out and return it to the studio. We were going to be TV stars. There was little doubt in our minds this would pay better than engineering and teaching. I made a copy for our friends.

The way it worked you went in for an audition. The premise of the game was they would separate the couple and ask the wife a bunch of questions. Then they would bring the husband back and see if he could guess his wife's answers. We didn't do so well. I think two right answers out of 10 was below average. We were relegated back to engineering and teaching.

Our friends were going in the next day, so they asked us what was involved. We told them the process and most of the questions that were asked. Turns out they asked the same questions therefore, our friends killed it and ended up on the show. They didn't do quite as well without the answers in advance and won zip but had a good time and were on a national TV show. Linda and I got a real kick out of seeing them on TV. Knowing we got them there we were sure they would invite us to the premier of their first movie. Sadly, their acting careers stalled after that, so they went back to being accountants. It was great to be part of show biz, albeit briefly.

I was assigned to the Hollywood District office of the bureau, so we lived in Hollywood and did have a few brushes with celebrities. The first one was at my job. The office was set up with a public area where there was a counter for dealing with said public, such as people getting permits or asking questions. Then there was the back room where we all sat at our drafting tables and designed stuff. We took turns manning the front counter. It wasn't a favorite duty. Engineers are not good at dealing with publics, being nerds and all.

Hollywood office of the bureau of engineering Sans Charlton Heston

It was my day for counter duty. About 10:00AM a limo pulls up in front and Charlton Heston gets out of the back and storms into the office. At first, I was star struck. That went away quickly when he demanded to know who was in charge in a loud and threating voice. He was an impressive man and even more so in person. Here I was having to deal with an angry Moses. I replied, "That would be me."

He leaned across the counter, locked eyes with me and said, "You clowns plan to put a storm drainpipe through the middle of the Hollywood Golf Course and that is not acceptable. I want to talk to the idiot who is designing that." Well, I was that idiot, but it seemed prudent to not disclose that information. Therefore, I informed him that that particular engineer was on vacation and would not be back for a week. I informed him I would be happy to pass on his concerns to the district engineer, who also was not in the office at this time.

He spun on his heels and snarled over his shoulder, "You guys better fix this or there will be hell to pay." He got in his limo and we never saw him again. The district engineer got out from under his desk, complemented me on my series of lies and said I handled the situation just fine. The storm drain went across the golf course a few months later. I assume Mr. Hesston was out of town at the time.

Another incident made the national news. There was a teen night-club called Pandora's Box. It was on a kind of traffic island on Sunset

Boulevard. We were putting a new storm drain in the street. The project made it necessary to tear down Pandora's Box. The kids who frequented the place went nuts and started a riot. There were thousands of kids protesting. In 1966 this was unusual. The national news organizations picked up on it and it turned into a major media event. The whole thing was on the evening news for several days.

The cops brought buses to the scene and started arresting kids and loading them on the vehicles. Not sure where they were going to take them. Linda and I lived about two blocks away, so we decided to go see what was happening. The next thing we knew we were being herded toward a bus. I pulled out my wallet and showed my Bureau of Engineering ID to the cop and told him I was one of the engineers on the project. He looked at the ID for a long time and then said, "Thanks a lot pal. When you get to your office tomorrow tell your engineering buddies, we don't appreciate being out here dealing with this." He then stormed off to grab some more kids. We went home and locked the door. This guy was a very careful driver after that. It was a sure bet if I got pulled over and the cop knew I was the Pandora's Box engineer it wouldn't go well.

Just getting to Los Angeles was problematic. We left Pullman in our new, used 1963 Chevy. It all went well until we got to Northern California. In a small town named Corning, the olive capital of the world, our engine quit on us. I had just bought this car a week earlier. We were towed to a garage where a mechanic looked it over. He said the engine couldn't be fixed and needed to be replaced. I explained we were on our way to LA for a job and had to be there Monday and didn't have very much money. He was a good guy and took pity on the newlyweds, advised us they could probably have the engine working the next day, but it wouldn't last much more than the distance to LA if that. We thanked him and went to look for a motel room.

Linda then informed me she wasn't feeling well and wanted to see a doctor. It was early evening by now, so the only option was the emergency room at the hospital. We walked there with her getting worse by the minute. When we got to the emergency room door she passed out. I grabbed her before she hit the sidewalk. There I was, my new car was broke down and my new wife was out of commission too. I picked her up and carried her into the hospital. The nurse told me to put her in a wheelchair and wheeled her away. I stood there wondering OK now what. This whole being married, graduate engineer starting a career, and Army officer thing wasn't going well. I contemplated returning to Ephrata and continuing my former career of hunting, fishing, drinking beer and chasing girls. It was looking really attractive, except for the draft board thing.

The next day we limped into LA and found an apartment. It seemed things were getting better, but that was when the country hick in LA factor kicked in. We needed to make a first and last month's rent payment in advance. I was prepared for this and had adequate money in my checking account. The landlady was perplexed as to how I figured she would take a check drawn on a bank in Pullman, Washington. She had never heard of Pullman and barley knew where Washington was. I was perplexed as to why she was perplexed. After considerable discussion she relented and took the check. We didn't have to sleep in the car that night. Not a good start on our new life.

On Monday we both reported for work. I was being paid $775 a month, she got $625. This was big money in 1966. The problem was neither of us would get our first paycheck for two months, an unanticipated complication. The first and last month's rent and car repairs had mostly cleaned us out. We had a serious cash flow problem. The only positive to our situation was that we were so low that there was nothing but upside.

My older sister, the wooden spoon witch, lived in Brea which was some distance from Hollywood. So, three times a week we would drive out to their house and have dinner with them. My Chevron gas card worked just fine in LA. The situation finally forced us to borrow money from a loan company. I think the guy's name was Guido. They gave us $300 with our paychecks as collateral. It got us through until we got paid, which was delayed for a week to sort out the lien the loan company had put on them. Once Guido was payed off, we had finally achieved financial stability, at least in the short term.

With our newfound wealth and a reimbursement from the car dealer in Pullman I got a new engine for the Chevy. A few months later we traded it in for a brand new 1966 Ford Mustang and a substantial monthly car payment. It was my first new car and I was so proud of that machine. It was washed and waxed twice a week. They say all good things must come to an end. It turns out that also applies to new cars.

Linda was driving the car home from teaching and literally a little old lady from Pasadena ran a red light and t-boned her. Linda wasn't hurt, but my beautiful new Mustang was smashed from headlight to taillight on the right side. It had 357 miles on the odometer. I was devastated. The lady's insurance paid for the repairs, but the car was damaged goods to me from then on. It was no longer a new car. We kept the Mustang for many years. It traveled to Alaska with us. I was working on the North Slope on a week on week off schedule. When leaving for a shift on the slope I told her to sell the car and we would buy a new one. She sold that 1966 Mustang for $300. I was re-devastated.

Being as how I am an outdoors kind of guy LA did not fit well with me. We would get together with our friends and drive out of LA to camp at a local lake. If you caught a fish or two in the course of the weekend it was a big deal. A fish over nine inches long was a monster. It just made me miss Ephrata.

In the fall I was at the office lamenting that all my buddies back home would be gearing up for hunting season and I was stuck here in the big city. One of the engineers said he and his pals went duck hunting north of LA every year and I was welcome to join them, I jumped at the chance. They were all southern California born and raised guys so, their concept of hunting was significantly different than mine. This soon became apparent. The trip was in six weeks and I was counting the days. About two weeks before the trip I asked about the details. It wasn't what I had expected.

Turns out their hunting trip involved going to a "hunting preserve." The facility had a pond where they fed the ducks. When the hunters arrived, they put a certain number of ducks in a cage and then hauled them some distance away. The hunters were put in blinds between the cage and the pond. They would release two or three ducks at a time and the hunters would shoot them as they flew back to the pond. You paid by the duck. I couldn't get excited about this deal and dropped out of the hunt. I was depressed even more.

Decided to call some of my friends in Ephrata and advised them I was coming home for a week-end hunting trip. They said everything would be set up at the appointed time. Now these guys seldom get things right, so this trip was a real crap shoot for me. Most of their decisions involve beer consumption and inattention to details. There were rare occasions when things didn't get screwed up, but they didn't involve these guys doing any of the planning or for that matter being within five miles.

Only a couple of minor details needed to be worked out. First Linda made it very clear I was not going to spend a bunch of money doing this, second, she wasn't thrilled about spending a weekend alone in the LA environment. Finally, there was no way she would agree to me taking the car. My options were narrowing by the minute.

The bus took too long, and air fare was too expensive so there were some significant logistical problems. Someone put me onto an outfit that moved cars between cities. I contacted them and cut a deal. It involved driving a car from LA to Seattle for $20 and then a different car from Spokane back to LA for another $20. Bus fare from Seattle to Ephrata was $15 and from Ephrata to Spokane $10, producing a $15 profit, which would cover the cost of the ammo. I took Friday off and headed for Seattle arriving in Ephrata at 4:00 AM Saturday morning.

We were in our duck blinds by 6:00 AM and had a limit of ducks by 10:00 AM. Then we went chuckar hunting and picked up a few pheasants. It just doesn't get any better than that, a great day with my friends and bagging a whole bunch of birds. I spent the evening with mom and dad, slept in my own bed and went to a movie with my little brothers. It was a good time. I left on the bus to Spokane the next morning and was back in LA late Sunday night. Most of my birds came home with me in my suitcase so we did have a couple of good meals. I love it when a plan comes together. The $15 profit was spent on beer, shotgun shells and junk food during the trip. My spending habits had reverted to my high school days. The only profit was the birds. A tidy profit if I do say so myself.

Troops and hippies at pentagon "riots"

CHAPTER TEN

FORT BELVOIR

I never warmed up to California so when I got active duty orders, in May of 1967, to report to Fort Belvoir Virginia, I was kind of pleased. Getting out of Los Angles was great, going on active duty in the Army? That jury was still out. Neither of us had ever been off the West coast so it was a big adventure. We drove across the northern states in our Mustang pulling a U-Haul trailer. Somewhere in Iowa we were passing an 18-wheeler when the trailer started fish tailing like crazy. I slammed on the breaks just as it broke loose and went rolling down the highway with our stuff flying in every direction. The trailer ended up in the ditch in a very distressed state. Our stuff was all over the road, we gathered it up between cars. Kind of like playing Frogger, except for real.

The truck continued its way without stopping. We got everything in one pile and then drove to the next town where I contacted the U-Haul guy. He gave us a new trailer and said he would go get the traumatized one. We returned to the scene of the accident, put our stuff, which was in a pitiful state, in the new trailer and continued our way. We really appreciated U-Haul's help.

I was to report to Fort Belvoir for engineers officers basic. This is an eight-week boot camp for mostly ROTC second lieutenants. We did have two captains and three first lieutenants from the Alabama National Guard. Their units were changing from infantry to engineers, so their officers had to take the engineers' basic. I had never been to the Deep South nor met anyone from there so there were some cultural issues with these guys that I had some trouble dealing with. There was also a language barrier of sorts. According to them you worsh your clothes, wrench em out and put them in the chester drawers. I never got to be good friends with them.

Being a brand-new butter bar lieutenant, I had to learn some basic lessons regarding being in the Army. I recall I was walking somewhere on post when a Sergeant Major approached me coming the other way. He saluted and I said, "Good morning, Sergeant." He immediately violated my personnel space and chewed me out for five minutes for referring to him as "Sergeant" and not "Sergeant Major." He then stormed off.

Lt. Bell on first day of active duty, Fort Belvoir Virginia.

I stood there for a while wondering as to how he could do that as I was an officer, and he was a non-commissioned officer. I concluded that he did it because I let him. I mentioned it to the captain who was in charge of the class. He agreed I did out rank a Sergeant Major and I could return the favor by chewing him out next time I saw him. He also pointed out that it would be a bad idea. The Sergeant Major was the right-hand man for the general in command of the post who needed his Sergeant Major much more than a second lieutenant in the officers' basic course. His suggestion was to call him Sergeant Major the next time I saw him and to smile while doing so. Lesson learned.

One of the other lieutenants in my class was the son of a Texas National Guard four-star general. I thought it was funny to call him and say I was General so and so and we would get a big laugh out of it. One day he gets a call and the person says he is General Jones. My pal proceeds to give him a bunch of guff.

The caller is not amused and then confirms he really is a general and is calling to tell him his dad is in town and would like to meet for lunch. Those gold bars on his shoulders immediately caught on fire. This caused my good friend to panic and say his friend Lieutenant Bell always calls him and pretends to be a general and he thought it was me calling. So, he threw me under the bus. We both lived in fear for a month. Nothing came of it.

After basic I was assigned to the 77th Port Construction Company located at Fort Belvoir. I reported for duty in July of 1967 and was assigned as the platoon leader of the second construction platoon. This was my first command and I was very nervous about how it would go, with limited exposure to enlisted personnel at this point. I assumed they were just like my buddies back in Ephrata, which I am not sure was a positive.

First, I was subjected to an interrogation by the company commander, "Who are you really? Have you ever been in a leadership position before? Do you have the intestinal fortitude to control Army sergeants?" etc. I soon learned this guy had a real Napoleon complex. He constantly tried to intimidate people but wasn't very good at it. Then a short but intense conversation with the first sergeant quickly followed, "You need to understand I am in charge here, do not even think about challenging my authority." The first sergeant was intimidating and was very good at it.

He then escorted me to the barracks of the second platoon where I was introduced to Sergeant Doland and Sergeant Tracy, both staff sergeants. Doland was the platoon sergeant and Tracy was his co-conspirator. Turned out those two were thick as thieves and far more devious. Sergeant Doland had the platoon fall out in front of the barracks and he introduced me as the new platoon leader. Their response was muted at best. I did a short "We need to work together speech" and Doland dismissed the troops. Seeing as how I had zip experience as a platoon leader and a total of eight weeks in the Army, in engineer officers' basic I just stood there like a bump on a log waiting for somebody to talk to me. Nobody did so I opted to wander around the company area to see where everything was located.

My platoon at Belvoir Sgt. Doland at left

I ran into Lt. Emery who was the first platoon leader and had been in the company for several months. He took me under his wing, and we adjourned to the officer's club. He filled me in on being a platoon leader. He suggested that the first thing I should do is get Sergeant Doland alone and chew his butt for not briefing me on the platoon or offering to show me around. He said it was a power play by the sergeant and I shouldn't let him get away with it. He also warned me to expect more of this type of thing from Doland and Tracy. So, the captain interrogated me, the first sergeant intimidated me, and my platoon sergeant power played me and it was not even noon on the first day. Those second lieutenant bars were getting very heavy. I was not in Kansas, well, Ephrata anymore.

That afternoon I asked Sergeant Doland to meet me in his quarters. He reluctantly agreed. I found his room to be quite messy and disorganized. You definitely could not bounce a quarter off his bunk. I doubt if you could have bounced a helium balloon off that thing. Kind of like my room in high school except with nicer stuff. It was obvious he resented me being there. I was in his space.

I started out gently by saying "Sergeant I think it would have been helpful if you had shown me around and briefed me on how things work with the platoon and the company." He replied that that was not his job. Wrong answer! I then said, "OK sergeant if you want to play it that way you stand at attention while I am talking to you, now!!!" He snapped to attention. I was suddenly feeling the power of those butter bars.

He was then informed that his job was what I said it was, taking a clue from Clyde the survey party chief. He seemed to agree. Hard to tell when he was at attention. The conversation was very one sided and went on for 10 minutes. I then told him that this little *tete a tete* would remain just between us. I then left the room with the good sergeant standing at attention.

The next stop was the platoon work area to see what the troops were up to. Most of them were working on equipment and many of them just hanging around, including Sergeant Tracy. He was invited into the construction shack and a similar conversation was held with him. I told the troops to fall in and explained to them that I had a construction background, and an engineering degree. My short time in the Army was noted, but I knew construction. They were also told that they were expected to work hard and efficiently and if they did, they could count on me to cover their backs. Also, if they had any concerns, they could come to me. I asked if there were any questions and there were none. The sergeant dismissed them, and they all got busy at various jobs. My authority was established with everyone. Turned out not so much.

At the end of the workday there was an operations meeting attended by the captain, the first Sergeant, all the platoon leaders and platoon sergeants. As I walked into the meeting all the sergeants were giving me the stink eye. It was obvious my

Platoon construction shed Fort Belvoir.

conversations with Doland and Tracy had not stayed in the room. After the meeting, the captain took me aside and asked what I had done on my first day to piss off the sergeants. I told him about my conversations with Doland and Tracy. He burst out laughing. He said, "Those two have had that coming for a long time. The last platoon leader was a complete wuss and they took total advantage of him. I am glad you had the guts to take them on. If you need any back-up, I am there for you. Welcome to the company." So, my first day had some up and downs.

On the second day my platoon was assigned a job to drive some sheet piling to form a wall along a waterway in Washington D.C. It took us two days to pick up the material and get all the equipment loaded up. We left right after morning formation. There was a 40-ton crane, a pile driver, several trucks and lots of sheet piling. I had no idea how competent these guys were at driving pile. My experience was nil.

The troops got the pile driver hooked up to the crane and were ready to drive the template for the wall. The first pile was set in place and the pile driver positioned on it. That is when Sergeant Doland informed me nobody knew how to use the pile driver. I was dumbstruck. I turned to him and said, "You are just now telling me this?" He just shrugged. My affection for this guy continued to dissipate. I went to the truck and found the manual on the pile driver and within an hour figured how to get it going. We finished the job late that night. Nobody was in a good mood when we got back to the barracks, especially me.

The next morning, I discussed the incident with the captain, he was not happy. He said he would get me a new sergeant. I started to agree, but then said maybe I would give it one more try. He wished me luck. So here I am, four days into being a platoon leader and already in crisis mode. Doland was invited into the construction shed and asked if he would rather be in Vietnam than Fort Belvoir? His eyes got quite big and he said was quite happy where he was. I then advised him that I was not happy as to where he was. Informed him he needed to make considerable effort to change my mind or he had a very long plane flight in his near future. He was also informed that Sergeant Tracy needed to find another platoon in another company in the next few days. You could hear the power shift in the room. Sergeant Doland and I had a very good working relationship for the rest of our time together. Lt. Bell was starting to learn what it is like to be in the Army. All macho and very little concern about feelings.

Dealing with Army NCO's is a difficult skill to acquire. A good example was the company Christmas party. The first sergeant was at the party. He had lost his right hand in Vietnam, therefore he had various hands he would use on different occasions. He was a very versatile guy. For this party he had a soft hand so he could shake hands with people. He had a hook like thing for everyday use. It was really strange, but we all shook hands with him. No one thought this was unusual. I was beginning to see the weird side of NCOs, not sure if there is another side.

The company would go to AP Hill, 50 miles north of Fort Belvoir, for weapons training. We would shoot rifles, grenade launchers, 90-millimeter shoulder fired weapons, and machine guns. The shooting range was a big circle about a mile across. The various ranges were situated around the circle. This meant that you might be shooting in the direction of another unit, but they were a mile away with lots of trees and stuff in between so there was limited danger of shooting anyone. At least that was the theory. I was beginning to learn that "In theory" was an Army term for "Probably won't work."

We were shooting the 90-millimeter weapons, similar to a bazooka only it has a longer range. The way it worked was the troop would put the tube on his shoulder and adjust the aiming sight to his eye. He would then put his right hand on his helmet, so it was away from the trigger. A rocket was then inserted into the tube and clicked into place. This would arm the device. Now you have a very anxious teenager with a tremendous amount of firepower perched on his shoulder that he knows almost nothing about. How could that go wrong? On command from the tower he would take his, slightly quivering, hand off his helmet, sight on the target and pull the trigger, a very simple procedure. The rocket would blast out of the tube with a great roar. The missile would scream down range and blow the target to pieces.

During the briefing they talked about some of the things that could go wrong such as a dud. One thing they mentioned was a "cook off." This is where the rocket doesn't launch but does generate enough heat to cook off the round in the tube thereby eliminating the troop from any further duty in the Army or the world, to include anyone within 50 feet of him. Not sure why they included this information in the briefing. If it did happen anybody involved would not be around for the debriefing.

Well, we had a dud, of sorts. The troop pulled the trigger and nada. They pulled the rocket and reinserted it and he pulled the trigger again. Still nada. By this point our guy is not concerned about hitting the target he has several other thoughts in his mind, none of them upbeat. The sweat was pouring off him like a locker room shower. They adjust the rocket again and the tower tells him to fire. This time it works, problem is he was no longer focused on hitting the target. He was busy trying to remember all the words to the Lord's Prayer. Turns out he had the tube pointed up at a 60-degree angle, so we all watched as the rocket disappeared over the trees. There was some apprehension about this, but no real concern. After all there was a mile of trees in front of us. The explosion was heard several seconds later. It was kind of a loud "whump" way off in the distance. Nothing to worry about there.

We got the next, very nervous, guy up to the line to continue training. About that time a jeep came to a skidding stop in the parking area and a very agitated major jumped out wanting to know who was in charge. Seeing as how I was wearing the lieutenant bars, unfortunately, that was me. He then informed me his unit was on an M-14 range when our rocket hit the 150-meter targets and blew the crap out of everything. Consequently, sending his panicked troops running through the woods at the back of the range. Obviously not a good thing. The major seemed inconsolable, so I didn't say anything. After he finally wound down, I explained what had happened. Didn't seem to mollify him. After chewing me and sergeant Doland out, he jumped in his jeep and left. He never filed a report, so we dodged that bullet. So did his unit except the bullet they dodged was a 90 mm rocket.

We had extra duty as a riot control platoon. There was a lot of unrest in the country in the mid. 1960s due mostly to the Vietnam War and, of course, the Pandora's box thing. So, it was necessary for us to practice riot control procedures. One formation was a V shape. Two squads would form a V with their M-14s, with fixed bayonets, pointed forward. The next two squads would be right behind them with their M-14s positioned between the men in the front squad. This presented a very intimidating double row of bayonets coming at you if you were a rioter. The idea being to persuade you to find another way to express your feelings.

My riot control platoon in training with Mock rioters

The platoon leader was positioned in the middle of the V. This put me right next to Corporal Tate an African American fire team leader with a tremendous, but weird, sense of humor. We were in the V formation and advancing on the barracks where first platoon was cast in the role of rioters. As we advanced, they started yelling and throwing empty soda cans at us.

I said to Corporal Tate, "Well, looks like we are in for some trouble."

He replied, "What do you mean "we," white boy?" Turned around and walked right out of the formation.

Everything stopped and it went quiet for a few seconds and then someone giggled. That set off the whole platoon and everyone broke up laughing. So, there we were laughing our heads off, in complete disarray, with tin cans raining down on us. This was not per the training manual. I looked up to see the captain storming across the field making a bee line for me, which is never a good thing. We had a somewhat unpleasant conversation after which we formed back up and continued the training. I advised Corporal Tate to keep his mouth shut. Couldn't get him to quit smiling.

This training was put in play twice in the next few months. First, we were deployed to the Pentagon riots. This really wasn't a riot as much as it was a party. We were lined up outside the building with our M-14s as part of a perimeter of troops protecting the facility from a bunch of stoned hippies having a really good time. They were putting flowers in the barrels of our weapons which presented an image the Army really did not embrace. Lots of hot chicks were in the crowd with their free love attitude and revealing attire. The biggest problem was keeping my troops from joining the party. I had some thoughts along those lines myself. I am sure there would have been serious consequences if we had given in to the temptations, but it was fun to think about it. I bet that would have made the national news. I could just see Huntly and Brinkley reporting on a platoon of Army troops consorting with the hippies as the platoon leader is being led away in handcuffs by the MPs.

We had been there for a few hours when we were replaced by an MP company so we could go get some rest and food. I was given a room number and told to go there. We walked into the Pentagon and started down a hallway. The inside of that building is very confusing resulting in our almost instantly being lost. After wandering the hallways for 30 minutes I told the guys to just sit down until I could figure this out. About that time a major general (two stars) came around a corner into the hallway where we were seated. I called the troops to attention. The general inquired as to why my platoon was sitting in the hall. I explained we were on our break but couldn't find the room, he patted me on the shoulder and said, "Follow me lieutenant." He then led us to our destination. Not often a second lieutenant gets escorted by a major general. Forgot to thank him.

Our supply officer, another second lieutenant, was assigned to get on the roof of the building with binoculars and report what the crowd was doing. So, he was perched on the roof watching all these hippie chicks many, as noted above, with revealing wardrobes. As he ogled the girls a voice behind him said "Are you getting a good look?" He then proceeded to describe the various cleavages, legs, and postures he was observing in great and appreciative detail. The voice then said, "I don't believe that is what you are up here to observe, Lieutenant." The thought in his mind as he turned around was, "This is not good." He found himself face to face with a four-star general. His very short military career flashed before his eyes as the sun reflected off all those stars on the general's epaulettes. He stammered for a few moments and then the general laughed and went on his way. Tom dropped to his knees and hyperventilated for half an hour. We did one more shift and returned to Fort Belvoir. Our role in the Pentagon riots was over. I became friends with one of those hippie freaks years later. He was an architect in Anchorage.

Our second deployment turned out to be not so much fun. The race riots had broken out across the country. Washington D.C. wasn't spared. I was called to a war room at Fort Belvoir. There were the officers of the battalion, the companies and the platoons all gathered in one room. I counted four companies and 16 platoons that were represented. The battalion commander got up and briefed us on the situation in Washington D.C. it wasn't good. Rioters were running all over the city looting and vandalizing businesses. We were being called in to supplement the local police. There was an ominous feeling in the room.

He informed us we would be armed with our M-14 rifles with bayonets, but no ammo. It was noted that if someone engaged us with firearms we should get on the radio and call the operations center and they would send us ammo. My company commander, Mr. Macho Man, stood up and said, "All due respect sir, but if someone starts shooting at us, we will be calling you from somewhere west of the Mississippi River." Everybody in the room was thinking the same thing, he was the only one who needed to say it out loud.

The room got very quiet and then the colonel replied, "These orders come from the Pentagon so I can't change them, but if you need to find a safe place to wait for the ammo I would support that action." Army talk for "Hell yes, get your butt out of there." Didn't make me feel any better about this deal. My troops had never been to war and I am sure many of them had never been in a fight involving more than two unarmed people. So, giving them loaded weapons in a very stressful situation may not have been a great idea at the time. Most of us ended up in Vietnam so this scenario did happen eventually but not in downtown Washington D.C.

My platoon, along with first platoon, were assigned to guard a high-end hotel in downtown Washington. We traveled there in army trucks. As we entered the city it was total bedlam. People were running all over the place, cars were on fire, and stores were being looted. We were pretty much ignored as our convoy traveled along the streets. After arriving at the hotel, we were deployed around the structure. Everyone was on pins and needles. This wasn't fun like the Pentagon. No one had attacked the hotel, but the stores across the street were being broken into by a small mob of rioters. It was a helpless feeling to watch this destruction and not be able to do anything. We had strict orders to not take any action except to guard the hotel. Some Virginia state troopers finally came along and ran the rioters off, but it was too late for most of the stores. What a shame for the small business owners.

We were replaced in the late afternoon and went back to the fort. I was sure glad to not have the night shift. The next day they assigned us one more shift and it was over. It was a sobering experience to see fellow citizens doing this kind of destruction to our capital city.

We were relieved of our riot control duties and then assigned a job to put some wooden bollards in a side road that came into the fort. They wanted to block off the road to keep bad guys out. Not sure why this was necessary. If I were a rioter, I don't think I would want to attack a fully armed army base with my baseball bat. But again, some of these guys were stoned hippies so probably not critical thinkers.

I formed up two squads and sergeant Dolan, gathered up some picks and shovels and drove to the location. We were given three hours to accomplish the task. There were four bollards to be installed. The dimensions were 12 inches in diameter and 12 feet long. They needed to be buried six feet into the ground. We started digging. The ground was very hard which required considerable pick work. The guys were tired, due to two days of guard duty, and the work was going slowly. At one point I grabbed a pick and started swinging. Somehow the job got done on time.

As we were riding back to the barracks, I turned Sergeant Dolan held out my hands and said, "We got it done on time and look I even got my hands dirty."

He replied, with a straight face, "What happened Sir, did you fall down?" I was going to reprimand him for that remark, but I started laughing so that option was no longer viable. Didn't hurt to let the sargent win one now and again.

During this time there was a program called McNamara's 100,000. The Army has a basic test they give to people about to enter the service, either draftees or volunteers. The questions are quite simple, such as "If you had two candles, one in the bottom of a glass and one with a glass turned upside down over it. Which candle would go out first?" surprisingly a lot of people failed this test. So, it was decided that the Army would take 100,000 of these folks anyway. The plan was that they would take classes such as remedial reading in the mornings and then serve as regular solders in the afternoon. One little interesting fact was a small percentage of these folks were college graduates. I can't imagine they tried to fail the test on purpose to get out of serving. Must have just had a bad IQ day. We never got one of those "college boys." I would surmise the units that did get them probably had some issues with their attempt to avoid joining the military fraternity. I am sure this resulted in several bad days for them, particularly in the remedial reading class.

My platoon got Private Spies. This was a good-hearted guy, but he couldn't read, write or do math. This made him pretty much helpless without his wife who could read and write. Spies had been working at a baseball factory in Chicago, putting the balls in their boxes. He was making good money. The Army swept him up and he landed with us. Within days of arrival he pleaded with me to arrange for his wife to come to Virginia. I found her a job in a mess hall, and she moved out to join him. With their two pay checks they could rent an apartment and live off base. He took the bus to the fort, all was good.

The two of them came to me one day and asked for my help. It seemed that they would run out of money each month and it was eating into their meager savings. I was asked to help them figure out their finances. Turns out she could read and write on a fourth-grade level but had no math skills. I told them to gather up all their bills and pay stubs and meet me at the library. It was an interesting experience for me. I had never had to deal with this level of economic survival, other than recovering from the railroad tie deal. We went over all their expenses such as rent, food, clothes etc. We then added up all the expenses and compared that to their take home pay. It showed they had $15 extra each month. They sat here looking confused. I then asked what else they spent money on. They went to a movie once a month, they bought some candy on occasion, and Spies had a beer each night when he got home. Thirty beers a month at 50 cents a beer was $15. Problem solved, no beer for private Spies. I also arranged for her to get some overtime at the mess hall. They were out of their financial crises. We would get together every month to go over the budget. It was my good deed for the month. I often wondered what became of them. Suspect he finished his hitch and went back to the baseball factory.

Another interesting education event occurred in the company. The supply section was run by Sergeant Bull. He was born and raised in a holler in the Ozark Mountains. It was often pointed out he was the best educated person in his extended family. He had completed third grade and then after a few years working in a coal mine, enlisted in the Army and got a bunch more book learning. As a consequence of his academic background and upbringing the good sergeant totally butchered the English language. An example was "police." For Sergeant Bull it is "Police pass the butter. It is the Po-lice that are cops." He also had a cliché for almost everything. "I am as nervous as a long-tailed cat in a room full of rocking chairs." The sergeant was very personable, and we all liked him.

During the Vietnam War you could avoid being drafted by joining a National Guard Unit. This significantly reduced your chances of ending up in Vietnam. At least at the beginning of the war. In the late 60s a lot of National Guard units got activated and shipped over. If you joined the National Guard you had to go on active duty in the regular Army for six months. We called them six-month wonders. They were not held in high esteem.

One of my fraternity brothers went this route. He dropped out of ROTC and joined a National Guard unit in Idaho. While I was home on emergency leave his unit was processed into Vietnam through our company. They went off to a remote location in NVA territory. He left a note for me saying if he got back to Cam Rahn Bay we should get together for a beer. I sent him a note pointing out officers don't drink with enlisted personnel. We exchanged a few letters. He made it home in one piece.

Well, we got in a six-month wonder who was an English Professor at Berkley. He looked normal, but we suspected he was a liberal. The professor reported in while the captain and I were discussing something in the orderly room. The first sergeant walked into the office and said, "I got a National Guard private out here who is an English professor, what do you want me to do with him?" The captain and I looked at each other and said, almost in unison, "Give him to Sergeant Bull!"

We all watched the interaction between these two with interest. To our disappointment the supply sergeant and the new supply clerk seemed to be getting along just fine. I was in the supply room a few weeks later and asked sergeant Bull how his new clerk was working out. The sergeant took me aside and told me the private was "enhancing his vocabulary." I was taken aback. Enhancing and vocabulary were words that didn't normally come out of Sergeant Bull's mouth. I asked what he meant by that. Sergeant Bull then explained that the professor was giving him two words a week to use as often as possible and this would "enhance his vocabulary."

He then volunteered that the two words for this week were "contemplate and defecate." So, for the next week Sergeant Bull would contemplate if it was a good time to defecate. The next week it was "fabrication and copulation." The weekly words always tended to have a sort of symbiotic (a Sargent Bull word) relationship to each other. The whole company looked forward the to next week's words for the rest of the time the professor was with us. I must admit all our vocabularies were improved by the time he left. I guess we were collateral scholars to Sergeant Bull's literary curriculum.

Because we were a port construction company, which has a diving section, Lieutenant Tom and I decided to get diving qualified. The class was at the Washington Navy Yard. We signed up and the next day the commanding general of the fort called us in to tell us he was very pleased we were taking this training. It was a big deal to him. No pressure there!

It was a six-week course run by a navy chief. The class was composed of 38 Navy ensigns and two Army lieutenants. Tom noted 38 ensigns to 2 Army lieutenants was a fair fight. It is an inter-service rivalry thing. Problem was the Navy chief was on their side and he was in charge. We concurred that this was not good for us. To our dismay this turned out to be quite true.

After considerable physical and mental testing, the training started. The first thing noted was that a hard hat diving suit weighed 23 pounds more than me. I was sure this would be significant, and it was. The tenders would put me in the suit then I had to go down a vertical ladder into the water. The ladder had seven steps. I remember that because each of them was agony in that suit. When only the helmet is above the water surface, they slam the face plate shut, bolt it down, and you are good to go. If the diver has any claustrophobia at all this is not what they want to do. Even without claustrophobia it is not really that much fun. By this point I had noted that "fun" wasn't an overused word in the Army.

There are two air valves in the suit. A valve above your left hip that you turn with your hand puts air into the suit. The other valve is in the helmet and you activate that with your chin to let air out. This allows you to regulate your buoyancy. Once you are completely submerged you can be very light on your feet, or not, depending on valve manipulation. Another fun thing is how you pop your ears. There is a ¼ inch rim at the bottom of the face plate. You use it to push your upper lip against your nose so you can blow to clear your ears. This not a fun thing to do when you are 20 feet under water. Now I have pushed my upper lip against my nose, but it was against the bar after drinking too much in college. There is a distinct difference between the two scenarios.

We were diving in the Potomac River where the visibility was about one-half inch on a good day. Therefore, you did everything blind. This resulted in several challenges for us. The chief's lesson plan was very consistent. He would tell us to do something, wait for us to screw up, explain what we did wrong and then instruct us on how to do it right. Seeing as how Tom and I were Army we were usually selected to go first. I don't want to say the Navy chief was prejudice toward Army officers, but I have to believe he was. He often used words like "Ground pounders and grunts" in referring to us but did so with affection. There may have been some insincerity in the affection part.

One of the lessons involved digging a trench on the bottom of the river. This is done by "jetting" which is using a high-pressure fire hose to blow the silt away making the trench. Now remember, the visibility was one half inch, a little less while jetting, which turned out to be a problem. The technique involves one guy holding the nozzle of the hose and the other guy right behind him holding the hose steady, both in hard hat gear. Of course, Tom and I were selected to go first with no instruction to speak of. "Take this big ass hose and go down there and blast a trench in the bottom of the river." That summed it up. No problem Chief we're on it.

We went down the seven steps from hell and descended 25 feet to the riverbed. I was "red diver" and Tom was "blue diver." I had the nozzle and he was behind me. I called to the surface and said, "Red diver to surface we are ready to begin, turn on the jet." The hose fired up and almost knocked us off our feet. We let air out of our suits so we could reduce our buoyancy to counter the push from the jet. I aimed it at the riverbed and began walking slowly ahead as the trench opened under my feet. The trench got deeper as we moved along.

Things were going great until I felt something rubbing against my elbows. Also, my forward progress was stopped by a wall or something. Perplexed, I called the surface and asked them to turn off the jet so we could figure out what was wrong. Once the jet stopped it only took us a minute or so to discover we were buried in the silt up to our armpits. That wasn't in our plan. We were jetting the silt up into the water and it was settling back down all around us. The chief had not advised us of this possibility, no surprise there.

I conveyed this information to the chief and requested instructions. His first response was for us to figure it out. One of the Navy guys told us later he was giving them a class on jetting and told them we would soon bury ourselves. He then went through the procedures on how to prevent this and how to get out of it if you were dumb enough to get yourself into this predicament. It was a nice lesson for them as they sat in the morning sun with a gentle breeze on their faces. While 25 feet below them, we struggled to free ourselves with no success. Being buried up to your armpits at the bottom of a river in pitch black conditions is not something you want to experience. Our blood pressure was hovering in the high 200s.

After several high-pitched requests for instructions the chief finished his lesson. He then told me to point the jet vertically right in front of my body to blow the silt away until I could reach the air in valve on my hip. This would increase my buoyancy, then continue to jet myself out of the riverbed and do the same for Tom. What he didn't tell me was to reduce the air in the suit, with the chin valve, gradually as I felt the silt letting go of me. An omission I am sure he didn't intend. I note this with considerable skepticism. We were told he then turned to the class and said, "Lieutenant Bell will soon be popping to the surface blown up like a Macy's Parade balloon. He was right. I had the air in valve wide open so as soon as I popped loose from the silt, I snapped into a spread-eagle stance and accelerated toward the surface with me pushing the chin valve for all I was worth. I popped to the surface and floated there for a minute or two and then the chin valve did its job and I descended back to the bottom. I jetted Tom out and he did the same cameo appearance on the surface. The Navy guys thought it was quite funny. We didn't. It was this sort of thing that endeared us to the chief and to the rest of those squids. Squid is an affectionate term for Navy guys.

Another of his lessons by trial and error had to do with sinking a ship. We were tasked with sinking an old derelict cargo ship parked in the river next to the Navy yard. It was probably 150 feet long and sitting in 30 feet of water. The plan we put together, with little or no input from the chief, was to plant shape charges on the hull below the waterline and then blow holes in the ship thereby causing it to sink. A simple plan by simple people. I had a nagging feeling it was too simple and with the chief not providing input the nagging intensified. It was out of character for him to be hands off on anything.

We determined we needed to place two charges on either side of the bow and the stern. These charges would blow four two-foot square holes in the ship sending it to the bottom. This is when the chief decided to give us some input. Red flags popped up in all our minds. He suggested that we needed to sink the ship fast so in real life the crew would not have time to fix the hull. He suggested ten charges on each side of the ship. Having never sunk a ship we went along with his suggestion. The nagging got more intense.

We spent all day getting the charges placed and wired to shore. It was almost quitting time when they were set off. It was a rather spectacular sight. Water shot up into the air, the ship rose about two feet and then sank to the bottom in less than five minutes. Only the antennas on the bridge were above water. We all did high fives and got in our cars and drove home feeling quite proud of ourselves. Should have known better.

The next morning, we assembled on the bleachers as we did every morning to find out what would be our next lesson. The chief informed us that we were now tasked with refloating the ship. We sat there in stunned silence. The nagging had been fully justified. The only saving grace was that this time it wasn't just Tom and me. All the 38 ensigns had been had as well. Didn't really make us feel better. Welding patches on 20 holes vs four was a much bigger job. It took two, two-man dive teams to sink the ship in one day, it took six (we only had six sets of gear) teams four days to patch it up. We put air bladders in the hold of the ship to get her to the surface and pumped out the rest of the water. Remember we did all this in water with one half inch visibility. When asked the lesson we learned on this exercise we all agreed the lesson was not to trust the chief. Of course, Tom and I already knew this.

Looking back on dive training I am not sure why I did it. If you go to Army Ranger school you get a ranger patch to wear on your uniform if you survive the training. paratroopers get a parachute badge to wear on their uniform. With diving school, you don't get a patch or anything else. Only you and the personnel officer know you are diving qualified. I did discover a few months later that you get diving pay of $115 a month if you are completely submerged once in the month. It was January so the swimming pools were closed, and the river was full of ice. I inquired if the bathtub would suffice and was informed that was not an option and to not call again. I did collect the $115 most months in Vietnam by walking off the end of the pier with witnesses.

My year at Fort Belvoir was coming to an end so I requested an assignment to Fort Richardson in Alaska. Somehow the Army misinterpreted my request and cut orders for Vietnam. I couldn't believe they screwed that up. Alaska was my first choice and Vietnam was my last choice. I had always said, "If they try to send me to Vietnam there will be three guys not there, me and the two Army policemen looking for me." Upon receiving the orders, I immediately drove to Washington D.C. to talk to the captain in charge of assigning army engineer lieutenants. I explained the error the army had made and inquired as to his rectifying said error. He stared at me for a short time and then told me to get out of his office before he called the MPs. I had hoped for a better response.

It appeared that a tour in the Jolly Green Jungle was in my future. A month later when picking up my port call there was an engineer lieutenant with the same resume as me picking up his port call for Alaska. He was from southern California and was complaining bitterly about being sent to a freezing cold state. I asked him if he wanted to exchange name tags and port calls as I was going to a very warm place. He declined, don't understand why.

We packed up the Mustang, got a U-Haul and headed back to Oregon where Linda would live while I was gone. We took the southern route going through the Deep South then Texas, New Mexico, Arizona, Nevada and Oregon. I managed to make the trip without killing any U-Haul trailers. We found a house to rent with a fenced yard for our German Shepard and did all the things necessary for Linda to live there. The house was in Salem where her folks lived. I was to report to McCord AFB on May 6 to catch the flight to Vietnam. I won't admit to being scared, but I was very, very concerned.

Vietnamese huts bursting into flames when gas went into stoves.

CHAPTER NINE

THE 497TH P.C.

We drove up to Tacoma, Washington May 5th and found a rundown motel near McCord AFB and spent the night. The next morning, I called my mom to say good-bye. She was crying the whole time I was talking to her, which didn't do much for my mood. Then my sisters did the same. My brother, John, kept his cool, but I could tell he was upset. So, I have all the women in the family bawling like they were at a funeral and John with his voice cracking. Somehow this didn't seem to relieve my anxiety significantly. The last person was my youngest brother Ed who was 13 at the time. He started the conversation by saying, "What is everyone crying about?"

I said that I was going off to the Vietnam War and it could turn out bad for me and everyone was concerned about that.

He said "Bob, you are the best shot of anyone I know, they should be crying for those Viet Cong guys not you." A rather profound statement for a 13-year-old, but for some reason it made me feel better. Didn't cancel out the rest of them but did help some. It is difficult to get upbeat about going to war.

The next morning, we drove into McCord. It was time to say good-bye to Linda. That was a hard moment for us. We had been talking around the dangers of this assignment ever since the orders arrived. Now it was real, and we had to deal with this. It was also when we fully realized that I was embarking on a very dangerous journey that I had no control over. Not a good feeling. I boarded the Pan Am flight that was full of army guys who were going someplace they didn't want to go and

151

had no idea of what they were getting into but were quite sure it was bad. Not a fun crowd. Nobody was singing or telling jokes. They just sat there in their seats and looked scared. We stopped in Guam to refuel and they let us off the plane to stretch our legs. We were on Anderson AFB and I recall the messages written on the walls of the toilets were all very dark and foreboding regarding our destination. I suspect they were put there by troops going home from Vietnam. They didn't help our frame of mind.

We landed at Cam Ranh Bay AFB in early afternoon. Upon reaching the door I noticed six Pan Am flight attendants standing in the galley watching us deplane. They were all crying. That also had an impact on our frame of mind. Between my mom, my sisters and now these airline chicks I had had about all the crying for me I could handle. We hadn't stepped on Vietnamese soil yet, but we were all dreading the next 12 months. If there was any upside to this deal it had not become apparent.

I had spent a year as a platoon leader in the 77th Port Construction Company so my orders were to the 497th port Construction Company located there in Cam Ranh Bay. I went to the MACV processing building, reported in and was told to sit down and wait until they could get to me. It had been about an hour when a major called my name. I reported to him and he said, "Lieutenant Bell you have been promoted to first lieutenant." He handed me the orders and two silver bars and, without further ado, walked away. The Army wasn't much on ceremony in those days. The other issue was we didn't wear metal silver bars in a combat zone, we wore black cloth bars. I didn't have any of those, so I was presented to the world as a second lieutenant for a few more days. The upside was my pay jumped up to $750/month from $715, a 5% bump. I was going to be living high on the hog now. An undernourished hog but, still high on it.

While waiting to be processed I called the 497th PC and talked to the company commander, Captain Straut, and filled him in about my orders to his company. He asked about my port construction experience. I told him about my civil engineering degree and experience as a platoon leader in the 77th PC. He was very excited about my qualifications.

None of his officers had an engineering degree or any port construction experience and so he could really use me. I was asked to keep him informed as I went through processing. He lamented about how the Army has a propensity to make dubious choices regarding assigning personnel. I thought back to the California lieutenant who didn't want to go to Alaska.

Shortly after the telephone conversation I was called into the processing office. There was a W4 warrant officer manning the desk. This is the highest rank for warrant officers. He was a grizzled old soldier. I sat down and handed him my orders. He pushed them aside and said, "Lieutenant you are assigned to the 318th Combat Engineers and they are located somewhere near the Cambodian border." WHAT???

Now let me put this in perspective. Cam Rahn Bay was one of, if not the most, secure facilities in Vietnam. The Cambodian border was the exact opposite of that; therefore, this wasn't good news. All that bawling by my Mom, sisters and flight attendants may have been justified. I needed to do some quick thinking.

I said, "Mister Lang, I have orders to the 497th not the 318th."

He said "you have the orders I gave you. Report back here tomorrow to get your port call."

We stared at each other intensely for a while with very little affection, then I picked up the orders and headed for the phone. This wasn't the assignment I was hoping for. The call to Captain Straut informed him of the situation. He said he was afraid that would happen and that he would deal with it. I was skeptical. Turns out captain Straut was a West Point graduate, and those guys get most anything they want in the Army. That came into play in this deal.

When I reported for my port call the next morning the general in charge of the 35th command group, also a West Point graduate, had contacted Mr. Lang and advised him that I was going to the 497th. When I showed up Mr. Lang informed me he was not happy about that on several levels. He asked if I was a senator's son or something. The next question inquired as to if I knew who General Westmoreland was, I answered In the affirmative. Then I was informed he was General Westmoreland's first sergeant when Westmoreland was a second lieutenant. The Army is a "good ole boy" system. He was letting me know where he fit in that system and that my place, in comparison to his, was somewhat subjective. The diatribe was completed by telling me it was inadvisable to get on his bad side. I flashed back to the sergeant major incident at Fort Belvoir. My reply was, "Chief, I didn't request these orders, so you have no fight with me." I got out of there as quickly as possible.

Reported to the 497th the next day. That call to Captain Straut may have saved my life. The 318th was constantly in a combat zone and took far more casualties than we did. At Cam Ranh Bay we didn't even carry weapons. The only danger we saw was when we got sent on bird dog patrols every month or so and that was minimal. There were very few hostile troops in the area. If you had to be in the Army and in Vietnam this was about as good as it gets. It was a different story when we were relocated to the Mekong River Delta where things were not so secure. More on that later.

I reported to Captain Straut and we had a nice chat about my experience and background. He seemed to be a bit standoffish, but he was West Point and I was ROTC so that was not unusual. Royalty talking to a commoner. He told me I would be taking over the 2nd Construction Platoon. At the time they were in a village 40 klicks south of us working on a pipeline from the coast to an American air force base. He suggested I drive down there and introduce myself to the men and platoon Sergeant Skidmore. He then dismissed me. I walked out into the orderly room and noticed a very large sergeant with a whole bunch of stripes on his sleeve.

He stood up and said, "Lieutenant Bell I presume?"

I replied, "You presume right Top."

"Top" is the informal title of the First Sergeant or top NCO of the company. He smiled and welcomed me to the company in a much more friendly way than the captain. He suggested I put my gear in the officers' hooch and meet him in the mess hall for a cup of coffee. You always accept this kind of invitation from a first sergeant no matter what your rank. He can be your best friend or your worst enemy, the former is better.

The only person in the officers' hooch was the mama san cleaning the place. She directed me to my bunk and dresser. My area and all the areas were decorated in early American army surplus with wooden walls and a concrete floor. The bunk was probably older than I was, and the dresser probably predated my grandfather, but the hooch was clean and organized. There was a piece of rebar to hang my clothes on. I did note the hooch had a bar attached which seemed well stocked with booze. I am thinking, "So this is home sweet home for the next year, hooya. The one-year part was, unfortunately, a bit optimistic.

I put my stuff away and walked over to the mess hall. Top was sitting at the officers table with two cups of coffee. I have to say it was the worst coffee I had ever experienced. I asked, "What is this stuff?" He laughed and said it was officer's coffee. If I wanted good coffee, we would have to move to the NCO table. We did and the coffee was much better. Not good, but better. I learned over the next few weeks this was true of everything in Vietnam. Nothing was good, but sometimes it was better. He had made his point that the NCOs get what they want, not so much the officers. Army NCOs are about as subtle as grizzly bears.

We talked for a while before he started to warm up to me. Once he determined I was an OK officer he became loquacious and started filling me in on the company, the officers and the NCOs. We talked for two or three hours. That talk saved me from a lot of missteps over the next few weeks. This was the exact opposite of the reception I got at the 77th P.C. I now knew who the good officers were, the mediocre officers and the worthless officers, same for the NCOs. Sergeant Skidmore was one of the good ones and Captain Straut wasn't. So, good news and bad news. It is always best, when in a combat zone, to know who you can count on to cover your butt when the chips are down.

When we were done talking, I went back to the hooch and started organizing my gear and wrote a letter home. About six o'clock the other officers started showing up. There are 13 officers in a Port Construction company and 350 men. This is a huge company, almost as big as a battalion.

I introduced myself to each of them as they came in making a mental note as to the Top's evaluation of each. After putting their stuff away someone grabbed a bottle of Jack Daniels and suggested a toast to the newbie (me). We adjourned to the bar where I learned that whiskey was $2 a fifth which resulted in lots of toasts for minor events and some toasts for no event at all.

After the bottle was gone, we went to the company operations meeting. Lieutenant Sarno was the company operations officer. He and Master Sergeant Pearce (the company operations NCO) conducted the meeting. Other than saying "Welcome to the company" they treated me like I had been there for months. Which made me feel all warm and fuzzy, but apprehensive about my responsibilities. They gave me assignments for 2nd Platoon that involved equipment and men I didn't know anything about. I didn't know where they were and wasn't familiar with the job sites. This made it problematic to plan the day. Typical Army M.O. After the meeting they left for the mess hall for dinner I followed along wondering what the heck I was going to do in the morning.

Me with my jeep, note spelling of platoon on tire

Lieutenant Sarno was sitting across from me at dinner. He asked about my background and experience and was very pleased to hear about my port construction experience. He then said, "I understand you are driving down to Phan Rang tomorrow."

I remembered that the captain had mentioned it, but I had no details. He said a motor pool driver would pick me up after reveille and drive me to the village. I was told to get an M-16, an M-79 grenade launcher, flak jacket, ammo and helmet. He explained that we got shot at frequently on this trip but assured me the Viet Cong were lousy shots and stopped shooting if you launched an M-79 round at them. I had just gotten off the plane and still hadn't adjusted to the idea of being shot at, even if it was a bad shot doing the shooting. I now had the details, none of which were good, I didn't feel reassured.

The menu was less than appealing. Not sure what most of the items were, but they all had no taste or bad taste. I got used to the food after a month or so. I think it takes that long for your taste buds to atrophy.

We had the weekly company officers' meeting after dinner. This meeting was run by Captain Straut and it was soon obvious to me that this guy was a real dip wad. The meeting had to do with personnel issues such as leadership changes (a new second platoon leader) and disciplinary actions. He said he was going to article 15 a spec. 4 because the troop had brought a pistol with him when he transferred into the company. I noticed all the other officer's kind of looked down when this clown was announcing this decision. It was obvious they did not agree. It is never good to go to work in a company where everyone hates the boss.

The troop had been transferred directly from Germany to Vietnam and had been told he could take his pistol with him if it was declared and turned into the company armory upon arrival. It would be locked up until his tour was over. He got in late at night, so he waited until morning to fill out the paperwork and turn in the gun. The first sergeant was fine with that, but Straut found out about it and had a fit. Article 15 is company level punishment dished out by the commanding officer. Straut ended up busting him to private. Welcome to Vietnam son. This whole thing soured my image of the captain and it never got better as time went by. It was bad enough to be here so having to deal with a jerk for a boss was salt in the wound. I could tell all the other officers had several salty wounds.

We adjourned to the officer's hooch and a few more bottles of Jack Daniels were promptly consumed. We had an interesting conversation about Vietnam and Captain Straut. Nobody liked either of them on multiple levels. So here I am with a new job, that included being shot at, sitting with a bunch of strangers who hate their job and the boss. Not a lot of upside with that. It was very informative for me. All unpleasant information, but still informative. We then hit our bunks. My home and family seemed very far away.

In the morning, after reveille, a motor pool spec. 4 showed up with my jeep. He was armed to the teeth, wide eyed and very nervous. I didn't take this as a good sign. When asked if he had made this trip before the troop said he had six of them under his belt, and he hated getting shot at. I could certainly relate to that sentiment. On the last trip they had taken a round through the windshield that missed his head by an inch or two. Doubts were expressed about how effective an army helmet was regarding AK 47 rounds seeing as how it was manufactured by the low bidder. Not what I would consider a positive attitude. My anxiety shot up several levels. I had been in Vietnam two days and was going on a leisurely drive through a shooting gallery with us being the little round tin target going from right to left. The learning curve in this job was quite steep and the consequences of screwing up were significant, but I was making $750/month. Somehow that didn't seem to even things up.

We set off with the driver's M-16 in his lap and me with the M-79 pointed out the other side of the jeep. This was very different than riding shotgun at the Winchester waste way. There was no pleasant conversation or sightseeing. We did see some ducks, but they were domestic birds. Anyway, an M-79 grenade launcher would probably be a little over gunned for ducks. 40 klicks are 25 miles. It took us one hour in actual time and about three days in perceived time. One hour is a long time to have your jaws clenched and your eyes darting from side to side. Particularly when you have a totally spooked driver. This is the exact opposite of a Sunday drive with the wife and kids. Being brand new in country I had no idea of what to expect but was sure if something did happen it would be bad.

To add to the drama there was a deuce and a half truck in front of us with a load of 155 howitzer rounds. These are very large artillery shells. The road was potholed, and they hit a big one which launched three howitzer rounds out of the truck. They came bouncing down the road right at us. No way to put a good spin on that sight picture. Now I knew the howitzer round is inert until you put the fuse in so I was mainly concerned about one of them hitting the jeep or worst yet, me. My driver, on the other hand, was not privy to the inert howitzer issue and assumed we were about to be blown to bits, consequently, he jumped out of the jeep when we were going about 25 miles an hour. I had not anticipated his actions which caught me off guard.

I grabbed the wheel and kept the jeep on the road until it rolled to a stop. In the process the loaded M-79 fell out of the jeep and went bouncing down the road. It was not inert, which caused me some additional concern. I took the jeep out of gear and then ran back to see if the driver was hurt. He had some scrapes and bruises, but nothing serious. His fatigues were torn in several places, so he was no longer a well-dressed solder. We found his M-16 and my M-79 which were dinged up a bit, but OK. The troops in the truck were policing up the 155 rounds so we continued our trip. At least nobody was shooting at us. Just another day at the office.

When we were about a mile from the AFB, he stopped the vehicle and said, "Sir, I am going to take a lot of heat if this story gets out. I plan to say I got scratched up helping get the howitzer rounds out of the brush. It would be appreciated it if you backed me up." I agreed, and he completed his tour, seven months later, with his story intact.

When we arrived at the base I found an Air Force sergeant wandering around and asked if he knew where my platoon was located. He pointed to a two-track road going into the jungle and said, "Your guys are on the beach at the end of that road."

We checked our weapons and drove into the tangled mass of vegetation that started outside the fence. It ended up being a two mile drive down a very steep slope to the ocean. You couldn't see ten feet into the brush, therefore if Charlie were in there, he would be so close he didn't have to be a good shot to ruin your whole day. This little Sunday drive we had embarked on wasn't getting any more fun. My adrenaline supply was approaching the low mark.

When we came out on the beach, I saw the men working on a huge motor. It looked like a locomotive engine. A 12-inch pipe was hooked up to the thing. The pipe ran through the brush up the hill to the AFB. You could only see the first 50 feet of the pipe due to the foliage.

I looked around, spotted Sergeant Skidmore and introduced myself. With a less than welcoming voice, he said he had been expecting me. I mentioned my civil engineering degree and my platoon leader time in the 77th Port Construction Company. He didn't seem to be impressed with my resume. It was pointed out that this was his third tour of duty in Vietnam and that he had joined the Army before I was born. The inference being his resume trumped mine, army wise. The sergeant noted he was happy to give me advice based on his experience, but only if that advice was followed. We stood there making intense eye contact with the testosterone valves wide open. The troops became very quiet. After a minute or two it dawned on me that this was a good offer and that anyone would be well advised to accept it.

I stepped back from macho land and replied, "Thank you Sergeant, I was hoping you would say that." An excellent relationship was formed that lasted the whole time we were together. His advice turned out to be invaluable. Some of which kept me and our men alive. I can't think of another situation where a 24-year-old recent graduate could form this kind of leadership status with a bunch of men. It involved a lot of trust.

The project they were working on was to convert a JP-4 (jet fuel) pipeline to a gasoline pipeline. This involved cleaning out the pipe and putting in place a new pump. The locomotive engine was the pump. JP-4 is not a very volatile fuel. It's similar to kerosene or heating oil whereas gasoline is very volatile. This fact turned out to be quite significant in the next hour.

The platoon had finished the job and were about to start up the pump to suck the gas out of the barge and push it up the pipe to the AFB two miles and 800 vertical feet away. This requires significant pressure. The pipe ran through thick brush, so it wasn't visible from the beach for most of its length. There were several huts occupied by Vietnamese civilians scattered throughout the hillside. It was a peaceful and quiet scene. Didn't remain that way for long.

Sergeant Skidmore ordered the pump started and it fired right up, high fives all around. A couple of minutes later one of the huts on the hillside burst into flame. A minute or two later another one caught fire. We were all standing there wondering what the heck was happening. Then two more huts blew up. Sergeant Skidmore yelled, "Shut down the pump!" It took a minute or two and three more huts before we could get it stopped. Once the pump was shut down the huts stopped blowing up, so we concluded there was a connection between the two events. The Army's job is to kill people and blow things up, so we were on task. The timing, location and demographics, in this particular case, were suspect.

With the exploding huts the AFB went on full alert with everyone adjourning to their bunkers. We were still trying to figure out what had happened when the Air Force Police arrived with several very pointed questions as to what we were doing. I advised them that we would fill them in as soon as we figured out what had transpired. They seemed a bit hostile and said that when we figured it out the base commander (a full bird colonel) would like me to report directly to him. I didn't perceive that this would a friendly chat. Sergeant Skidmore looked away and remained silent. Where was his highly touted advice? I had been in country three days and already in trouble with the brass. My first lieutenant bars were feeling quite heavy, even if they were made of cloth.

It turned out that over the last couple of years the Vietnamese folks who lived near the pipeline had run metal tubing underground from their huts to the pipe, then taped into the bottom of the pipe so the tube was concealed. They were using the JP-4 for cooking and heating. All very convenient and cheap, until today. When the more volatile gasoline hit their stove, it set everything on fire. All the civilians managed to escape with no injuries, but their huts and belongings were all burned up. They weren't very happy about this situation and were expressing their displeasure rather forcefully. Only one of them spoke English so he interpreted for the others. Didn't really need him as their opinions were quite obvious by their body language and the pitch of their voices.

Sergeant Skidmore suggested we come up with a story, for the colonel, very quickly. Only thing I could think of was to present the facts and hope for the best. I soon learned this was bad policy in the military.

Armed with this information we reported to the base commander's office. After waiting for an hour, he finally called us in. We came to attention in front of his desk, saluted and I said, "Lieutenant Bell and Sergeant Skidmore reporting as ordered, sir."

I felt we needed to be as formal as possible considering the circumstances. He gave us an at ease and then explained that he had been on the phone with his boss, a major general, trying to explain why his base had gone on full alert. Resulting in several combat missions being delayed. He hoped we could help with that task. We explained what had happened in great detail. He seemed mollified and dismissed us. As we walked to the jeep Sargent Skidmore turned to me and said, "Oh, by the way, welcome to second platoon." I didn't get a warm and fuzzy feeling from the comment.

That night after dinner I introduced myself to the troops. It was different than my introduction to the platoon at Fort Belvoir. With more experience as a platoon leader it was easier to convey to them my background, also that I would do everything possible to look after them and expected them to return the favor. I knew I had to earn their trust and intended to do so. We spent the next two days disconnecting all the taps into the pipe and repairing it. We then convoyed back through ambush alley to Cam Ranh Bay without incident. Had to wonder how I could keep this up for 361 more days and stay alive and sane.

We got in late at night, so just went to bed. The next morning, after reveille I was summoned into the captain's office. He wanted to know what had happened with the huts. He didn't seem to be in a magnanimous mood. Our colonel had received a rather testy call from the AFB commander and then called Straut and expressed his concerns. I was chewed out big time for causing all this trouble, with no opportunity to explain what had happened. At the end of his tirade I was told to report to battalion HQ. It was an unpleasant drive to the colonel's office. I decided to do the coming to attention and Lieutenant Bell reporting as ordered routine. He told me to sit down and tell him what happened. It only took a minute to explain what had gone down.

When I finished, he laughed and said, "Those blue suiters are a bunch of wimps." He then said he was glad to meet me and looked forward to working together and sent me back to the company. I was off to a less than auspicious start with only 360 days to go.

Over the next few months, we had a bunch of rather mundane jobs. Building showers, setting buoys for ships, sheet pile walls etc. I developed a good working relationship with Sergeant Skidmore and the troops. Also being firmly entrenched in the captain Straut is a dip wad crowd, which was pretty much the whole company. The platoon was made of 44 men. Most of them were between 18 and 25 years old. They were from lower income families and hailed from all over the United States. It was a cross section of blue-collar America. None of them were happy about being there.

It was a clash of cultures in that mix of people. When troops are excited and, in a hurry, a young man from southern Arkansas yelling instructions to a kid from the Bronx can have communications problems. It is even more pronounced when there are bullets flying around. Being from the Pacific Northwest I noticed that the guys from the Northeast, and in particular New York, talked fast and precise. "Come here when you're done." The guys from the South talked slow and obscurely. "I recon I will be rat cheer when yawl git back from over yonder." There were many other accents, but those two seemed to be the most diverse. These guys got along just fine but did have some problems understanding each other. I acted as interpreter when needed. I did note one time when I visited them at the NCO club that beer helped them communicate better.

Me and my platoon in Cam Rahn Bay with basketball trophy

We had lots of equipment to include a 60-ton lowbed, six deuce and a half trucks, my jeep, two front loaders, four dump trucks and a D-6 cat. Our floating equipment was a 60 foot by 120-foot barge with a hooch and a 40-ton crane. It was powered by two 185 horse Sea Mules. We also had a bridge erection boat, a diving barge and an amphibious Duck. This was a lot of equipment to care for so, the motor pool was a busy place.

Our Duck driver rotated back to the world, so we needed a new driver. Spec. 4 Rodriguez, a Latino guy from Texas, volunteered to take that job. He was driving a deuce and a half with less than average success. I asked him if he could swim and he said "Yes sir" so I sent him to the motor pool to get up to speed on the Duck. He worked out fine for a few weeks. Seemed like he had found his calling.

We were installing a huge buoy several hundred feet from shore in the main bay. The Duck was hauling people and equipment between the barge and shore. On one trip the engine room flooded and then the whole thing sank.. Everyone jumped off the vessel and swam to the barge, except Spec. 4 Rodriguez. He was flailing around in the water screaming for help. One of the divers swam over and towed him to the barge. I confronted him immediately. "spec. 4 Rodriguez you told me you could swim!" "I can swim LT; it is just I can't swim when I am scared, and I get scared when I am in water over my head." Rodriguez was one of those guys you can't help but like even if he does screw up almost every job you gave him. We found a new Duck driver. LT was the way the men addressed me. It was a sign of acceptance.

The company had an engineering design section. At the time, the officer slot for that position was vacant. Since I had an engineering degree, I was the defacto design engineer. We received a work order to design and build an LST (landing ship tank) landing facility. I was given the design and construction responsibility. This is a far cry from designing a storm drain in a golf course in Hollywood. Upside was very little chance of Charlton Heston dropping by to discuss the project. The spec. 5 in the design section said he knew how to design it, so I turned that part over to him. The facility was to be built on a sand beach and was a concrete structure composed of a ramp with side walls. A very simple design. The way an LST unloads is to drop its anchor a couple of hundred feet offshore and then run up on the beach, drop its bow ramp and unload its cargo. It then pulls itself off the beach with its anchor winch. These ships weight 4,800 tons and are 64 feet long. They hit the beach with a lot of force.

Upon reviewing the design drawings, I noted the concrete was quite thick and had lots of reinforcing steel. Looked very stout to me, but then what did I know? The spec. 5 said he was comfortable with the design. This was the third one he had done and the other two were working just fine. Hard to argue with that reasoning. Turns out I should have done some arguing. We proceeded to build the facility and then lay asphalt across the sand from the main road to the ramp. It was all set. The LST would run up to our superb facility, drop its ramp and everything would roll off the ship and down the road. Piece of cake. One little factor my design guy had not considered was his other two ramps had been built on rock, not sand. This turned out to be a significant issue.

LST ramp under construction.

The first LST arrived. Sergeant Skidmore and I went down to witness the landing, feeling quite proud of ourselves. We had even put a 497th PC flag on the ramp side wall so everyone would know who built it. The ship dropped its anchor and came steaming to shore. Sergeant Skidmore commented that the boat seemed to be going a little fast. I noted that they knew what they were doing. They hit that concrete ramp like an NFL lineman. The ramp probably weighted five tons the ship was 1000 times as heavy. The result was spectacular. The ship pushed the whole structure ten feet straight back which caused the road to buckle and fall apart, it was a complete and catastrophic failure. We stood there in total shock. This caused some problems with unloading the ship. They had to pull themselves off the beach and get unloaded by cranes at the dock. They weren't happy sailors. Within an hour I got a call on the radio that the colonel would like to have a word with me at my convenience. I suspect the convenience part was sarcasm. The Air Force hut burnings flashed through my mind. Would he remember that? Sergeant Skidmore demurred regarding accompanying me to this meeting.

When I walked into the colonel's office and before I could report and salute, he started explaining to me what batter piles were and that you used them to keep a structure in place, such as a concrete structure on a sand beach. It was obvious he was referring to my project. I started to explain that my design experience was designing storm drains but thought better of it. The more he talked the more the pitch of his voice got higher, you could have defined it as squeaky bellicose. I have been involved in some unpleasant conversations, but I am sure this one was in the top five. I stood at attention and looked very somber. He finally wound down and told me to fix it and do it fast. I told him I appreciated his input and would get right on it. He didn't seem to have a lot of confidence it that assurance. The pleasant conversation we had had a couple of months earlier about the hut issue was a vague memory.

It was a unpleasant drive back to the company area as I knew Captain Straut would be waiting for me with both barrels loaded. He was in front of the orderly room when I drove up. The good captain said, "Hey Lieutenant Bell, how did the LST landing go?" The colonel had not told him! I replied, "We had some problems with the footings, but we will get it taken care of before the next ship." He wandered away happy as a clam. I rushed over to Sergeant Skidmore's hooch and told him to keep his mouth shut as he, the colonel and I were the only ones to know what happened and the colonel wasn't talking.

We managed to get batter piles driven and the structure secured to them in the next two days. We swore the platoon to secrecy, and they managed to honor that, Straut never found out. Every time an LST was scheduled the sergeant and I would go watch. They were all good. I was now a fan of batter piles, still am to this day. Never did find the 497th flag we placed on the ramp.

Another interesting project was a dock for the boat that brought the local workers from across the bay to the base. Every morning they would off load on this rickety old dock which was a serious safety concern. We were tasked with building a new one.

We had just finished a barge offloading facility and, as usual, we referred to it with an acronym. In all our reports it was referred to as the BOLF (barge offloading facility). In Vietnam, as with many wars, we had derogatory names for the local people. One of the less offensive terms was "zips." Not sure where that came from, but it was in common use when I arrived in country. So, naturally the new dock was the ZOLF. This was a politically and socially marginal term. To say we were politically incorrect would be an understatement. Hey, it was who we were at the time. Probably more politically ignorant than incorrect. Anyhow all our reports to battalion and up the line to group referred to the ZOLF.

One day the battalion operations officer, a rather humorless major, asked me what ZOLF stood for. I filled him in on the acronym. He went pale and then advised me that our Vietnamese Army counterparts would probably have some problems with that description. The reports had gone to them also. It was suggested quite strongly that we come up with different meanings for the letters. After some thought we came up with zone of operations loading facility. Everybody below the rank of lieutenant colonel, other than Straut, knew what it really meant, but remained mute on the subject.

Unloading locals on old ZOLF

There was one instance, when I ignored Sergeant Skidmore's advice that had spectacular results. There was a POL (petroleum) pier that needed to have the cross members replaced. This was underwater work with depths up to 20 feet. We put the divers down in SCUBA gear to inspect the cross members and figure out what we needed to do regarding repairs. They were only in the water for a minute or two when they surfaced and quickly climbed up the ladder onto the pier. The chief diver informed us there were some very large (six feet long) barracuda down there and he was concerned about their safety, the divers not the fish. He inquired as to how I wished to proceed. After thinking about it for a few minutes I concluded that we needed to make the big ugly fish go away. I told the troops to get some concussion grenades from the barge and throw a couple in the water to scare the barracuda away or to kill them. Either result would solve our problem.

Sargent Skidmore expressed some reservations regarding my plan. I brushed him off before he could express his thoughts and told the chief diver to proceed with the munitions. The good Sargent simply stepped back, assumed the parade rest stance and remained silent. After this incident I recognized that this posture was a major red flag and that I needed to deal with it ASAP or bad things would happen, most probably to me.

I had the troops toss four grenades spaced evenly along the pier. Water and various forms of sea life shot into the air; it was quite spectacular. The explosions also stirred up the sediments on the bottom making the water very cloudy. We waited for about 15 minutes for the water to clear up and put the divers back in. Skidmore, ominously, remained at parade rest and silent. I had to be totally socially tone deaf to not see this huge red flag. Turns out I was.

The grenades had done a couple of things. They had made visibility quite poor and they had killed or injured a whole bunch of fish, none of which were barracuda. This became apparent as the divers descended into the water column, they found themselves in the middle of a barracuda feeding frenzy. The dead and wounded fish were attracting them like bears to honey. A six-foot barracuda probably weighs 50 or 60 pounds, 20 pounds of which is teeth. When you have a dozen or so of them swirling around you, in murky water, gobbling up everything in their path it can cause you to have some concerns. This is the situation in which our divers found themselves. There was an instantaneous decision by all the divers to exit the area. How do you write a Purple Heart citation for getting bit in the butt by a commie barracuda?

Standing on the pier we couldn't see what was happening below the surface. The next thing I know the divers are swimming up onto the beach at a high rate of speed. Some of them didn't stop swimming until they were 30 feet from the water. One guy stopped when he was in about 12 inches of water to take off his fins, big mistake. When he did, a barracuda charged up, grabbed his foot and stripped all the meat off his little toe. We didn't get him shut down for a couple hundred yards. Other than that, it all worked out just fine. Sergeant Skidmore remained at parade rest the whole time.

I did have another, somewhat less than obsequious conversation with the captain. We couldn't get in the water for another week and then had to have a barracuda guard posted. Sargent Skidmore never said a thing to me, didn't need to. The toeless diver was back to work in two weeks. He never seemed to have much trust in me after the incident.

One project we were assigned at Cam Rahn Bay was a pipeline from the fuel pier up to the Air Force Base. The pipe was constructed on dunnage laid on the sand consisting of a 12-inch line for jet fuel (JP4). The route went up through some hills that were covered in brush with occasional open spaces. It was several miles to the AFB.

We built a two-track road to haul the pipe and other materials. This was the biggest job in the battalion and was very high profile with the brass. Which is never a good thing for the guy in charge of building it, in this case that was me. All these guys with eagles or stars on their shoulders were following the activities of a first lieutenant intently. I felt like a germ in a petri dish.

Now this was 1968 so the term "environmental protection" wasn't well known. Upon completion we filled the pipe with several thousand gallons of low-grade diesel and did the pressure test, which did have some exciting moments like when a coupling would fail thereby spewing diesel a hundred feet into the air. All the brush and ground within 150 feet would be coated in diesel. No big deal we just left it that way. I am sure it all went away eventually.

When finished we opened the valve and let all that diesel flow out into the ocean at high tide, the outgoing tide took it away. There is the old saying, "The solution to pollution is dilution." Some of it ended up on the beaches of the islands out in the bay, but it was gone in a couple of months. Nobody used those beaches anyway. All the eagles and stars seemed to be fine with all this. I suspect there would be consequences if we were to do that today.

One day, we were inspecting the pipe prior to turning it over to the pipeline company. My driver and I were in the front seats of the jeep with Sargent Skidmore in the back. I was carrying my AK 47 with two 30 round clips taped together. I wasn't supposed to have this weapon, but the Army's M16 was a piece of crap. It would jam if you walked by a piece of dirt. If we were going to get in a shooting match with Charlie a rifle that worked was preferred. The AK worked.

As we drove into a patch of brush a whole herd of wild pigs busted out and took off across a big patch of open sand. Don't know why, but I told the driver to stop and I stood up and gave those pigs two 30 round blasts from the AK 47. Pigs were going in every direction, sand intermixed with pig parts was flying all over the place and bullets were ricocheting off into the hills. AK 47 casings were bouncing off the hood of the jeep and the pigs were squealing like crazy as pigs are wont to do when shot. Gun smoke hung in the air like a gray fog. The sand was soaked in pig blood and I suspect my jeep driver's shorts were soaked in some other liquid. AK 47 casings were scattered far and wide. It was quite the show.

The result was several dead and wounded pigs and a shell-shocked jeep driver. Sargent Skidmore did not say a word. He just got out of the jeep and finished off the wounded pigs with his M16. It didn't jam once. I couldn't help with this task as I was out of ammo. He then turned to me and said, "So, LT, are we having a BBQ tonight and every night for the next couple of weeks?" On reflection, I think there was a hint of condescension in his voice.

I didn't answer as I was still contemplating what had just happened. Is there an army regulation regarding shooting pigs? Is someone going to investigate this and take my AK 47 away? Is this serious trouble and have I put these two guys at risk? My jeep driver had not moved or blinked since the first round went off. So, he probably wouldn't be able to recall what happened. It then got very quiet. Sargent Skidmore wasn't in parade rest, but it seemed like he should have been. He picked up the radio mic called the first

The great pig shoot of Cam Rahn Bay.

sergeant and told him what had happened. It was requested that he drive over to the Vietnamese village and have the locals come up and get the pigs. They showed up about an hour later, gathered up the pigs and went back to the village. They really were very pleased to get the meat and we were equally pleased to be rid of the evidence. We didn't have a BBQ. As far as I know the three of us and the first sergeant are the only people, other than the villagers, who knew about the Great Pig Shoot of Cam Rahn Bay. It became part of the unwritten history of the Vietnam war.

When you are involved in an armed conflict you tend to be stressed on occasion, but you also get very bored. We were working 14 to 16 hours a day, seven days a week. The Army doesn't pay overtime, nor do you get extra compensation when Charlie or the NVA (North Vietnamese Army) shoot at you. There is very little upside to this schedule. There was also the food situation. Dehydrated steaks (taste like cardboard), powered eggs and reconstituted milk were some of the high points of our culinary repast, which results in an abstemious dinning culture. Then there were the C-rations which were one or two steps lower on the dining enjoyment scale. Due to our anti-gourmet diet and mind-numbing work schedule, we took advantage of any break in either category.

We were getting the barge ready to drive some piling. The guys were setting the anchors and rigging up the pile driver. Suddenly, the barge was completely surrounded by millions of mullet. These are a fish about 10 inches long that, obviously, travel in huge schools. They are also quite tasty. Much better than dehydrated steaks or C-rations. We were presented with a culinary opportunity if we could figure out how to take advantage of it.

Our first thought was how do we catch some of these fish? We didn't have any nets or fishing gear. One of the troops suggested shooting them, but that was a natural reaction for an army troop. The best solution to any problem is to shoot it. They are trained that way. We rejected that out of hand.

I then came up with a brilliant plan. The company commander did question the brilliant part later. We once again broke out a box of concussion hand grenades. Those puppies don't have any shrapnel. They are just a high explosive device used mainly under water. They seem to have barracuda issues, but generally are effective in killing fish or bad guys. Sergeant Skidmore wasn't in parade rest so it was a go.

I had one squad (11 men) line up along the edge of the barge with two grenades per man. On my command they pulled the pins and threw them into the water among the fish. The result was spectacular. Twenty-two domes of water rose about five feet, like you see in the movies when the Navy sets off depth charges, only smaller, and with mullet flying in all directions. An impromptu flight of non-flying fish. It was a sight to behold. When things settled down, there were hundreds of mullet floating on the surface and thousands more lying on the bottom of the bay 30 feet down.

It is not often when one of my plans comes together. Producing a good, but rare, feeling of accomplishment for me. Sargent Skidmore nodded his approval.

The platoon was put into the water to gather up the floaters. We filled three 55-gallon drums with mullet. The whole company had fresh fish for dinner three nights in a row. Everybody was happy, except the Captain. He had gotten the, "What the hell is going on out there?" phone call from the colonel. I think he was just upset because he didn't get any of the fish. I was advised, in very strong language, not to do anymore high explosive fishing of any kind. This reprimand was delivered by the captain over a plate of fresh mullet so the impact on me was somewhat muted.

Troops in water getting fish

We sent someone to the village to tell them they could have the fish on the bottom of the bay. About 30 mama sans, each with a young girl, showed up in dug out type boats and the girls free dove down to get those fish. It took two days to collect them all. Thankfully, they encountered no barracuda issues. There were fish drying all over that village. I like to think that everyone in the village appreciated Lt. Bell for the pigs and fish, Vietnamese surf and turf. They say you are here on earth to do good for others. What the others are here for I have no idea. In this case, I was just doing my part for General Westmoreland's pacification program. I don't think he ever thanked me.

We did have one other fishing adventure. An Army port construction company has a diving section. It has scuba, Jack Browne and hard hat diving gear. I was a diving qualified officer, so I could use the gear if I wanted.

On one occasion Captain Lee and I gathered up scuba gear and went to inspect the sea floor where we were going to place the anchor for a large buoy. We swam over the barrier reef on the surface and then went down in about 40 feet of water. The work site was about 100 yards from the reef. The bottom had lots of large rocks scattered around but was mostly coral with patches of sand and gravel. As we swam along, I noticed a langouste (lobster). Then I saw another one, then two more. They were all over the place. Another culinary opportunity had presented itself.

After we inspected the site we surfaced, and I told the C.O. about the lobsters. He had seen them too but didn't know what they were. He was from Nebraska. They don't have a lot of ocean there. He attended the University of Nebraska and told me the football team had a big N on their helmets. He said the N stood for knowledge. I just nodded. Anyhow, he wasn't real up on sea life, so the lobsters weren't something he had seen in the wild. The captain did concur that this was an opportunity to supplement our diet as long as it didn't involve explosives. Apparently, there was still some sensitivity about the barracuda and mullet incidents. A plan was devised. It involved going back to the company area and getting one of the barrels from the mullet episode and picking up some bags from the diving section made from net for carrying things under water. About 10 lobsters would fit in each bag. Then we would head back to the lobster beds.

We placed the barrel in the back of a ¾ ton vehicle and filled it with sea water. Now that we were geared up it was time to launch the lobster collection program. It took us a few hours swimming back and forth with bags full of lobsters, but we returned to the company area with a lobster for every man in the company and ten more for the colonel. This was in lieu of another scolding phone call. I think he was OK with us catching lobsters if it didn't involve any ordnance. It was hard to tell as most lieutenant colonels don't have any emotions. In fact, this guy was a West Point graduate and his dad was a four-star general, so he was most likely on his way to "generalhood." I suspect if you cut him, he would bleed olive drab. Any infraction of Army protocol wasn't something he wanted on his record, but, boy, do those lobsters taste great! I suspect the acceptance of the lobsters was a difficult judgement call on his part.

That night we lit a fire under the barrel and boiled those crustacean puppies. The mess Sargent prepared the side dishes. It was the best meal any of us had the whole time we were in Vietnam. The only downside was those dehydrated steaks tasted even worse after the lobster experience. Our taste buds had been born again after months of bland food. Took a few months to shut them down again.

We didn't go lobster fishing again because a memo came down from group HQ that the village had complained about us catching their lobsters. Seems like the mullet and pigs didn't buy us much goodwill after all. Should have given them some lobsters.

I had a real surprise when I received a call from the Red Cross advising me that my dad was coming into Na Trang harbor in a week. He was an officer on an American Merchant Marine troop ship hauling Korean troops to Vietnam. His real estate business had gone broke, so he joined the Merchant Marines to get a paycheck. They sailed from Japan to Korea then to Vietnam and back to Japan. I got permission to go visit him as he was in port for two days and one night. Our motor pool warrant officer, Mr. Tanaka wanted to go with me, so he drove the jeep. The roadway between Cam Ranh Bay and Na Trang was called ambush road due to the frequency of being sniped while driving that route. I reflected on the trip to Phan Rang a few months earlier. No sweat. Consequently, we were in full battle attire for the trip, which was made without incident. We did sweat like crazy, in the 90-degree heat, due to our wardrobe.

Dad's ship was anchored in the bay with a large loading barge tied to her. We jumped on the liberty launch and were delivered to the ship. When we got to the barge there was a large unit of Korean soldiers formed up. I would suspect several hundred of them. They were part of the White Horse Division. The troops were standing at parade rest facing the ship. There was no way to get to the ship except to walk right through the troops. So here is a U.S. Army officer and a warrant officer walking through these Korean troops coming from behind. The White Horse Division were very disciplined troops and extremely conscious of rank. The result was as we were noticed by each line of troops they would snap to attention. Of course, once that started to happen there was no turning back. We arrived at the front of the unit with all of them at attention. A Korean Captain approached us and asked if he could do anything for us. He seemed a bit curious as to what the heck we were doing with his men. We explained we were just trying to get to the ship. He laughed and noted the protocol was for us to have the liberty launch call ahead when officers were coming so he could have his troops prepared. We said we would do that next time, shook hands with him and headed up the ramp to the ship.

Dad and I on his ship in Na trang.

Dad was waiting for us in the galley. He had a nice lunch laid out. I introduced Mr. Tanaka and we sat down to the first meal in a long time with food that actually had some taste, other than the lobster and mullet meals. It was a great start to a pleasant two days.

After lunch dad gave us a tour of the ship. I had never seen engines as big as the ones on this ship. The stainless-steel drive shaft going to the prop was like six feet in diameter. I was really impressed. Mr. Tanaka, as our maintenance officer, was fascinated. It took an hour to get him out of the engine room. The whole ship was impressive. I don't remember the total capacity, but it was several thousand troops. The bridge was a little disappointing. I expected a bunch of sophisticated equipment and high technology. In fact, it was just a wheel to steer, a bunch of phones, the throttle and a few more knobs and switches. Much less impressive than the engine room. Even the captain was a funky old fart with the personality of a hippie.

Dad had some duties to attend to, so he took us to our quarters. They were a bit cramped, but clean and tidy. We took a nap. Dad showed up around 4:00PM and said the plan was to go ashore to have dinner and a few drinks. It was back on the barge, sans Koreans, and then the liberty launch to town. Mr. Tanaka said he had some Green Weenie (Green Berets) friends stationed at the 5th Special Forces headquarters at the base. He went to hook up with them. We went to the Na Trang Hotel. There was a dive bar on the roof. Dad ordered a mixed drink and I had a Ba Muoi Ba beer, brewed in Vietnam. It was an awful tasting beer, but I was used to it from when the booze ship was late. Taste buds were numbed anyway so no big deal.

Our table was located so we could see the people on the street below. While catching up on what each of us had been up to, Dad suddenly said "Damn, that is one of my crew." I looked down and saw an American guy staggering down the sidewalk totally drunk. He stopped in front of a building across the street and was suddenly pulled through the door by somebody. Was he just kidnaped? Paid the bill as we ran down the steps and across the street. The door was partially open, so we just walked it. Found ourselves in a sort of hallway with the walls made of tarps hung on a wire. At the end of the hallway was a beat up old desk with a very imposing Vietnamese lady siting there scowling at us. It wasn't a welcoming environment. About that time a U.S. Army guy came out from behind a tarp, took one look at me in my officer's uniform and yelled "Raid." He then took off running down the hallway and out the back door. I was initially perplexed. What the heck was going on here?

Pandemonium broke out at that point. G.I.s were bailing out in all stages of undress and heading for the doors. Vietnamese women, dressed similarly, were suddenly everywhere yelling something in Vietnamese. I am sure it wasn't them welcoming us to their house. It was obvious we had stumbled into a house of ill repute. After a quick search we found dads guy sprawled out on the floor. We dragged him out of there with the madam beating on our backs and yelling insults. She seemed to have a good grasp on American cussing protocol. We took him to the launch and sent him back to the ship. Doubt if he had any valuables on him at that point.

After that little adventure it was off to a tour of the city. Got pictures of monks, ancient buildings, the university and other points of interest. We then went to the Green Weenie officers club, located Mr. Tanaka and his friends, one of whom was a captain, and had dinner which was delicious. The Green berets were such a storied outfit that the Army gave them anything they wanted, including good food, when they weren't out in the jolly green jungle eating bugs and roots. After dinner we adjourned to the bar. We had a few drinks, maybe more. The captain got very inebriated, the master sergeant with him didn't, so he kind of took charge.

The conversation turned to procuring stuff you needed to do your job. The sergeant noted that they had been trying to get a quad-50 machine gun for two months with no success. I perked up and said, "I have one." Our company area was on a hill overlooking the main supply yard for Cam Rahn Bay. Not only did a huge amount of material come in through that yard, but a lot went out including damaged tanks, APC (armored personnel carriers) and other broken equipment. Every morning our supply officer would review what came into the yard with his binoculars. It was his way of shopping for equipment and supplies. We also needed quad-50s for our barges, so if he saw one on a damaged vehicle, we would go retrieve it that night. The company had a specially trained team to procure items from the supply yard, sans paperwork. It just so happened we had two extra guns at the time.

The first question I had was what they had to trade for it. The sergeant replied that they had two pallets of mahogany plywood, a pool table, a ping-pong table and two Czech made AK 47s with 2,000 rounds of ammo. He said I could pick what I wanted. I picked all of it, which caused the negotiation to go on for some time. The sergeant finally settled for everything except the ping-pong table. He told me to deliver the quad-50 and pick up the merchandise in two days. I suggested that it would be better if they delivered as they were better suited for Ambush Road. Negotiations were renewed. We finally got him to agree to deliver, but I only got one AK 47 instead of two. He then picked up his captain and left. Dad, Mr. Tanaka and I did a high five and then drank ourselves stupid. Don't remember going back to the ship.

Late the next morning we were on the barge waiting for the liberty launch. Another Korean unit was formed up same as before, except they had been warned we were coming. There was a Korean colonel who had an air conditioner on the deck next to him who spoke English. I asked him where he got the device. He said it came from Japan on the ship. I turned to Dad and said, "You can bring an air conditioner?" Dad said he would have one on his next trip. This was a huge deal. An air conditioner provided not only comfort, but considerable status. We then drove back to the company. About halfway there somebody took a shot at us and put a hole in the spare tire. We didn't stop to investigate. Neglected to put the tire in for a purple heart.

I was amazed when the Green Weenies showed up in our company area two days later. Captain Straut had been reassigned so that somebody didn't frag him and was replaced by Captain Lee, who was a good guy. Everyone was delighted with the change. He didn't even ask about the trade deal. We built an addition on the officer's hooch with the plywood and installed the pool table. I took the AK 47 for my weapon. It was far superior to the M-16. A pool room with mahogany walls wasn't something you would expect in Vietnam. As noted above life in Vietnam was never good, but now life wasn't as bad.

Dad's ship was back in Na Trang the next month. I drove up to meet him and pick up my air conditioner. We did the Na Trang Hotel thing again, sans the whore house. As we were standing on the barge with my new air conditioner waiting for the liberty launch, we were approached by a Korean major who inquired as to who owned the air conditioner. Being cautious we asked as to his intentions. Turns out he and other Korean officers were in the market for air conditioners. Dad asked what they would pay for it and without hesitation he said $300 American. Dad countered with $500. The major said $450. I am thinking well, "there goes my air conditioner." My new and improved status was about to be eliminated. I was saved when Dad said this one was for me, but he would be back in a month with four of them that he would sell for $450 each. The man just never quits selling.

The launch showed up and I loaded up my air conditioner and headed to shore. I turned and waved good-bye to Dad as he stood on the barge. It was the last time I saw him alive. He died of a heart attack three months later. Vietnam was a bad experience for me, and this was one of the worst things that happened. The danger and harsh conditions were bad enough, but for that place to be the last time I saw my dad really sucked. I have often reflected on that moment over the years. Life is so unpredictable. He was only 56 years old. I assumed we would both be back in Ephrata in less than a year and we would be going fishing or bird hunting. Instead I was home on emergency leave three months later to attend his funeral.

I was in a White Horse Division officer's club several months later and noted the air conditioner was the same brand and model as mine. I asked, but nobody knew where it came from. I suspect they bought it for $450 from an old guy on a troop ship in Na Trang.

One of the odd little quirks in Vietnam was that we all used outhouses. There was one half of a 55-gallon drum situated under the seat that caught the sewage. With the high temperatures in Vietnam your daily constitutional was never a pleasant experience air quality wise. Every day at 5:00 PM throughout the country the drum was pulled out from under the seat, diesel poured on the contents and then ignited. It was a duty performed by civilian employees or a troop who had really screwed up big time. We built a 22-seat outhouse which I am sure was some kind of record. Not sure if the Guinness record book covers outhouses. It was much larger, but with fewer technological features as Smith Hall at survey camp.

As noted above, our supply officer surveyed the base supply yard every morning. One day while we were at breakfast, he noted that he had observed two porcelain toilets in the yard. We all perked up. Hadn't used one of those puppies since we left home. We had to have those toilets. That night our specially trained team procured the appliances.

As we were an engineering unit, we had the men and equipment to construct a sewer system with relative ease. We installed one toilet in the officers' hooch next to the shower and one in the NCOs' hooch. Got to keep those guys happy. The troops had a high end 22 seat facility for their use. The company was located on a hill about 500 feet above and 1,500 feet away from the ocean. It was decided to go with a

Cam Rahn Bay Vietnam

holding tank and gravity system. The sewage would go into a 500-gallon tank. When it was full a valve opened into an eight-inch pipe that would deliver the contents down the hill and fifty feet offshore into 30 feet of water. Nobody but a few fish knew it was there. The result was our commanding general pooped in a metal drum and we pooped in a real toilet. How is that as a status symbol?

As noted above Cam Rahn Bay was a very secure facility. If you had to be in Vietnam this was the place to be. The only danger we experienced was an occasional bird dog patrol, but even these were relatively safe. There was not a lot of enemy activity in the vicinity. Most of the patrols were just a walk in the woods in 100-degree weather with 50 or 60 pounds on your back, wearing a flak jacket and a steel pot on your head. These factors made the walk less pleasant. We did get shot at a few times by some Viet Cong with antique guns. Charlie was well known for being an extremely bad shot. They confirmed that assessment every time we encountered them. We returned fire with several thousand dollars' worth of ammo. The exchange was very lopsided. This caused them to exit the area or exit this world depending on the accuracy of our return fire. We recovered a couple of the weapons which probably dated back to their war with France in the 1950s or even before that. Charlie was far from a well-trained or well-equipped troop. They were mostly farmers who took a pot shot at the Americans every now and then, part time solders. I guess they were the Vietnamese National Guard.

When we were relocated to the Mekong River Delta area, we found ourselves in the war, big time. I took the safety of these guys, as well as my own, very seriously. When on bird dog patrols or when we were in fire fights, I would take control of the men and Sargent Skidmore followed my orders without question. There was no time to discuss options, somebody had to be in total charge and that was me. It was a tremendous and frightening responsibility. I am proud to say none of us got killed. We collected a few purple hearts, but nobody got dead. There is a lot of truth to the saying that American soldiers are the best troops in the world. I know because I witnessed them in action. My pride in having served with those guys is beyond description.

Me, Tom, and Allen between NVA attacks Near the Mekong Delta.

Cruising the Mekong River with quad 50

CHAPTER ELEVEN

LONG BIEN

Our pleasant life was totally ruined when we moved to the Mekong River Delta. Some colonel showed up and gave us orders to relocate to Long Bien. We had no idea this was coming. It was a huge task. Half of our equipment floated. Therefore, the barges and boats would have to go by sea, our trucks etc. would go by highway and the rest would fly. They gave us five days to move 350+ troops and all this equipment half the length of the country. The CO put me in charge and flew to Long Bien to "set things up." He was really good at setting things up, particularly me.

We lined out the barges and boats with a route, made arrangements for Navy escorts, procured fuel and food and sent them on their way. We had a considerable amount of construction material such as steel beams, navy cubes, a concrete mixing plant etc. We could only haul about half of it in our trucks, so I went to the base supply and asked them how to return all this material. They said they had no way of accepting the stuff so it was up to us to deal with it, but we couldn't leave it behind in our area. Their lack of assistance made us feel better about stealing all that stuff from their yard.

I solved the problem by having one of the cats dig a deep hole next to the stockpile and then push everything in and bury it. I suspect there was 20 or 30 thousand dollars' worth of material in that hole. Wonder if it is still there.

We formed up in a convoy, hooked up with our escort, a grunt (infantry) unit, and headed south. It took five days to make the trip. The grunts had a few shooting incidents, but I suspect they were the only ones doing the shooting. They probably killed a few monkeys. In my conversations with the infantry officers about their lives I realized just how good we had it and how that was about to change for the worse. When we got to Long Bien the CO had everything "set up." He had scoped out the base officers' club and had stocked our officers' hooch with booze. The company area was in great shape with facilities in good condition, sans a mahogany walled pool room. I concluded this would not be so bad after all. Those grunt officers had it all wrong. At least it seemed that way at first. We quickly settled into our new home with a false sense of security. Fact is, in Vietnam any sense of security was false.

It took a couple of days to get everything up and running. We were unable to bring our toilets with us, so it was back to the outhouse. Definite downside to the move. The barges and boats were docked on the Mekong River about three miles away. There was no security there, so we had to post guards at night. Not one of the more sought-after assignments. Charlie would take a crack at them every now and then, but never came close. Still, anytime somebody is shooting at you it tends to be stressful

Normally a Port Construction Company is attached to a group, but once again we were given to a construction battalion. The 92nd Engineer Battalion. The commanding officer was a good guy, but his operation officer, a major, was a real dip wad. We had just gotten rid of one of those, now we had another one. Shortly after arriving in Long Bien our operations officer went back to the world, so I was promoted from platoon leader to operations officer. The promotion didn't involve a raise in pay or status. My duties involved overseeing all the construction projects, the equipment maintenance and facilities. In essence this put me in charge of all the other lieutenants and their NCOs', a whole lot more work and responsibility. The captain took care of personnel issues, command duties and "setting things up."

My staff consisted of two spec fours and a spec five. Two design/drafters and a clerk. I also had an operations sergeant. He had the same rank as the first sergeant. He referred to the stripes on his sleeve as "Three up and three down." His name was Patterson and he had been in the Army for 25 years, nine of which were, at various times, in the 497th Port Construction Company. He was a very competent man and not somebody you wanted to cross. I developed a very good working relationship with him as quickly as I could.

Every day at 6:00 pm Sergeant Patterson and I would attend the battalion operations meeting run by Major Dip Wad. Since we had much more equipment than the other companies in the battalion the major would assign my equipment and operators to them as needed. We got last priority on our own equipment. None of their equipment was ever assigned to us. This was a one-way street. I think the battalion didn't really think of us as part of their organization. We were just "attached" to them. We were the red-headed stepchild in the family.

I complained bitterly about this in our company operations meetings which took place after the battalion meeting. Because we didn't have all the equipment we needed, many of our projects were delayed and we were held responsible for the delays. The colonel would berate our CO who would pass it on to me. The whole thing was not conducive to good morale.

One day on the way to the battalion meeting Sergeant Patterson said he had a plan to keep our equipment away from the other companies. Upon being asked what the plan was he advised me I didn't want to know. I nodded and we continued to the meeting.

The first thing the major said was that we needed to send two of our four dump trucks to Bravo Company. Sergeant Patterson said that all four of our trucks were on red line (in need of repair) and produced the red line report. The major scowled but moved on. The plan, I didn't know anything about, was working like a charm.

On the way back to the company I asked to see the red line report. It was obvious that all the needed repairs were quite simple to fix, such as a flat tire. By the time we got back to the company all the repairs had been completed. The sergeant did let the major have a piece of equipment on occasion to not be obvious. I never felt the need to check the red line list after that day nor did our captain. The major never caught on. I am sure his operations sergeant was on to the "red line scheme" but he drank the same brand of whiskey as Sergeant Patterson. I know this because I paid for that extra booze.

Another favorite story I have on Sergeant Patterson had to do with my platoon leaders and his platoon sergeants not staying on the job sites to supervise the work. They would be off doing personal stuff or just goofing off. One day after the company operations meeting, I told Sergeant Patterson that I was going to get all the platoon leaders together in the officers hooch and chew them out about not being on the job and suggested he might consider doing the same with the platoon sergeants. He didn't say anything, but just nodded. I very seldom gave Sergeant Patterson an order. He responded much better to suggestions.

We had our meeting and it wasn't pleasant for the lieutenants. I ended my dressing down by asking which of them would rather be on the job site or in some combat engineer unit on the Cambodian border. They all seemed to lean toward staying where they were. I then decided to go sit in the operations office for a while so they could talk among themselves.

While sitting at my desk, in the dark, I heard the platoon sergeants gathering up outside office. They couldn't see me through the screen, so I just sat there and kept quiet. They were asking each other what was going on and the common answer was "I don't know, Patterson said to be here, so I am here."

About that time Sergeant Patterson showed up and told them to form up and come to attention. There was some hesitation until he yelled "Now!!!" They quickly formed a line and snapped to attention. He then put them at parade rest. My admiration for my Sergeant went up several notches with his next statement. It was, "I want each of you to count the stripes on your sleeve." He waited a few seconds and then said, "Now I am going to count mine." Of course, he had more than they did, so he quickly had confirmed his dominance. It was awe inspiring to watch.

He then hit each of them in their weak spot. Sergeant Gonzales, the first platoon sergeant, had retired as a staff sergeant. The Army contacted him and told him if he would reactivate for a tour in Vietnam, he could retire again at sergeant first class grade, but he had to complete the full one year tour in order to retire at the higher grade. This meant a substantial increase in his retirement pay. He joked that it put him in a new tax bracket. Sergeant Patterson addressed him first by saying, "Gonzales if me or Lieutenant Bell show up on your job site and you are not there you better have a damn good reason, or I will send your butt home on the next plane." The world came to a stop for Sergeant Gonzales. The sweat was immediately glistening on his forehead. He then turned to Sergeant Cole, the motor pool NCO, who fancied himself a tough guy and was always threating to beat somebody up. The threat was, "The next time I come to your work site and you are not there I will wait for you to come back and then beat the crap out of you in front of all your guys." He went right down the line and had an unpleasant scenario for each of them, they were then called to attention and Sergeant Patterson walked away.

They stood there for some time until someone said, "Is he gone?"

Another sergeant said, "I think so." They left without saying a thing to each other. It was a well-run and constructive meeting unless you were one of the sergeants. He had defined the problems and listed the action items necessary to resolve them.

I suspect that conversation wasn't something they taught in NCO school, but I must admit it was quite effective. I never arrived on a job site after that meeting that the platoon sergeant wasn't there. The lieutenants were there also, but they did not have nearly as much fear in their eyes as the sergeants. Officers run the Army; sergeants make it work.

Long Bien was also a fairly secure post. Not quite as secure as Cam Rahn Bay, but still much better than most of the country. Problem was, most of our work was up and down the Dong Nai and Mekong Rivers which were far from secure. Chugging along at two knots in a large work barge you're a very tempting target for Charlie or an NVA unit. We were constantly getting sniped at from the shoreline. There was no upside to this. It has a negative impact on morale, damages equipment, and interrupts the tranquility of floating along the river. We resolved this issue by mounting two quad-50 machine guns on each barge. These puppies put out about 2,000 fifty caliber rounds per minute or a little more than 33 rounds a second. You could turn the jungle into silage with these things. We kept two guys on each gun as we leisurely cruised up and down the rivers. If Charlie took a shot at us we would pulverize him and everything within 100 feet of him in less than a minute. This made it a lot less fun to shoot at us, so the snipping fell off dramatically. The quad-50's didn't help much with the tranquility thing, but you sometimes have to make sacrifices.

One of our jobs was ten miles up the Dong Nai River from Long Bien. We were building a pier protection system. This involved putting an underwater chain-link fence around the piers of the bridge and then filling the area between the fence and the pier with concertina wire. Which made swimming in the area problematic. This was to keep Charlie from setting charges on the piers and bringing down the bridge. Second platoon had the job, so they were there with their barge and 40-ton crane. The diving section was also there as most of the work was under water.

I drove up to see how things were going. Lt. Dave was the platoon leader and Sergeant Skidmore was still the platoon sergeant. When I arrived, they were in the process of removing a steel piling that was imbedded in the river bottom. It stuck about ten feet out of the water. They had tried to pull it out with no success, so the plan was to attach a shape charge where it went into the riverbed and blow it loose. As with most Army plans it was a simple and straight forward scheme.

A shape charge is a piece of C-4 explosive material with a V cut in one side. The V directs the explosion to a very thin line on the pile, so it cuts the steel like a cutting torch, except it also produces a very big explosion. A big explosion while using a cutting torch, on the other hand, is never a good thing. Lt. Dave was also a diving qualified officer, so he was determining how much C-4 to use. When I got there, he had somehow decided to use two pounds. The diving chief was concerned about the amount of explosive material and Sergeant Skidmore was in his parade rest pose which told me he wasn't on board with this deal. I approached Lt. Dave and inquired if he had referred to the manual on underwater blasting, he advised me he had and was damn tired of everybody questioning his plan. I said "carry on" stepped back and joined Sergeant Skidmore in the parade rest position. It was then suggested we move the work barge further away from the blast site. The diving chief had already moved the diving barge. The only thing near the piling was the 600 CFM compressor which was tightly strapped to a ten-foot square float. We moved the barge and the divers set the charges. What happened next was truly spectacular.

A huge dome of water erupted out of the river and that 12-inch-thick, 500-pound, steel piling shot out of the water dome and into the air like a missile fired from a submarine. A mini tidal wave flipped the 600 CFM compressor over, so it was now under the float and then hit our barge with enough force to almost knock us off our feet. It was lucky we were at parade rest as that is a very stable stance. The piling went up about 50 feet and then splashed back into the river. We stood there speechless for a few seconds and then Sergeant Skidmore said, "Well that is taken care of, let's get started on the fence." Once again, I noticed a hint of sarcasm in his voice.

Several dead fish soon floated to the surface and the people in the village jumped into the river to retrieve them. So, there was an upside to this Deal, albeit a small one. I checked out a few other things and was preparing to leave when Sergeant Skidmore walked over and said "I sure miss you LT."

I responded, "You had to break me in, I am sure you can do the same for him." He nodded and went back to work. The work report never mentioned the steel pile missile incident.

Vietnam was a good experience for me engineering wise. I got to design and supervise construction on lots of projects that a young engineer two years out of college would never be put in charge of back in the world. I also had some major screw ups, such as the LST ramp, that were learning experiences without the consequences found in the private sector. It gave me a head start in my career when I got home.

I met some great people and developed a strong comradery with them. Other than family, I don't think I have ever developed that kind of fellowship with anyone. We truly were brothers in arms.

All the other aspects of Vietnam were negative. We worked 16 to 18 hours a day, seven days a week. People were shooting at us and trying to blow us up. We were shooting back trying to kill them and we didn't even know who they were. The food was terrible and the accommodations even worse. Our employer (the Army) had very rigid work rules, lousy pay and benefits and job safety, particularly during combat, was less than ideal. This is a job description that would go begging for applicants in the private sector. Not even sure such a job would be legal. If it were not for the fact that we were American soldiers answering the call of our country, we probably wouldn't have taken the job. Well, the draft might have had some influence on that decision.

The worst assignments we got were the bird dog patrols. When we were in Cam Ranh Bay these little extra duties were not bad. They would send us into an area to look for bad guys and we would occasionally have a Viet Cong sniper take a shot at us, but not very often and, as noted earlier, they were lousy shots. He would fire a 25-cent bullet and we would respond with several thousand dollars' worth of ordnance. The economics were in Charlie's favor but, we always won the fight. The big deal, as noted above, was crawling through the brush with 50 or 60 pounds on your back, wearing a flak jacket and a steel pot on your head in 100-degree weather. There is no fun component to that deal.

The purpose of the bird dog patrol was to find NVA (North Vietnamese Army) units point them out and then call in artillery or gunships, hence "bird dog." When we got to the delta the bird dog patrols got much more stressful. There were a lot more bad guys in this area and they were better trained and equipped. It was on one of these patrols that I found myself in the situation depicted at the beginning of this book.

It was Lt. Dave and my turn to take a patrol. We took a barge upriver about 20 miles. I was to take two squads and cover an area west of the river and Dave would take two squads and do the east side. It was relatively flat topography, but thick brush, trees and tall grass.

There are 11 guys in a squad, so I had 22 men and Sergeant Skidmore. We had two M-60 machine guns, four M-79 grenade launchers, five ATW (anti-tank weapons). Each man had his M-16, ammo, 4 hand grenades and one smoke canister. My radio man carried the prick 25 radio (about 25 pounds) as well as his weapons. I had my AK 47,

100 rounds of ammo and my 1911 pistol. Two troops carried machine gun ammo to supplement what the machine gunners were carrying. Each of us also carried extra water and personal items. We were loaded down as usual. Of course, it was 90 degrees with 85% humidity. Not good conditions for a pleasant hike in the Vietnamese countryside.

The patrol was to cover a specific area. This was before GPS, so we figured out where we were by noting topographic features on the map and using a compass. I figured it would take us about eight hours to complete the patrol if we didn't get delayed by Charlie or the NVA. It was thick jungle terrain, so slow going for us.

When you are on these patrols you never walked on the trails as they were often booby trapped. You had one guy on point (in front of the column) and one flanker on either side of the column about 50 to 100 feet to the side and 20 or 30 feet back from the point. This made an alert triangle for the rest of us. The name of the game was to be very cautious as there could be bad guys anywhere and it was best to see them first. If they saw you first, they would disappear into the brush or, if they had a good position, things could go very bad very quickly. Being loaded down with gear in 90-degree heat while being totally stressed out about bad guys is not good for your mental or physical health.

The patrol was an uneventful slog through heavy brush and swamps. We were within a half mile of the river on our way back when we came to a large clearing about a quarter mile across and two miles long. The clearing was flat with grass about 18 inches high covering most of it. The troops were all exhausted, hungry, and thirsty. We were within a half hour of the barge if we crossed the field or more than two hours to go around it. There was a low ridge behind us that we hadn't checked out.

The safe thing to do was to stay in the brush and go around the clearing. I turned to Sergeant Skidmore and asked what he thought about crossing. Before he could speak the troops on either side of me express their desire to cross as they were pretty much used up and needed to rest. Skidmore looked skeptical but nodded his head. I then made the worst decision of my military career and almost the last decision of my life. I opted to take the easy, but less secure route. We moved out into the clearing with the point and flankers going out first. The rest of us were right behind them.

It was near the middle of the field when the first shot was fired. We should have sprinted for the brush on the other side, but I assumed it was a lone Charlie taking a pot shot at us, so we stopped and returned fire. That was when all hell broke loose. We had engaged an NVA battalion of over 400 men who were up on the low ridge looking down on us. The NVA were in a very defensible location, we were not. The bad guys outnumbered us 20 to 1 and had a lot more firepower. They not only had machine guns they had mortars and AK 47 rifles. We were immediately pinned down in the middle of the field laying in the grass as described earlier. The radio man was next to me, so I called the artillery guys to blow the NVA up. They responded that they were under heavy attack and couldn't help us. The next call was to the Cobra helicopter unit who said it would take at least 30 minutes to get to us from their base. I told them we would all be dead in 15 minutes. My radio operator seemed disturbed by that comment.

So, there I am thinking we are all about to die and I couldn't think of any way out of the situation. If we got up to run, they would mow us down. If we tried to crawl through the grass, they would see the grass moving and concentrate their fire on us. I was thinking that if we all threw smoke canisters and grenades in front of us it might give us enough cover to run 100 yards of the 300 yards to the brush so that a few of us might survive, but not likely. My mind was going a mile a minute, the panic was welling up into my chest and the intensity of the NVA fire was increasing. It was a no-win situation for us. We were all going to die in that field, far from home and family. I can tell you that is a very bad feeling.

What I didn't know was that Dave had arrived back at the barge and was listening to my radio transmissions and could hear the sounds of the battle. It was obvious we were in deep trouble. So, he did what solders do, he did his duty and took his men to flank the bad guys and opened up on their position. This distracted them from us, as they engaged him, so we could fall back to a defensible position on the other side of the field. We then opened up on their other flank which caused some confusion on their part. Between the two of us we kept them busy until the gunships got there and hammered that ridge. A couple of Air Force F-4s also joined in with napalm. It was an army mad minute that lasted several minutes. We were told later that over 20 NVA were killed. Body counts in Vietnam were notoriously overstated, but I am sure a lot of NVA were taken out that day.

My guys suffered a few wounds, but nothing life threatening. Lt. Dave and his guys were not so lucky. Five were wounded three of which were hauled out by the dust-off guys. All three had million-dollar wounds (Bad enough to get you sent home). Two would not be going home, ever. My troops and I owe every day of our lives to those guys. We will never forget.

I remember after that fight sitting on a mound of dirt surrounded by devastation and death trying to understand why. Some young men from North Vietnam and some young men from America, who didn't know each other, had just finished a battle where several of them died and many more were wounded. This took place in a little patch of jungle nobody wanted. A bloody battle that would make no difference in the war and would soon be forgotten, except for the participants and the families of the dead. Then what had just happened really struck home. I was overcome by negative emotions like fear, hate, dread, sorrow, and shame. Suddenly all that mattered to me was to go home. I had to get away from this awful and dangerous place. I wanted to hug my mom, laugh and joke with my brothers and sisters, kiss my wife, pet my dog go fishing with my friends and go to Saint Rose of Lima church and sit in the pew I had sat in while growing up, surrounded by family, friends and neighbors and to finally feel safe. I had never wanted anything so much in my whole life.

When we got back to the company area, I was informed that this was my last bird dog patrol as I was too short to be assigned another one. So just like that my combat duties were over. It seemed anticlimactic. I laid in my bunk that night thinking about what had happened and all those guys who had died. I realized that every day was now a gift as I should have been one of them. I resolved to make the rest of my life count for something good. Not sure what, but something good. I went

Me in my dress greens the day I got home in May 1969

back to being an engineer officer instead of a part time infantry officer. My tour in Vietnam ended two weeks later and I went home to my family and friends. 58,220 of my fellow solders did not, including two very close friends.

As the years go by the memories of my buddies and my men, of blowing up fish, and shooting pigs have dimmed, but the stark terror of combat is still vivid in my mind. War is a terrible thing for anyone to have to experience. It is totally arbitrary (who gets killed) and destructive. A few years ago our youngest son, FT, got married at a beautiful lodge in Alaska to a wonderful young lady, named Seina, whom we all love. I was sitting at the edge of the crowd after the ceremony watching my kids, grandkids and friends talking, laughing and having a good time and feeling very happy and content. Suddenly a dark thought entered my head. If I had not survived that day in Vietnam, my four kids and six grandkids would not exist. America would have nine less wonderful and productive citizens. So how many kids and grandkids don't exist due to 58,220 of us not making it home? War has far reaching impacts and none of them are good. To find out we were there the last two years due to Johnson and McNamara's political ambitions makes it even worse.

The plane ride home was much more cheerful than the ride over a year earlier. We all cheered and clapped when the wheels lifted off the runway. The wide-eyed green troops I traveled to Vietnam with, who were scared to death, had been replaced by hardened soldiers most of whom had seen way to much violence while living in deplorable conditions. I think the cheerfulness was only skin deep. So many veterans end up homeless or mentally messed up. This is a major failing of our society. They got mentally and/or physically injured serving our country. We need to do a lot better for our vets, particularly for those that need help.

We landed in San Francisco and were bussed to Oakland to be processed out of the Army. I checked into the BOQ for the night. The next morning, we were bussed to a big warehouse with all these stations scattered throughout. One station for medical one for finance etc. you went from table to table to get processed. The processing was very casual. For instance, at the medical table they noted you were breathing and walking, good enough, next? At the last table, a lt. colonel asked me what it would take to get me to re-insist for four more years. I told him two things, an assignment to Alaska to which he replied he could do that but couldn't guarantee I wouldn't be back in Vietnam within a year. The second thing was a promotion. He said he could promote me to captain right there, to which I replied that I was thinking brigadier general. There was an awkward moment of silence and then he told me to move on in a cold as ice voice. As noted previously lieutenant colonels have no sense of humor.

After the last table I was directed to a door. There was a WAC spec. 4 standing there. She said, "Can I have your ID card sir?" I gave her my card and she motioned for me to go through the door. I then found myself standing on a street in Oakland. Two years of my life and damn near getting killed and no one even said thank you. At first it pissed me off, but then it dawned on me that my butt was back in the world, not dead, and out of the Army. I didn't owe anyone any money and there was $5,000 in the bank. All I needed to do now was get back to Oregon, pick up my wife and dog and head for Alaska. Things were looking up. Two more lieutenants stepped out behind me and had the same initial reaction of being upset but got over it quickly for the same reasons. Vietnam set a very low bar, so any place was better, even a back street in Oakland. We all concurred that the best thing about the Army was being out of it.

At the BOQ we were advised to not wear our uniforms when we went to San Francisco airport to catch our flights home due to antiwar groups harassing people in uniform. Welcome home guys. I packed my dress greens; the fatigues went in the dumpster. I did keep my jungle hat. We shared a cab to the airport. While I was waiting in line at the ticket counter, I noticed two hippie freaks eyeing my duffel bag and scowling at me. The guy ahead of me was an Army sergeant in civilian clothes. I must admit I was almost hoping those two creeps would do something so we could beat them down, but they didn't so we went on our way. Fifty years later the resentment on how we were treated still lingers. You step up when your country calls on you and then get slapped in the face when you get home. Vietnam vets are thanked for their service now. Too little too late.

I got to the house in Salem at about 9:00 PM. There was a small traffic sign on a pole at the edge of the sidewalk. I put my duffle bag down next to it, sat on the bag and leaned back against the pole. Sat there for a long time staring at the front door. Not sure if I was savoring the moment, but I think I was also letting things unwind a little before another emotional event. Linda was ecstatic to see me and Lady (my dog) went totally nuts. Not sure how to explain it, but it took a long time for me to feel like I was home. I just had to shed Vietnam and it took some time. Never did shed it all. It is interesting to note that nobody, even my family, thanked me for my service until 25 years later. It was just not talked about. I was running for the Anchorage Assembly (city council) and was soliciting support from a local pastor when Vietnam came up. He thanked me for serving in that war. It was the first time someone had thanked me. I went back to my car and sat there and cried for 10 minutes. Not sure why, I guess I was letting some of the Vietnam pain out of my heart.

Co-pilot checking for wheels down and locked status

CHAPTER TWELVE

NORTH TO ALASKA

A few months later it was time to realize my lifelong dream to live in Alaska. We packed up everything, visited all the relatives and took off to Seattle where we shipped the Mustang and all our stuff to Anchorage and got on a Western Airlines flight. By the way, Linda was pregnant, which I suspect occurred about an hour after I got up from my duffel bag in front of the house.

I had a job with the Alaskan engineering and surveying firm, Tryck, Nyman and Hayes, but no place to live. Anchorage was busy in 1969 so it was very difficult to find a house or apartment. We weren't sure what we would do when we got there. The flight was uneventful except when we were on final for the airport. The co-pilot came back and lifted a trap door in the aisle and fiddled around with something and then went back to the cockpit. He did this three times, which didn't give any of us warm and fuzzy feelings. Finally the pilot comes on the speaker and advises us that "the little green light that tells him the landing gear is down and locked won't come on so he is not sure if the landing gear is locked in place or "the little green light" was burnt out. The former being much more significant than the latter. I looked down and saw all the emergency trucks lined up along the runway with their light flashing which didn't Inspire confidence. I was thinking, "So you struggled your way through college, survived Vietnam and now you are going to die in a plane crash just as you finally get to Alaska. God must be really pissed at me." We landed without incident, other than the green light deal, so God and I were back on the same page.

Suspect Western Airlines was out 10 cents to replace the bulb in the little green light.

Curley and Thelma Bell (cousins) met us at the airport. They were my parents' age. I had only met them once or twice in my life. Thelma was born in Anchorage in 1916 and Curly moved there in 1935. He owned a bar called the Union Club. It was a little rough and tumble, but he didn't let the drug dealers and prostitutes in so it was popular with the old time Alaskans. I spent many evenings in the Union Club listening to stories of Alaska's past, some of which may have been true.

They drove us to a delightful little one-bedroom house one block from my office. This was a huge deal as housing was so tight in the town. We were overwhelmed with gratitude. They chatted for a while and then Curly said there was a car behind the house for us to use, gave us the keys and left. We soon discovered they had stocked the cupboards and refrigerator with food. What a great welcome to Alaska. We were to learn this was typical Alaskan hospitality.

I didn't report for work until Monday, so we spent the weekend exploring the area. First thing we noticed was the cost of food was like 50% more than Salem and the rent on the house was double the one in Oregon. In addition, our winter clothes were no match for Alaskan winters which meant a whole new wardrobe. Plus, we had another mouth to feed in a few months. I thought I had negotiated a nice fat salary of $1,250 a month. It wasn't looking so nice or fat now.

I had been hired by Frank Nyman so on Monday I walked into the office and asked for Frank. He was in Sitka until the next day. No one had any idea who I was or what I was doing there. I found this a little upsetting. They escorted me to Charlie Tryck's office who also didn't know anything about me. There I am, I have $3,000 left of my stash, I have a pregnant wife, rent to pay and no job!! Now what? Thankfully, Charlie got Frank on the phone. Frank told him he had hired a young engineer but didn't remember his name. Seeing as how I was the only young engineer claiming to have a job there, he deduced it was me. Thus, began my engineering career in Alaska.

The next issue was what to do with me. I am sure Frank had some ideas, but he wasn't there. Charlie took me downstairs and handed me over to John. He was a senior engineer who designed sewage treatment plants. He had a less than welcoming personality. My experience was storm drains and port facilities. John was not impressed with my resume. He noted "Army experience doesn't count because they screw everything up." Sounded like a rather global assessment. I was put to work designing a small parking lot for a sewage treatment plant in Kodiak. A less than auspicious start, but better than no job.

The next day Frank Shows up, calls me into his office and tells me the firm had just got a big job from the school district to design school sites all over the city. He wanted me to take on that project. I said that would be great and I would do the best I could. He then briefed me on the client staff I would be working with. They were all named Bill. The superintendent, the design manager and the construction manager. This made it easy to remember their names. Turned out they were all good guys. This was my first big engineering project in Alaska.

In order to get registered as an engineer you take the eight-hour engineer-in-training exam when you get your engineering degree. Then you practice engineering for four years under the direct supervision of a registered engineer. Finally, you take the 8-hour professional engineer exam. If you pass both you are registered by the state you live in at the time. These tests were extremely important if you wanted an engineering career. We had dedicated at least eight years of our lives to the cause at that point so failing these tests was like a star running back blowing out a knee in his last college game before going to the NFL draft, except less physically painful.

One of the engineers I worked with, named Les, was scheduled to take the professional engineers' exam at the same time as me. Les was born and raised in Hope, Alaska, a town of about 30 people. He was a nice guy but had a very dry personality. He enjoyed sharing Alaska with me, the new guy. Three months before the exam we would stay at work an hour and a half each night and study. Reminded me of study desk at the fraternity. It was about a week prior to the test Les and I were studying away when Frank walked by. He asked what we were doing, and we told him we were studying for the exam. He said, "Don't worry about the exam, we have never had one of our employees fail that test." No pressure there!!!

The big day came and Les and I showed up at the University of Alaska prepared to give it our best shot, Frank's comment heavy on our minds. Another employee named Ed was there to take the professional surveyor exam. We were escorted into a large room with the typical student desks. An old metal desk was located at the front of the room for the monitors. It was a stark and foreboding environment. Few things in the engineering world are dramatic other than bridges falling down or buildings collapsing. We try to avoid those things as much as possible. Well, walking into that room with what was on the line was dramatic. Some of us were displaying some signs of emotion, such as worried looks and nervous twitching, which is frowned on in the engineering world. This was it, the big game. The engineers were seated in the front of the room and the surveyors in the back, which seemed appropriate to us engineers. Not sure the surveyors took note. Nobody spoke so it was quiet and foreboding.

This was before handheld computers, so it was all off the top of your head. No reference material was allowed. For some reason, the surveyors were allowed to bring Curta calculators. These were little cal-culators the shape of a beer can, but half as big. They had a handle on top that you turned to get it to do the calculations. It was a mechanical device, so it made a whirling sound when you turned the handle. This immediately became an issue with us engineers as our slide rules were silent devices. We are trying to concentrate while being serenaded by 15 or 20 Curtas. Les was the first to express his opinion on the noise closely followed by all the rest of us. A riot broke out. Now in the engineering world a riot was three or four guys quietly expressing their concerns about something. I am sure if the situation had been reversed and it was the surveyors being impacted the response would have been different. They would have had a vehement and bellicose dissertation on the subject. Boy, that was a Sergeant Bull sentence. Anyhow, the monitors were stunned by this outburst.

Typical of most engineering functions, this test was highly regu-lated. There were two monitors (One registered engineer and one land surveyor) who were in charge. 15 minutes into the test they have a rebellion on their hands. Well, the surveyors were quite content, but they were the source of the problem. The test was stopped while they sorted out the issues. the proctors decided to ban the surveyors to a different room and each monitor would take a room. This prompted a heated discussion as to whether the test should be started over or restarted at the 15-minute mark. The exaiminees wanted to start over and the examinors weren't sure. Another 30 minutes were expended resolving the dispute. We started over. Muted mob rule had prevailed.

In the early 70s each state composed and gave its own exam. Now it is a standard exam nationwide. The Alaska exam was one of the toughest in the country. The pass rate was 31% and that was with some people taking it for the second or third time. This was more than a little intimidating and with Frank's comment it was even worse. The stress level was through the roof, I even saw one guy take a deep breath.

The exam was divided into two four-hour sessions, neither of which was any fun. The morning session was mostly straight forward engineering questions such as calculating the maximum load on a beam, a few engineering economics and math questions. For most engineers this was just another day at the office. I breezed through this section with confidence. The afternoon was a full-blown engineering interrogation. You were given eight questions and you had to answer six of them. I vividly remember the first question. If you had a city of 150,000 people and a stream was flowing nearby with a flow rate of 100 cubic feet per second and a dissolved oxygen content of 2%. Design a sewage treatment plant to serve the city that will not reduce the dissolved oxygen in the stream to less than 1.5%. WHAT!!!! The confidence thing went right out the window.

This is a project that a staff of ten engineers could accomplish in a year or so. I moved on to question two with considerable concern. I got through five of them with varying degrees of confidence. My professional life was on the line and I wasn't feeling upbeat about this deal. Two of the remaining questions I had no idea of how to solve. There was 15 minutes left in the session. I went back to question one. After thinking about it for a few minutes it dawned on me they didn't want me to actually design the plant they wanted me to tell them how I would go about doing the design. I would assume 150 gallons of wastewater a day per person in the city and if storm water and wastewater were combined etc. set up the parameters of the design, not do it. This could go well, or not. I left the room at the end of the day not feeling warm and fuzzy about my chances. Les wasn't a happy camper either. He didn't even try on question one. We walked out of the building, threw up on the grass, and went home to drink heavily. Ed was very confident he had passed. We didn't appreciate his attitude. He had a Curta to lean on.

Four months later three letters showed up at the office from the Board of Engineers, Architects and Land Surveyors addressed to me, Les and Ed. There was a small round table in the front office and the letters were neatly placed on said table. We were then summoned from our offices to get our mail. The three of us stood there by that little round table and looked at each other waiting for the other guy to open his letter. Nobody moved. All the other employees were avoiding the area like it was radioactive. The front office receptionist just sat there looking at her lap. Those letters appeared to glow with the tremendous impact they would have on us. Everything seemed to be moving in slow motion.

Finally, Ed picked up his letter and went back to his office. Les and I followed suit. When I got to my office, I knew I had to open that letter fast because if it were bad news, I could prepare myself for being the loser if one or both of the other guys passed. My whole career flashed before my eyes, it only spanned four years, so it did not take long.

I carefully open the envelope and removed the letter with trembling hands. It was very short. I took a quivering deep breath and read the text. It was good news! I almost passed out from the huge burden being lifted off my shoulders. Life was good, again. A few minutes later Les poked his head into my office looking very solemn. When he saw my smile, he started to do a little dance and then we heard a whoop from Ed's office, we had all passed. The other employees all came out of hiding and congratulated us. Frank just said "I told you so." Just like that I was a registered professional engineer.

It was near the end of the workday so Dan, one of our senior engineers, suggested we call our spouses and have a celebratory dinner at the Green Dragon restaurant. All three of us were flattered that they would do that for us. Should have known better.

We adjourned to the restaurant and were met by our spouses. There were about 20 people all told. Dan coordinated the whole thing. He was a take charge kind of guy and as it turned out a rather deceptive one. We all sat at one long table and he ordered the various dishes that were doled out family style. Some fine wine was ordered, and we had a very nice meal and great conversation. Things were really going well, all was right with the world. We had taken a major step in our careers and our fellow employees were celebrating with us. All good stuff. When they delivered the check, Dan announced that it was our party, so it was our bill and they all got up and departed leaving the three of us siting there in shock. It was obvious that the whole thing was orchestrated, probably by Dan. I think the bill was $250. We were each making a little over $1,000 a month net, this was a big hit. Our wives weren't happy with the financial ramifications of this deal, so the pain just kept coming. We wrote checks and limped home while being browbeaten with considerable enthusiasm by our wives. All the happy at passing the exam became muted.

The next morning, I advised Dan that it would have been nice to have had some warning as to the bill policy. He said it was a tradition in the office. He pointed out that all three partners were in attendance and just assumed we knew what we were getting into. We did not. Our options were to take the hit and shut up or pitch a fit and then take the hit anyway. We went with the former. Over the next few years, it was nice to be on the other side of this tradition. Everyone enjoyed the scam, except the new guys. Having received my Professional Engineer license allowed me to then apply for a land surveyor license which I obtained a year later. This made me a two-fer in the design business. I could now plan to start my own firm and realize my dream from that first job with the highway department when I was 18 years old. Don't you love it when an 18-year old's life plan comes together? I suspect this was the first time in human history.

Angry tenant attacking our survey crew

CHAPTER THIRTEEN

BELL HERRING AND ASSOCIATES

The first job I stamped as a professional engineer was Crescent Harbor Park in Sitka in 1972. I continued to work for TNH until 1974 to get to know the state and the business. I was sure I wanted my own firm but was a little shaky as to how to go about starting a company. This was far more complicated than Bell's killing service. The big plunge took place when I left TNH and took a job with ARCO as a facility engineer on the North Slope of Alaska. It was a one week on and one week off schedule. I got together with John Herring LS, the chief surveyor at TNH who was unhappy with his employment and, after discussing it for over an hour, we decided to start an engineering and surveying firm. Due diligence was a concept we hadn't embraced, the fact is we didn't know what it was.

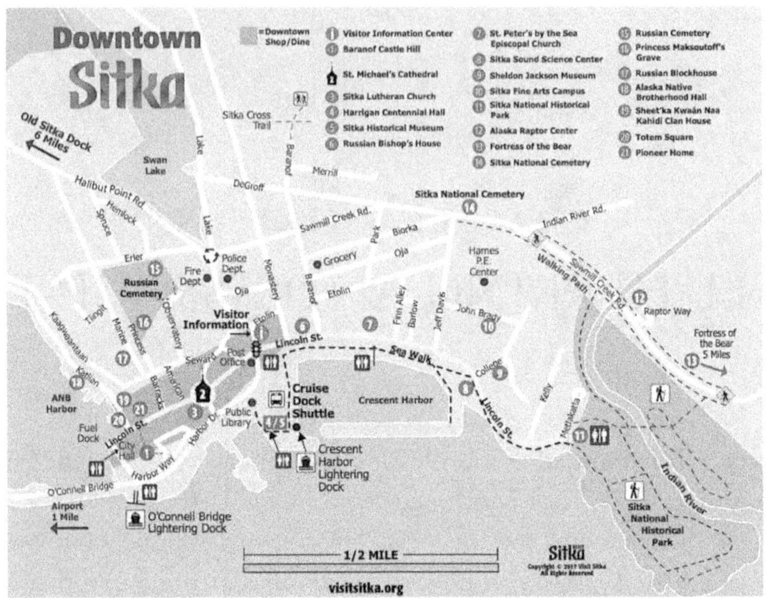

Crescent harbor park

We pooled our funds and came up with the impressive sum of $1,500, we may have been a little undercapitalized. The deal was John would be full time at the company and I would be there every other week. My ARCO pay would be split with him. As far as financing house payments and families this was a very skinny financial plan, but we went ahead, and "Bell, Herring and Associates" was born. Maybe hatched would be a more appropriate term. We didn't have any associates but anticipated getting some as soon as some clients were located. So, no clients, no employees and very little money. As far as business plans go this one had some significant challenges. That didn't really bother us as we didn't even know what a business plan was anyhow. Ignorance and bliss can sometimes be assets. In our case it allowed us to proceed with our endeavor. Logical and prudent people would have bailed out. We didn't even put on the parachute.

Our first job was an as built of the home of a friend of mine. We went to the Stake Shop and rented a transit and bought some supplies. The transit was placed in the back of my 1971 Chevy pickup, not a good plan as it turned out. Two blocks before we got there the truck hit a bump and the transit went banging around in the bed. The instructions on the transit recommended avoiding this sort of thing. Needless to say, it was damaged. I had a flash back to Cap dropping the transit off the log at survey summer camp.

The as-built fee was $75 the transit was worth $1,000. Our profit and loss statement wasn't looking good. We returned to the Stake Shop got another transit and accomplished the job. The

Ole Blue In 2015 after being rebuilt

transit repairs were $225 so net profit was minus $150 plus rental and supplies. This wasn't an auspicious beginning for our business enterprise. Over the next few days several more as-builts were ordered which got us back into the black by over $50 assuming John and I worked for free. The business plan needed some more tweaking. I left for the slope for my week on so we hired a friend of mine, named Bob, who worked for the city to help John while I was gone. He was a civil engineer, but John used him as a surveyor. They had a tenuous relationship but managed to get the work done. John wasn't a fan of "government people."

There was a little incident involving Bob that caused him to pause as far as continuing to work for us. We were doing an as-built survey for a tri-plex on a winter day. The snow was two feet deep. As we were pulling the tape from a building corner an enraged man came boiling out of the unit screaming at us. He picked up a snow shovel and charged Bob, who was standing in the driveway like a deer in the headlights. This had the potential of turning out poorly for him. I was off to one side about halfway between the two. As the aggressor ran toward his victim, I jumped into action and threw a cross body block thereby knocking him flat on his back in the deep snow. This gave both of us an opportunity to exit the area very quickly, but with very little dignity. We returned the next day, with a cop, to finish the survey. That was a well-earned $75. Bob continued to help out for several more years, but he always seemed nervous.

So, we start out by breaking a transit on our first job, then having a crazy guy chasing a part time employee around with a snow shovel. The trials and tribulations of running a small (very small) business was beginning to become apparent. The ignorance and bliss were still firmly in place, so we plodded on with the endeavors.

We had rented a spacious office of almost 400 square feet and sublet 200 feet of it to a one person drafting service. This required some detailed planning regarding office furniture layout. Seeing as how we had one desk, two chairs and a drafting table there were very few options. At least we were saving the cost of an interior designer. We took the modesty shield off the desk so John could sit on one side and me on the other. Because I was the engineer, I got the side with the drawers. It was a status thing. I suspect John used my side of the desk when I was on the North slope.

First office of Bell, Herring and associates Upper right corner

The owner of the building was a developer. One day as I was coming into work, he asked me to step into his office. Turned out he had an 800-acre tract of land he wanted to subdivide into five acre lots with gravel roads and onsite utilities. He asked if we could do the engineering and surveying for the project. I didn't hesitate and told him I thought we could work it into our schedule. I think we had two as-builts (about four hours work) to do that week so the "working it into our schedule" wasn't difficult. When I got to our office and filled John in, he got a kind of panicked look on his face but said, "Let's do it." The next day I negotiated a contract where we got paid $25/hour for engineering and $30/hour for a survey crew. This included all pay and expenses. We had our first big contract. It was named Hidden Hills Estates. Now all we had to do was avoid bumps in the road and crazy guys with snow shovels, along with a myriad of other things we didn't even know about.

I managed to get the roads and utilities designed in three months by working 16 hours a day the days I was home from the North Slope. This didn't do much for my family or social life. The latter being limited before going into business. John did all the platting work. We got the project through the Matanuska Borough platting board and started doing the field work the next summer. In the meantime, we were picking up other work such as more as-builts, parking lot designs and open to entry remote land surveys. The business plan was starting to come together. Still not sure what it was, but it seemed to be working. They say, "Even a broken clock is right twice a day." Not sure we had as much business sense as a broken clock, but the work was coming in and we were getting it done.

At the end of our first year we managed to realize the princely sum of $1,800 as a net profit, $300 more than we started out with. This didn't cover house payments or family expenses, which had a high priority with our wives. The ARCO money was keeping us afloat, but just barely. I continued as a facility engineer in the arctic. Statistically, 70% of small businesses fail in the first year. I think we had failed a couple of times in that year, but didn't know it, so we just kept going.

It is interesting to reflect back on those first years and what things were significant then, but not so much later. I recall the company finally had enough money to have some stationary printed. We were getting more sophisticated by the minute. I came up with a logo and then took the design, the address and phone number to the printer. A few weeks later it was ready to be picked up.

I was dismayed when I noticed the address was messed up. It had the wrong street number. The sophistication factor was declining. The printer showed me the sample I had given him, and obviously it was my error. When I got back to the office it got worse. John noted that the address on our new stationary was the massage parlor/house of ill repute across the street named The Body Shop. I should note that we were not located in one of the high-end business districts of Anchorage. In fact, this area was still working hard to achieve a low-end business district status. There are some issues when the neighborhood business leader runs a house of ill repute.

We had paid $100 for 500 sheets and envelopes, 27% of our first year's profit. That was big money for us. There is a solution for most problems, unfortunately not all of them are good. We tended toward the bad ones, so decided to just change the number on the address by hand as the stuff was used. Now this could have been a reasonable solution with a proper protocol. We didn't have one. The first issue was we changed the address on the letters but neglected to change the envelopes. The second issue was the new office person we had hired to answer the phone and type letters wasn't informed about the address situation. John and I were so busy working on Hidden Hills Estates to notice the impending disaster

The new stationary had been in use for about a month when we got a call from The Body Shop advising us, they had a bunch of our mail. We then had a very contentious discussion as to who was going to go get the mail. The new, and first, employee was a devout, 19-year-old, Mormon so he wasn't an option. I made the argument that being seen going into a house of ill repute would be much more damaging to the reputation of an engineer than it would be to a surveyor. White collar vs blue collar. That didn't work. It went back and forth for some time until I finally settled it by promising John a six pack of beer to go get the mail. If reasoning does not work, then use a bribe. Worked on my kids.

John was a crusty old coot. He was a surveyor's surveyor. He loved the profession and the people he worked with. He swore a lot and drank too much. He and his buddies could empty out a dive bar just by their obnoxious behavior. John really did not want to walk across the street and into The Body Shop, but he did. Of course, we were all watching from the office window, there was only one. Could he out obnoxious a madam?

John had put on his coat with the hood up and a hat under the hood, the best he could do to conceal his identity. He managed to cross the street, but then his courage failed him. He just stood on the sidewalk in front of the place with his hands in his pockets and his shoulder hunched up looking lost. Not sure this was a good plan regarding anonymity. After a few minutes, the door opened and a pleasant looking middle-aged woman stepped out and spoke to him, he then followed her inside. John was in there for half an hour. We were all speculating as to what was going on. Finally, the door opened, John came out, shook hands with the lady and returned to the office with our mail. We had several questions for him at that point. He looked like a conquering hero.

John said she had come out and asked him if he was looking for his mail. He said yes so, she invited him in. He was very apprehensive about that plan but accepted the invitation. Once inside she introduced herself and asked if he would like a cup of coffee as she had just made a pot. They had a very pleasant talk about the neighborhood and the stationary mix up, he gathered up the mail and left. After that she would call when mail came in and John would go get it without any debate, or bribes. It turned out the woman was a very successful businesswoman and ended up owning a lot of real estate in Alaska and Texas. My oldest daughter, Jennifer, when she was in High School, went to her downtown office and interviewed her as a class project. The interview covered all her businesses and property, but the Body Shop never came up. Jennifer never knew about her nefarious business enterprise. I have often wondered if her teacher knew about it when the project was turned in.

The upside of The Body Shop was that it was very well known in Anchorage. Nobody knew where we were. Our office was on West 27th Avenue, but it was only one block long, so it was hard to find. We solved that problem by saying "Do you know where The Body Shop is? We are right across the street." That put us on the map. One day some house movers came and picked up the Body Shop and moved it over to Spenard Road. Then we would say, "Do you know where The Body

Shop used to be?" that only worked for a year then memories faded, and we were hard to find again. Name dropping in the business world is tentative at best.

The developer/landlord hired us to do the engineering and surveying on a new bigger building he was going to build on the corner of Arctic Blvd and Fireweed Lane. The architect wasn't the most competent guy in the business. When they started construction, the city came along and said the code only allowed a building half as wide as this one on that lot, consequently, they built half a building. This resulted in a hallway on the first floor that ran down the side of the structure instead of down the middle as in most buildings. So, you had a hallway with outside windows along its length. When the building was completed in 1976, the developer moved there, and we followed a couple of months later. We increased our office space to over 600 square feet with none of it sub-let. We were now a major factor in the very small engineering firm community. Well on our way to being in the medium sized engineering community.

Hidden Hills Estates was completed, but following in my dad's footsteps I began selling the lots to my friends up in the Arctic, for a commission. That helped the bottom line. We also had a lot more work, so we hired our first professional employees. One was a civil engineer I had worked with at TNH and the other was an architect fresh out of college, and Louisiana, as a drafter. He used a Leroy drafting kit, so we called him Leroy Artichoke. We also hired a receptionist/bookkeeper who was drop dead gorgeous and a part time model. She was born and raised in Alaska and had lived most of her life in remote areas. Therefore, the young lady was also tough as nails. Her name is Mitchie. She is a truly delightful person.

The modeling agency she worked for did fashion shows at high-end bars in the evenings. Whenever Mitchie was doing a show we would all go and cheer her on. After the show she would join us for a drink or two. Other guys in the bar were green with envy. We loved the perceived studliness. Engineers don't get that much.

It was in the middle of the winter when she did a show at a hotel bar near our office. After the show she had a drink and then said she was going home. We said our goodbyes. About a half hour later the hotel manager came to our table and asked if we knew her. I said that I was her boss. He then asked me to come with him. He was very solemn. This was a bit unnerving.

We went to an office behind the check in counter where I saw Mitchie sitting there with all the hair on one side of her head soaked in blood. I was taken aback by this sight. When asked if she was OK the reply was "It's not my blood." She was explaining to a cop what had happened.

After going out to the parking lot, which had no lighting, to get in her pick-up there was a problem. When she opened the door, a guy pushed her into the cab and jumped on top of her. He was intent on rape. Mitchie kept a steel bar under her seat so she reached down, grabbed it and then hit him across the bridge of the nose. I am sure that smarted and tended to reduce his sex drive a bit. The cop asked what happened next. She replied "He took off across the parking lot. I was wearing high heeled shoes so I couldn't catch him." She was hoping to knock him out with the bar so the cops could arrest the creep. Alaska women rule big time. The idiot came back into the bar a few hours later with a compress on his nose. The hotel manager called the cops and they picked him up. He went to jail for a long time. Alaska criminals are just as dumb or maybe dumber than most.

Mary, the Lonely Camp manager, telling us there is no room at the inn

CHAPTER FOURTEEN

GROWING A BUSINESS

In the second year we turned a profit of $85,000. Hidden Hills was a money maker. John and I were returning to Anchorage from Palmer where we had just got a sub-division through the platting board. We decided to stop at a strip club for some culture and a libation. This was a real classy joint named "The Booby Trap". The name contributed to the class. There were cases of beer stacked against the back wall of the stage. The sign in front of the stage warned you not to touch the girls because they would kick you in the face if you did, more class. Everyone in the place was drunk or passed out. The bartender was a huge sweaty slab of a man with hairy arms and a big cigar in his face. The waitress looked like an escapee from a detox center with the personality of a pit bull. So, this was the cultural part of the joint. How can you not enjoy yourself in an establishment like this?

We found a table and John said he would buy the beer. He had never done that before, so I instantly became very suspicious. What was he up to? The entertainment was somewhere between tolerable and just plain bad, so we struck up a conversation. John pointed out that we had made a profit of $85,000 last year and it looked like we would do as well or better this year. I concurred. This is when I found out why he was buying the beer. He said, "I think it is time for you to quit the ARCO job and be full time with our company. If you don't, then I am done and will go back to work at TNH."

All of a sudden, the entertainment seemed much better, so I just sat there and stared at a truly ugly woman gyrating on the stage in front of the beer cases, sincerely hoping she didn't plan on taking off any more clothes. John broke the spell by telling me I had a week to make up my mind. That seemed like a rather short time to make a life altering decision. We finished our drinks and went home. As noted above I had dreamed of running my own engineering firm since I was 18. Problem was that all that dreaming had taken place prior to me having a wife and two daughters and all the financial obligations involved. Your priorities change when you have two little girls depending on you for room and board. ARCO was the safety net.

Linda wasn't a big fan of the idea, or for that matter most of my ideas. She pointed out we couldn't keep going with the income we had now as all the savings were gone. I was hoping for a more positive response. It was a tough decision, but I decided to just jump in with both feet and all my other body parts and go for it. My family, her family and all our friends thought it was a fool hardy decision, but John didn't so, ignoring common sense, which we had become very good at, we launched. They say every arrow not shot is a miss. This was a very big arrow shooting at a very small target. We would need a lot of luck and hard work to pull this off. I really had no idea what we were getting into nor did John. As noted, before, they say ignorance is bliss. Well, this time we had plenty of the former and none of the latter.

At the beginning of my next tour I informed my boss that I was dragging up. He said, "Bob I just got you a promotion and a substantial raise."

I replied, "Hoyt, don't tell me the amount of the raise as it will just make me feel worse, but won't change my mind." The die was cast. I stayed on for two months so they could find a replacement. He was a bit of a dweeb but did eventually fit into the job. As I looked out of the airplane window flying back to Anchorage that last time, I could not help but think, "What did you just do?"

The next year we bid on doing the surveying and field engineering for Husky Oil on the Naval Petroleum Reserve (now the National Petroleum Reserve). We didn't get the bid because our prices were too high, but in the process, I did get to know the construction manager for

Husky. The next year he saw to it we got another chance. We sharpened our pencils and won the contract.

So here we are a company of four people, including John and I, which had just been awarded a contract with a major oil company to provide about 80 field engineers and surveyors to a project in the High Arctic in one month. No stress there!! We were only 76 people short. Turns out there were lots of other things we were a bit short on.

This was in 1977 and no internet so, it was in person recruiting. John managed to hire about half of the surveyors already working on the project with the departing firm. We put help wanted ads in the Anchorage, Fairbanks and Seattle newspapers and started calling everyone we knew in the business. It paid Davis-Bacon wages which were very high. So that helped.

There were no construction engineers currently on the project requiring us to find all new people. Finding 12 engineers who are willing to work in the Arctic based in a place named "Camp Lonely", 80 miles from the nearest road, had some issues. Then with a six week on two weeks off schedule involving 12-hour days, seven days a week at down to 40 below zero, had some HR challenges. The pay was very good with free room and board, but still it was a hard sell.

I managed to get a couple of local guys I knew to give it a try and the newspaper ads did begin to bear fruit. The trouble was many of those who applied had never been to Alaska let alone the Arctic. I was running all over the country interviewing people. We ended up with a rag tag bunch of field engineers who were all single guys, some of whom had dubious resumes and extensive police records. This had the potential of being as organized as a bunch of cats in a room full of mice.

When it was all said and done, we had the 80 people, 45 of whom we didn't know prior to hiring them, which is always a crap shoot. They were put on two charter flights to Camp Lonely. I went with the first group to get everything squared away. It was bedlam when we got there. The camp manager hadn't been told we were coming. 40 people showing up at your doorstep in minus 20-degree weather with no notice can cause some coordination issues, particularly in a remote camp that was already full. My marginal managing skills were about to be put to the test.

The camp manager's name was Sally (a retired Army WAC) who had the personality of a discontented prison guard with a toothache. I explained that we were the new technical folks and needed room and board for the night and flights in the morning out to the four remote construction camps. It was also noted that we would need office space for three people. At this point I detected some hostility on her part. Her expression was something between disdain and disbelief. Her reply was that she did not really care what I needed, we would get what was available, and it was up to us to figure out how to make everybody fit. I didn't perceive this response as cooperative. Miss Sally became even more hostile when informed that we had 40 more folks arriving the next day. She looked me in the eye and said, "That is not gonna happen." This caused me to have some concerns with the welcoming committee. She suggested we retire to her office and call the Husky Oil construction manager who had sent us here. His lack of communication had caused this situation in the first place. She reluctantly agreed and marched off down the hallway with me in tow.

When we entered her office, I noticed plaques on the wall regarding her service in the Army as a sergeant, which helped explain her demeanor. I immediately informed her of my service in that same Army. I did not mention the being an officer thing. This caused her to soften up a bit. She was now like a just plain ole prison guard. We got the manager on the phone and he said we had to have all the people on site as planned so just figure it out and hung up. Lots of help there.

We sat there looking at each other for a few minutes and then I said, "We can't sleep outside so what do we here." She told me to get out of her office, take everyone to the mess hall and wait for her to figure this out. I guess she didn't feel I could help with the planning. We sat there for two hours before Sally showed up. Her disposition had not improved. The morale in the room was in free fall.

By doubling up people already in the camp she had rooms for 20 people with two to a room. Only one single size bed in the rooms so we would have to figure out who slept on the floor. There were seven spare mattresses. The rest would sleep in the common area and the mess hall on blankets laid out on the rug. I had better accommodations in Vietnam, and it was a lot warmer there.

So, there I was with 40 new employees, only two of whom I knew, explaining to them we would be sleeping on the floor, and that I wasn't sure what happens tomorrow. The plane had left, and the wind was blowing the snow past the windows at 20 below and there were no roads for over 80 miles, so their options were limited. I am sure if they had a way out, they would have been gone in a flash. I was getting some very skeptical looks.

Thirty seven of the folks would be flown out to the remote sites in the morning and the second flight from Anchorage would arrive at 2:00 PM. Sally advised me there was a cat train with 30 bunks in it located in the parking lot, but it would take the contractor 24 hours to dig it out of the snow and fire up the heating system. She also informed me that I would be returning to Anchorage on the return flight as there was no room for me in the camp. End of conversation. I got the impression she blamed me for all this inconvenience. Now I have someone I just met making major decisions for me. This just kept getting worse.

The next morning, I had some personnel problems, particularly from the folks who were first time Arctic adventurers and were having second thoughts regarding the living conditions. I got them calmed down and assured them that at the remote camps the conditions will be much better. They were not, but once dropped off at the camp, it would be 50 miles across frozen tundra to the next human being, so leaving wasn't an option. They had become indentured servants, except with excellent pay. I advised them there was a pot of gold behind every tree at the camps. One of the Alaska guys pointed out there wasn't a tree within a hundred miles of here. So, I had to back up on that promise. Mentioned the Davis-Bacon wages at every opportunity. With the overtime those guys could make $5,000 to $7,000 a month. That was real money in 1978. Didn't see a big increase in morale. They settled in for the night.

There were only two, five passenger airplanes available so it took most of the morning to get everybody to the camps. I checked on the cat train and the contractor was running behind schedule due to needing parts for the heating system. Nothing I could do about that. The situation had disintegrated about as much as possible so things should start to get better. I rode out to the airstrip to meet the plane and fill in the second wave of folks on the situation. They headed for the camp hoping for the best and I got on the plane. It was a surprise to find a surveyor sitting in one of the seats. I asked him what he was doing there. He replied that when they landed, he looked out the window at the snow blowing across the runway and everybody in parkas, face masks and gloves and said, "No way am I getting out of this plane." He flew back to Anchorage with me. I didn't have much to say to him. He returned to California the next day. He wrote to me later asking to be paid for his time. I didn't reply.

That night I got a call from my chief of surveys telling me the cat train heaters didn't get going until 7:00 PM so after dinner when it was time to turn in, the choice for half of them was to sleep on the floor or get into a bed at minus 15 degrees and wait for the heater to catch up. Not a couple of good options. He noted that there was some apprehension on the part of several folks as to their odds of survival and if the pay offset those concerns.

Most of them chose the cold bed. They kept their parka, insulated pants and wool hats on and got under the covers. As the room slowly warmed up during the night, they would shed clothes as needed. The rooms were warm by 4:00 AM. By that night everyone was where they were supposed to be, and they all had a warm room and bed. Morale inched up a little bit to low instead of extremely low. We now had 80 new employees, with less than enthusiastic attitudes, scattered across most of the arctic coastline of Alaska in the dead of winter. No management challenge there.

In a few days everything was running smoothly. A few weeks earlier we had proposed on the ARCO survey contract in Prudhoe Bay. No word from them so assumed we didn't get it. Well, we did get it and needed to have six three-person survey crews, three union and three non-union on the slope Monday. They called us on Friday evening, so I had the weekend to find 18 surveyors and have them on the last flight Sunday night. So much for things running smoothly. When I dreamed about running my own firm none of this was in the dream. It was rapidly turning into a nightmare. There was no way to contact the union business agent, so we had to wing it. John and I called everyone we knew and hit every bar in town Friday and Saturday night. We managed to get the three union crews together but could only find two non-union crews, so we stole one from Husky oil by sneaking them out of Camp Lonely and putting them on a chartered plane to Prudhoe. You do what you have to do to get the job done. We sent a new crew to Husky a few days later. They never noticed.

Monday morning, I called the union and gave them the list of surveyors we had sent north. The business agent wasn't happy with the deal, but he dispatched all but one guy who wasn't a member. The union guy and I never did get to be close. I had to send a replacement up on the next plane and bring the imposter home. He insisted on being paid for his time flying back and forth. That didn't work out for him any better than the guy who wouldn't get off the plane.

So now our firm had gone from four to 98 in one month. This generated a multitude of problems. The most significant was the fact that it is an American tradition that you pay the people working for you and that requires having money to accomplish that function. We had money, but it was about 2% of what we would need to make the first payroll. There was also the issue that we wouldn't get a check from Husky or ARCO until after the second payroll. This is what is known in the business world as a cash flow problem. Seeing as how we had no cash to flow, we needed to borrow some from our friendly banker. Should not be a problem because banks have lots of money, right?

The meeting started off poorly. We advised Ken we needed $400,000. He stared at us for a minute and then started to laugh, it was not a happy laugh, never a good sign. He had been our banker since we started and was keenly aware of our financial status or lack thereof. Between the two of us we had a net worth of a little less than nothing.

He then inquired as to why we needed this astronomical amount of money. We filled him in on the big contracts and the impending payrolls. He said he understood but didn't know if he could give us that big of a loan, with no collateral, without putting his job at risk. We said we were willing to take that chance. He didn't see the humor. We were told to come back in two days to meet with the loan committee to see if it could be done. We didn't know what a loan committee was, this seemed a bit ominous, but our options were limited. A bank loan or not pay our people. Not paying them would most likely have a negative impact on our human relations factor.

It turns out one of the loan committee guys was a good friend of mine. He called me that night with the "What the hell are you guys doing?" question. I explained the deal to him. He advised me it would be a tough sell. Not what I wanted to hear. I asked if it would help if we put the contracts up for collateral. That seemed to gain some traction. The world of finance was a confusing and strange place for me. I had considerable reservations about wandering into it with little or no knowledge as to how it functioned. It is hard to imagine why any normal person would want to make a career of it.

Two days later we walked into the bank conference room in our brand-new suits and ties carrying our brand-new briefcases. We had decided to improve our image with most of the little cash we had left. All the bankers had suits from a much more expensive line, so they weren't impressed. $85 wasted on clothes and accoutrements. We all shook hands, but I didn't feel the love. This was a very somber group of humorless executives not subject to circumlocution. The room got very quiet. Other than having a bank account and one small loan for a survey instrument, that Ken handled, we had zip experience dealing with bankers or loan committees. This is a significant resume shortfall when asking for a $400,000 loan. The room seemed to get smaller and hotter by the minute.

The chairman, very formally, introduced the members of the committee, including their titles, and we introduced ourselves, sans titles. We sat there and looked at each other. Finally, my friend said "Mr. Bell and Mr. Herring would like to explore the possibility of securing a loan for some large contracts they have recently acquired. Mr. Bell would you please present your proposal." "Proposal?" What proposal? Nobody told us about a proposal. We needed $400,000 to make payroll, end of story. I started out by explaining the two contracts and the financial terms of those contracts. They asked for copies which I had in my brand-new briefcase, written on our defective stationary. I passed them out and they all sat there and leafed through the papers. Sometimes they frowned and sometimes they nodded in the affirmative. The time crawled by. My deodorant failed after a few minutes. My new dress shirt was being broken in big time. John had checked out of the deal after the handshakes and was just contently staring out the window. This was all my show. I have had some socially stressful moments in my life when I didn't know what to do, such as when my girlfriend in the back of my brother-in-law's Edsel said she wanted to "go all the way." This was far more frightening.

Finally, they started asking questions like what the rates of pay were vs billing rates, what was the gross margin and net profit etc. I was a little shaky on the financial terms so needed some prompting from the committee. Such as telling me the gross margin was profit before indirect expenses. Didn't know what indirect expenses were so that wasn't much help. This went on for an hour, one of those hours that takes a year to pass. Looking back on this meeting I can see they were trying to help us but didn't want to appear like they were. There may have been a tiny bit of compassion in the group.

We were summarily dismissed and told they would get back to us in two days. The first payroll was due in 4 days. Not much of a lead time if they turned us down. Of course, if they did the whole thing would go up in smoke anyway. Therefore, time wouldn't be a factor. We were called back and told they would grant the loan if both of us put up everything we owned to include our houses, cars and bank accounts. They also required that the contracts show them as being in first place for all payments. They noted there would be no negotiations. Take it or leave it. So much for the tiny bit of compassion.

So, we put up everything we owned in the world, as miniscule as it was, had our clients send the checks to the bank and then the bank determined how we would spend that money until they were paid off. I felt like I was negotiating with a firing squad after the leader had already said "Ready, aim." At least they didn't require we give them our first born. Jennifer was a cute little girl, but if she had to go live at the bank for a while so be it. I assumed they would pay for her room and board. We considered all the ramifications of this deal for about 30 seconds and then agreed. We had payroll covered until the checks started arriving. We also had a new partner in the firm who would have his foot on our neck for some time.

I didn't realize just how intrusive the bank was going to be regarding where the money was spent. We found ourselves in Ken's office two or three times a week justifying expenditures. In one meeting I had to show him John's and my mortgage payment slips and household expenses so we could draw money out of our own bank accounts for those things. Big brother was totally controlling our lives and he was determined to protect his interests above ours. So here we have an engineer with very little business experience trying to explain the operations of an engineering business to a banker with no experience with engineering companies. It was an inefficient and frustrating process. I thought I was back in the Army. Where is Sergeant Patterson when you need him?

One day after a long meeting with the Husky oil staff on our North Slope operation the construction manager asked me to stay after the meeting, usually not a good thing. He took me to his office, shut the door, and said he wanted to give me some "off the record advice," which is always a red flag. This was our biggest client, so I said "sure" and smiled as my stomach churned like a rip tide in Cook Inlet.

He pointed out that my grasp of business and accounting terms and processes seemed a bit lacking. He was being gentle. The bank was much more brutal in this regard. He said we were doing great work in the field, but they were making more concessions to our lack of business acumen than could be sustained. Even with my limited business experience I knew this wasn't a good thing for my biggest client to be saying. I just sat there like a deer in the headlights. He advised me that he was enrolled in the Engineering Management Master's Program at the University of Alaska Anchorage. It was strongly recommended that I should consider enrolling in the program. I called the University the next day. I was going back to college at the ripe old age of 34. UAA did not have a chapter of Delta Tau Delta so I would have to set my own study hours.

I took two classes that semester, The Legal Environment of Business and Management Accounting, followed by a whole bunch of other business courses in later semesters. The Husky guy was right, these courses cleared away the fog I had been looking through regarding the business side of the firm. I also found these business classes to be much easier than engineering courses. In fact, the classes were enjoyable. Never did find the class on intimidation that I am sure the loan committee guys took. Must have been a Ph.D. course.

One incident that really showed the value of this education in real time had to do with the unions. Our operation with Husky Oil was non-union. Most of my surveyors were members of the Teamsters Union but were working for us on the Husky project non-union. The Teamsters weren't thrilled with the arrangement. They seemed to get a little testy when you use union members on non-union jobs and were not shy about expressing their displeasure. They were a major financial and political force in Alaska at that time.

One day the surveyor business agent for the union landed in the Teamster jet at the Lonely airstrip. He got a ride into camp and was waiting for our surveyors when they came in that night. I was in Anchorage, fat and happy. He suggested, rather forcefully, that all the surveyors sign "green cards." These are cards asking for an election to go union on the job. As noted above, many of our guys were members of the union so the implication was, sign the card or don't get called out of the union hall ever again, a rather strong incentive to cooperate. He only needed a simple majority to get the election and that was accomplished. It was not a free and confidential vote. The die was cast for an election, which would be a secret vote.

The next day I get a call from the business agent advising me he had the signed green cards and wanted to come over and discuss what we wanted to do in that regard. A seemingly mundane request. Well, it turns out I was taking the course "Personnel Administration" and had just read the chapter on union organizing tactics. One of their tactics is to get the cards signed and then contact the employer and draw him into a meeting. If the employer does meet with the union, by law, they have recognized the union and there is no need for an election, the job is now union. It seems this would totally abrogate the rights of the employees. I referred him to our lawyer, my cousin, Jess Bell. So, the university course served its purpose almost instantly. I was getting smarter by the minute. You have probably noticed that I just admitted we have a lawyer in the family. Over the years we have had that cross to bear. To make matters worse, he spawned another one when his son went to law school. Luckily, the son saw the error of his ways and went back to college to get a medical degree.

The election was anti-climactic. We were paying more than the union wages so none of the guys wanted to go union. It was not in their best interests to disenfranchise the union, so they need to find a way to abrogate the threat anonymously. I was told a few years later that chicanery was employed. They got together and decided who would vote yes and who would vote no with the no's being the majority. That way the business agent wouldn't know who voted which way. All of this did not endear me to the union, even though I didn't participate in the plot. Never did get a Christmas card from them.

Six months into the loan deal and things were going well, except for the constant meetings with the bank. To our surprise we were awarded the BP contract for the Western half of the Prudhoe Bay field and the Kuparuk field. This added 15 more people to our staff and $30,000/week to the payroll. We were overwhelmed with both good and bad news. I made the long trip back downtown to the banker's office with no idea as to how this would turn out. Ken was dumbstruck. I think his exact words were, "Are you trying to kill me?" Even though it had crossed my mind a time or two I replied in the negative. Two days later I was back in the room with the loan committee in my newly laundered dress shirt, explaining how this was a good deal for us and them. I have to admit that I was a little weak on the latter. John opted to stay at the office. Again, I was asked to come back in two days. A pattern seemed to be forming.

In that meeting the chairman explained to me, in somewhat force-ful terms, that while we were using their money, they needed us to tell them when we were bidding on more work, thereby needing more of their money. The whole group of high fashion suits were in complete agreement with him, including my friend. They seemed a bit myopic to me, but they had all the business experience. We assured them that would be the case in the future. I even used some of my business terms just learned at UAA. They granted us the additional funds. None of the committee members seemed happy. Looking back on this, with considerably more business experience, I can see the bank was in the position of us being so far into them financially that they couldn't let us fail.

Our staff had increased to 145 people on the North Slope and 12 in the Anchorage office. We were picking up design work around town such as sub-divisions, parking lots, utility systems etc. so the Anchorage office was growing. We didn't think this staff increase needed to be reported to the bank as it was just a bunch of little contracts. Besides the checks for this work didn't have to go through the bank. Problem was soon the town staff was 25 people, all of whom expected to be paid on a regular basis. Ken finally noticed the payroll acceleration and inquired as to what was going on. This resulted in another meeting with Ken where he just hung his head and said, "Why me?" He opted to let it go and not bring the loan committee into the situation. Not sure if it was fatalism or he was beginning to warm up to our business style. His demeanor didn't seem warm, so I suspect it was fatalism.

It took another 18 months for the checks from the clients to catch up with the payroll so that we had the bank paid off. They then granted us a line of credit, for a considerably smaller amount, we could use as needed. We were on our feet financially. Jennifer never had to go live at the bank.

It was shortly after this that the company picked up the contract with Conoco Oil Company which added 12 more people to the payroll. We now had all the survey contracts for the North Slope from Barrow to the Canadian border. There were about 200 people on staff and making more money than we could comprehend. By God, my dream had come true and there was a financial component to it I hadn't anticipated. That 18-year-old kid was right on.

I remember walking into John's office one day after meeting with our accountant and saying, "John, do you know we are making a profit of $1,000/day?"

He said, "The Company is making that much?"

I said, "No, each of us is making that much." He nodded and went back to work on a survey plan. It didn't appear to register with him. John never was a money guy. He just wanted to survey stuff. That was big money in 1980. Fact is it is big money now.

At this point we were the 195th largest engineering firm in the nation according to Engineering News Record. My dream of having a firm in Alaska had come true big time, but boy did I have a tiger by the tail or vice versa.

Surveyor working in the arctic

CHAPTER FIFTEEN

BUSINESS OTHER THAN OIL

Besides our North Slope work we were increasing our footprint throughout Alaska. One job was to set section corners for a few thousand acres of federal land up near Nome. The property was going to be transferred to the NANA Regional Corporation as part of the Alaska Native Claims Settlement Act.

This was before GPS, but a new technology had come out. It was called an inertial system. In essence it was a box, the size of a footlocker, full of gyros that you could move from one place to another and it would tell you the distance and the bearing. For setting corners that are a mile apart out on open tundra this was the way to go. We would load it in a helicopter and fly it from corner to corner. No problem there, other than putting a very temperamental machine, the inertial system, inside another temperamental machine, the helicopter. Then sending it off into extreme weather in a remote Arctic location. How could that go wrong?

Turned out there were lots of problems. First, the BLM (Federal Bureau of Land Management) wanted a hard dollar bid. This kind of bid is where you say we will do this work for X number of dollars no matter what it costs. If you bid $100,000 and it ends up costing $110,000 you lose $10,000. If that wasn't enough to bring my stress level up, the bid included a lot of helicopter time. The helicopter companies required we pay by the hour with a minimum of four hours a day. So, if bad weather keeps us on the ground, we pay four hours for each of the birds. When they fly, we pay for however many hours with a minimum of four. Then we had the box of gyros. They required we pay for a specific number of days for this contraption, if we needed those days or not. If we ran over the number of days, then we paid double for the extra days. If we used it for less too bad, we still paid for those days. On top of that if the thing broke down, we had to pay for the technician to come up and fix it as well as pay the daily rate on the box while it was broken. I think Hannibal Lecter's contract manager designed that contract. Finally, we had to pay Davis Bacon wages which were much higher than the company normally paid. Our hard dollar bid was composed of a bunch of subcontractors on cost plus profit deals. We took all the risk. You had to be a complete idiot to take this deal, we were, and we did.

Let me put this all in perspective. We had to figure out how many days it would take to do the work, how many helicopter hours would be required, how many days of inertial system, surveying hours, equipment and camp costs. Then guess at how many weather days and other delays would be needed, add it all up and give the BLM a hard dollar bid. We put the bid together, I took it down to Saint Patrick's church and had the priest sprinkle holy water on the document and delivered it to BLM.

We were low bidder. John and I were not sure if we should celebrate or cry. BLM wouldn't tell us what the other bids were, so we didn't know if we had screwed up or submitted a good close bid. Would a big chunk of that $1,000/day profit go away with this contract? All my newly acquired business savvy was telling me this should work out. If it didn't what recourse would I have against the University of Alaska for giving me that savvy? Well, that very savvy told me none. It was pucker time. I signed the contract, with a very shaky hand. I remember our accounting manager standing there watching me sign the contract with her arms crossed and a scowl on her face. Kind of a Sergeant Skidmore pose. I wondered if she knew something I didn't. Fact is she knew lots of things I didn't, but, regarding this contract, not so much. We were flying blind.

The job started the next spring. We made a deal with the helicopter company to lease the birds at their hourly rate, but we would hire our own pilots who had to be approved by them. A Cessna 185 was purchased to use as a support plane. We mobilized to the village of Kiana, northeast of Nome. John was excited because it was a whole new type of surveying with the gyros. I was totally stressed, HARD DOLLAR.

The job went well with a few hic-ups. One was the people who agreed to rent us rooms in the one-story hotel located in Kiana, a remote Alaskan village, neglected to tell us the hotel had been boarded up for three years and none of the utilities worked. A rather large oversight on their part. We spent two days, at Davis-Bacon wages, getting everything working. They rejected the suggestion that the rent should be reduced. This wasn't good regarding the budget.

Another little problem came about one evening, about four weeks into the job. We had moved to a new location and were in a tent camp. It was at the end of the day when everyone was back in camp. An Air Force helicopter landed, and two Secret Service guys got out flashed their badges at me and asked for one of my helicopter pilots. Can't say this gave me a comfortable feeling. Without a word to me they put him in their bird and flew away. Never heard from that guy again. Don't know if he was gunning for the president or spending funny money. I suspect the latter. This left me short one pilot. The four-hour minimum on the pilotless bird was a costly issue. So, with the hotel deal and now this we weren't off to a great start. The words "hard dollar" kept pounding in my brain.

The owner of the store in a nearby village told me he had heard there were some helicopter pilots in Nome who had just finished a job. The next morning, I borrowed his Cessna 172, our 185 was in Anchorage for repairs, and flew to Nome and inquired at the terminal about the pilots. The folks there said, Indeed, three recently out of work pilots had been drinking at The Board of Trade bar in town for two days. This bar has been around for many decades and has a colorful history.

I got a cab and arrived at the bar around noon. At the time, the doors into the bar were those old-fashioned swinging type that you watched John Wayne push through going into the saloon to confront bad guys. My entrance had nowhere near the flare of John Wayne. I asked the bartender if there were any helicopter pilots in the joint. He replied, "Those three jerks over there and if they are yours then get them the hell out of here." This statement seemed to indicate the pilots hadn't endeared themselves to the bar staff. I denied ownership but said I would see what could be done to thin the herd for him. He didn't seem mollified.

I observed that one guy had his head on the table and appeared to be passed out, one was leaning back in his chair studying the ceiling intently or he was maybe in a dark place. The third guy was regaling the other two with a story not noticing his audience was in another place mentally. It was a table of drunken stupor. So, which of these guys would you trust to fly your airplane? There was no good choice, but I was desperate. I needed to make the least bad choice.

When I approached the table, the dude talking shut up and stared at me like he was sure my being there was significant but had no idea why. When asked if he was a chopper pilot he nodded slowly. When I inquired as to if his companions were also pilots he nodded again. I then stated that I was looking for a pilot to work the summer and fall. This seemed to register with him as he kicked the guy with his head on the table and yelled at the other guy which brought both of them back from wherever they had been, but just barely. The conversation was becoming more labored by the minute. The bartender looked on with mild interest.

I now had three semi-conscious pilots staring at me while trying to re-engage their brains with limited success. The other patrons of the bar were all tuned into the drama hoping for some excitement. I asked if they were certified in a Jet Ranger helicopter and all three raised their hand. Only one pilot was needed so which to choose, this was like trying to decide which of the Three Stooges to pick for your financial advisor. It was obvious that I was not going to get detailed resumes from these guys which made it a total crap shoot. If I picked a loser, he could be brought back and then I could pick a different drunk. I said, "We only need one pilot and there is a cab waiting outside. First one of you to get to the door is hired." The talker was the only one who made it to the door even though he was on all fours at the time. The other two couldn't get out of their chairs. The track star's name was Joe. The bartender didn't thank me for thinning the herd.

We took the cab back to the airport, picked up his gear, stuffed him into the 172 and flew back to the camp. I got him into the mess tent and poured several gallons of coffee down his throat. By the next morning he was walking and talking, semi coherently. He did ask how he got there and why. Joe turned out to be the best pilot on the job. We remained friends for 30 years. Sometimes you win a crap shoot.

I went back to town the next week and John took over running the job. They moved from village to village, as necessary. The last place they ended up in was at an abandoned FAA facility called Moses Point, several miles east of Nome. Nobody lived there and the FAA buildings had been boarded up for many years. Our guys fixed them up as best they could and moved in. There were no utilities, so it was camp stoves, cots and propane heaters. Luxury accommodations for field surveyors. They named the place Bell Herringville.

We completed the job right on budget. Therefore, we had a tidy profit. This was due to good management and luck. Luck being the major factor. I contacted a local air freight company about flying all the remaining food, appliances, cots etc. from Moses Point to Anchorage. They said it would cost $16,000. When I called John and told him this he said, "This stuff isn't worth $16,000." I asked if he could sell it up there. We discussed it for a while and then he said he would get on the single side band radio and announce to everyone from Nome to Unalakleet that we were having a "going out of business sale" and listed all the stuff. The next day two boats showed up and bought a few things. The sale was off to a bad start. The next day boats started coming from everywhere. It took a day to get from Nome and Unalakleet to Moses Point so that accounted for the delay. John sold everything we had right down to the unused toilet paper.

I was sitting in my office when he walked in with one of those canvas bankers' bags clear full of checks and cash. $21,500 worth. I couldn't believe it. We saved $16,000 in freight and netted $21,500 more. The profit on the job just went up by 50%. There was one small problem.

The cash was about $5,000 the rest was checks that were mostly welfare, unemployment and personal checks that had been endorsed five or six times. In essence they had been used as currency in the villages. I will endorse my check over to you to buy your boat, then you endorse it over to someone else to buy something from them. Sitting there looking at these old wrinkled up faded checks I had a bad feeling as to their legal tender. There was also some apprehension as to how this was going to play out with Ken the banker. He always seemed to get nervous when we walked into his office. None of my UAA courses covered this issue. I suspect this type of transaction is rare in the business world.

Rather than cause him any more stress I would just fill out a deposit slip and give it, with the cash and the checks, to a teller and that would be that. It wasn't. The teller almost had a heart attack. "Mister Bell the bank can't take these checks, I have never seen anything like this." Her eyes got really big and she picked up the phone and called Ken. I saw him coming out of his office with that "what now" look on his face. There was a small pang of guilt, but it passed quickly. You can't show compassion to bankers because it confuses them as they don't know what it is.

Ken sorted through the checks with a look of incredulity on his face. He then turned to me spread his arms wide and said, "What have you done now and is any of this legal?" I stated that it was quite legal and explained how we came about getting these checks. His chin dropped to his chest, his shoulders slumped, and he whispered, "Follow me to my office and bring this stuff with you." We adjourned to his small, but well adorned office. He explained that he was only a couple of years from retirement and he was concerned that I would dash that hope. I assured him I would make every attempt to avoid any dashing. He didn't seem convinced. I observed he had developed a rather noticeable tick on the right side of his face, I chose not to inquire about it.

After considerable discussion he agreed to take the checks but would only credit our account as they cleared. We returned to the traumatized teller who took the checks and deposit slip with very wide eyes and shaky hands. All but one of the checks cleared, I couldn't believe it. Ken did retire a couple of years later. He didn't invite us to the party. I am sure it was an oversight. Oh well, the loan committee would have probably been there, and they didn't impress me as party animals. So, it would have been boring anyway. Besides, I couldn't remember where I had put that suit I bought for the committee meetings.

`While we were building the business, I was also building a family. Our daughter Jennifer was born in 1970 and Gretchen came along in 1972. The relationship between dads and daughters is really special, at least until they turn 13. Then they go from being daddy's little girl to a teenager who can't stand to have you in the same room. Fact is they own you, lock, stock and barrel. I remember one night we were at the dinner table and Gretchen was about four with blond hair down to her waist. This was a super cute little girl, as was Jennifer. She had done something wrong and I was scolding her about it. In the middle of my tirade she put her chin on her chest, looked up at me, with big blue eyes, and said, "But daddy, I am just a little girl." How do you deal with that other than just caving in? Dads have no chance of coming out ahead in the world of young daughters. Both girls grew up and managed to get college degrees and are good citizens. The world is a better place because they are in it.

Gretchen managed a restaurant and bar in Girdwood, a suburb of Anchorage for 25 years. It is a ski resort community. Her degree in early childhood development served her well in dealing with the bar flies when she tended the bar. She is now a flight attendant for Alaska Airlines.

People often say to me that Gretchen is Bob Bell in skirts, except 30 years younger and considerably better looking. I can't argue with that assessment.

Jennifer gave me my first grandkids. Emma, Brice, Ryan and Ethan. They are all good kids and we have lots of adventures together.

I was a full-fledged family man. We bought a spacious 1,000 square foot three-bedroom ranch house in South Mountain View. This was not a high-end neighborhood, but it was pleasant and relatively safe. When I say relatively safe that can be a matter of perspective.

We lived on South Park Street. One night a man named Bob Bell who lived on North Park Street was shot and killed by his wife. He obviously had screwed up somehow, at least in her mind, Well the front page of the morning newspaper announced Bob Bell of Park Street had been killed by his enraged wife. Of course, all the people at the office thought it was me as I was the only Bob Bell they knew who lived on Park street. Most had read the paper before going to work and, of course, I was late that day due to a discipline issue with the girls.

The reception I received when I walked into the office un-shot and alive was mixed to say the least. Our receptionist was in full sob mode when I came through the door. She went through a disbelief, happiness, confusion, and relief process in five seconds. Then she went back to crying without saying a word. As I hadn't read the paper I was somewhat confused as to what was going on. About this time a couple of other employees came into the room to see what the commotion was about. They went into shock and then began shaking my hand and saying how happy they were to see me. This was a very different reception than I had received all the other times I had come to work so I figured there was more to this than their high regard for me. I said, "I know you guys love me, but what the heck is going on here?"

Someone handed me the newspaper so I could read the headline. I said, "I don't remember getting shot or being dead." Nobody appreciated the humor. It took me an hour to get back my stapler, tape dispenser and other things that had been appropriated from the "dead guy's" desk. They were sad about my demise, but engineers tend to be pragmatic and office supplies were in demand. Linda was somewhat confused to find out she had killed me. Even though I am sure she had considered it a few times.

We bought a bigger house in 1973 in Chugach Foothills. It was two stories, twice as big as the Mountain View house and much more expensive. This was less than a year before John and I decided to start the business, so the timing was problematic to say the least. You triple your house payment shortly before quitting your job. Not a well thought out financial plan, even for me.

The fact that I was gone every other week on the North Slope and then working 60 and 70-hour weeks when home was taking a toll on the marriage. Linda and I decided to divorce in 1982. It is difficult to really nail down why a marriage goes bad and we were no exception. I reflect back on that night, when getting home from Vietnam, as I sat on my duffel bag in front of the house staring at the front door. Was I savoring the moment or debating going through that door? I had been thinking about not going back to Linda when in Vietnam, but after that day we were pinned down all I wanted was to get home and have everything the way it was before leaving. So, I went through the door. Still not sure why. Seventeen years and two kids later it came home to rest. We all have failures in our lives. This was a really big one for me, I am sure it was for her also.

With most divorces someone ends up homeless, in this case it was me. A good friend of mine owned a gravel pit where he kept his mobile home. He invited me to move in with him and I gladly accepted. My accommodations have now gone from an upscale home in a high-end neighborhood to living in a very old mobile home in a gravel pit. There is no way to view this as anything but a significant downgrade in my quality of life. My business life was going well, but my social life had some issues. Fritz was also a successful businessman, but very frugal, hence the trailer house. His social life was akin to mine, less than optimum.

We did a lot of bar hopping, but both of us were reeling from a divorce so we didn't want to get involved in a relationship with anyone. Our standard line when asked what we did was to say we worked for the city sanitation department. Fritz drove the garbage truck and I was the guy on the back. In most cases interest waned at that point, but not always. At least we didn't have to deal with gold diggers.

I had been at a bachelor party that ran until the wee hours of the night. For me it was one of those parties where someone takes your keys and sends you home in a cab. Don't know who did it but appreciate their concern. I arrived at the trailer shortly before dawn and staggered through the front door. Fritz was laying on the living room floor lightly clothed, as in buck naked, surrounded by empty beer cans. Next to him was a similarly clothed woman who was covered in tattoos. They were both out cold. This was a social event I didn't want to participate in no matter what. I stepped over them, retired to my room and passed out on the bed in the exact opposite attire than them. Didn't even get my shoes off. Woke up bright and early the next morning around noon and found Fritz still passed out on the floor. The tattooed lady was gone, so was a whole bunch of our valuables. Two of his guns, my coin collection, a gold watch Mom had given to Dad when they lived in Naknek, etc. all gone. It was reasonable to assume Fritz's companion was the likely suspect.

I woke Fritz up and inquired as to his friend's identity. He said he thought her name was Silk but wasn't sure. With this information we determined the possibility of recovering the items was slim at best. We never saw any of that stuff or her again.

This incident convinced me of the need to give up the high life of living in a trailer house in a gravel pit and find other accommodations. I bought a nice condo with a kitchen, living room and a loft bedroom. It was quite small, but bigger than my room in the mobile home and in a nicer neighborhood. Sticking to my real estate protocol the condo was purchased in 1984 just before the real estate market totally crashed. I paid $85,000 for the condo. One year later it was worth $29,000. Not the kind of result those ads on TV portray about real estate investment.

My social life kind of sputtered along. I did have a relationship with a spectacularly beautiful woman who had been the Miss World contestant from New Zealand sometime in the 1960s. She was also very rich. I met her in San Francisco.

I had travelled to San Francisco, California with my chief of surveys Scott for a meeting with British Petroleum. One night we were in an Irish bar named O'Toole's. Scott and I were at the piano bar when two women came in. One was spectacular and the other was not. They sat down next to us. I soon struck up a conversation with Alene and we were hitting it off great. She noted she was spending the night with her friend and returning to her condo in Marina Del Rey the next day. I perceived this as a hint that she might consider other arrangements.

It was getting to be closing time, but we were not done partying. Alene said she knew of an after-hour's club we could go to. Her friend didn't buy in to that plan. She wanted to go home. I told her to go and Alene could come home in a cab when we were done partying. Never did call that cab. Don't know what happened to Scott that night, but I had a really good time.

That started a strange relationship. Alene travelled extensively. She would be in France and call me and say she would send a ticket so I could come join her for the weekend. A month later it was Bombay. I had a business to run, couldn't just be running off to the four corners of the earth on a whim. In most cases I demurred. A gorgeous, rich woman sending you a ticket to join her at an exotic location, only a socially challenged engineer could turn that down and unfortunately, I was one.

One trip was to Mazatlán, Mexico. Alene called and said she and a friend of hers were going there for a week. The friend was a centerfold model for a French magazine. She wanted to know if I would like to join her and inquired if I had a friend for her companion. Don't know an unmarried man in this world who would turn that deal down. I replied with an enthusiastic "Yes." After an extensive vetting process Fritz was selected from a large crowd of my single male friends. We were off to Los Angeles to meet the ladies.

We were sitting in a Los Angeles airline lounge when the two women walked in. As they approached us Fritz said, "I don't know which one is Alene, but the other one is fantastic." Several notches above the tattooed lady and far less likely to steal our stuff. We were off to Mexico.

Once we got there, I noticed Alene spoke Spanish. When asked about that, she said she used to live in Mazatlán. A few days later the subject of her living there came up again and she asked if I would like to see her "place" in the suburbs. She was divorced from a very wealthy man who owned a bunch of smelters. They had built a very elaborate estate on the edge of the city. We went to see the "place."

Alene and I in Mexico

There was a staff of six people, a pet leopard, a pool and about 20,000 square feet of house. It was surrounded by a barrier wall with an armed guard. I was impressed. This beat the hell out of a trailer house in a gravel pit. The ex was not in country at the time, so she was OK with bringing us there for the afternoon. As women go Alene was in the top 1% for a single guy with no desire for a permanent relationship. How could it get any better that this? I was a stud muffin and loving it. A whole new experience for me. Should have been written up in engineers weekly social hero section.

We had a wonderful week and headed back to California. Fritz took off for Alaska, but Alene asked me to stay and have dinner with her. While we were dining in a very posh restaurant, she suggested that I should drop everything and just travel the world with her on a full-time basis. Well, can't say that was expected, having never been a kept man. I pointed out that I had a business to run. She said she would buy the business and turn it over to someone else to manage. To say I was taken aback would be an understatement. After stuttering for a minute or two and gulping down my drink she suggested I think about it for a while and then get back to her. Her suggestion would involve a rather significant lifestyle change for me.

Upon arriving home and thinking about that for a long time. I realized having no purpose in life and being a kept man wasn't for me. I flashed back on the Tina thing in college. My girls were here and so were all my friends as well as my business. It was with a heavy heart that I turned her down. She never called again with an invitation. I never regretted that decision.

The family before grandkids

CHAPTER SIXTEEN

HERS, MINE AND OURS

In the early 1980s the company formed a joint venture with a large Alaska native corporation. This gave us access to a lot of work. They hired a lady to take over their accounting department shortly after we formed the joint venture. She made an appointment to come over and inspect our accounting department. Turned out that was one of the most important meetings of my life.

Her name is Candace and she is the most intelligent, personable and beautiful woman I have ever met. When she came into my office I was smitten immediately, and I am not easily smitten. A week later I launched my campaign to get her to go out with me. It was a well-organized and intensive effort but to no avail. All my advances were gently rebuked. Finally, by working through her co-workers I got her to agree to have a drink with me, and them, at a place called Harry's. She showed up and we had a nice conversation, then she said she had to go pick up her son and left me there with her co-workers, who I berated for not making this work. As the drinks had already been paid for by me, they saw it as a win. Self-interest is an ugly trait.

After considerable work and the devious manipulation of several people, I finally got her to agree to go fishing with me. It was a beautiful summer day when we got in my airplane and flew over to Lake Creek to fish for king salmon. I am a very skilled fisherman, at least that is what I tell anybody who will listen. Candace wasn't. In fact, this may have been her first salmon fishing experience. She was destined to have many more. We were using spinning poles and casting from shore a technique prone to problems. When you hook a 50-pound fish and it takes off downstream, keeping up with it while crawling through the brush and holding onto the fishing pole has some challenges. She almost immediately got tangled up. I graciously stopped fishing and got her gear untangled. She went back to fishing while I retrieved my pole. Before I could make a cast, she was tangled again. Once again, I untangled her. I was trying to impress her with my patience and my untangling skills. I also intended to impress her with my fishing skills if I could get a chance to fish.

As I was going to get my pole, she hooked a king. It was an epic battle, with considerable advice from me, but she persevered anyway and landed a nice 25-pound king, without the riverbank running process. Now if you read the fishing laws carefully it says the limit is one king a day per person. My interpretation of this is that if there are two of you, you get two kings. It doesn't specify who catches those fish. The "per person" can be interpreted a couple of ways. I am sure if you read all the text it might clear this up, but I never got to that part. Therefore, I told her to keep fishing. We went through a few more tangle episodes and then she got another king of about the same size. We were limited. Now I had worked hard to get her to go on this trip so I couldn't pitch a fit and roll around on the ground screaming because a rookie fisherperson had skunked me. I put that off until I got home.

I did manage to parlay the negative of being out fished, by a total novice, into a positive by saying that she had to give me chance to redeem my fishing reputation by going fishing with me again. I was astounded when she agreed. When we got back to Anchorage, we fileted the fish and I put hers in a plastic bag with some ice, she gave me a kiss on the cheek and drove away. Well, it was a start. Not much of one, but a start. On the next trip she was left to deal with her tangles, and I caught both fish. We were even and I established that I was not a total suck-up. She took it in good spirits.

On the next fishing trip Candace brought her son Christopher. I hadn't met him before. He was 10 years old and seemed like a nice young man. I considered it significant that she brought him to meet me. Maybe there was an outside chance of her taking me seriously. He wasn't any better at fishing than his mom, so I spent most of the trip untangling lines. A pattern was developing that had a negative impact on the number of fish I was catching. My fishing legend was being sullied, but it was worth it to get to spend time with Candace.

Our relationship slowly grew stronger. We went out to dinner a few times and went dancing at the Whale's Tail bar, which was the "in" place in town. I made excuses to come by her office "on business" whenever possible. The more I got to know her the more I respected her and began to have some serious feelings in her regard. Having a marriage fail is a very bad experience. This makes it difficult to dance around that flame a second time. She was such an exceptional woman that flame burned very bright for me. The flame dancing intensified.

The relationship went from casual to center stage. I managed to introduce her to my girls who were hesitant at first, but soon they were all good buddies. Sometimes it seemed like Candace liked them more than me. I got to know Christopher much better and soon discovered he was a lot smarter than me by several times over. You may opine that this was a low bar, but it still put him very close to genius level. Things were going well making me a happy guy. Life was good and I felt centered again.

I have a cabin on a remote lake named Shell Lake. There were a bunch of characters who also had cabins. There was Junk Food John, Dave the Torch, Gentleman Jim, Scooter, Champagne Ann, Kenny, who was the Shell Lake marshal, and many others. I was Bad Bob and Candace was Dandy Candy. We would all fly in on Friday night and party hardy until Sunday afternoon. Most of the partying took place at the Shell Lake lodge. We were all quintessential Alaskans and thoroughly enjoyed each other's company.

One of the more fun events was the trial of Junk Food John. I was the prosecuting attorney for the lake and Gentleman Jim was the defense attorney. Junk Food had been charged with two counts. Count one was sleeping at a party and count two was wasting a three-man moon, both considered major offenses. The crimes occurred at a party in the lodge. Junk Food fell asleep during the festivities. Probably brought on by the consumption of mass quantities of beer. Scooter rounded up three, of the more rotund, guys to stand in front of Junk Food's chair and flash a, wide ranging, three-man moon, at which time he was awakened. He glanced at the moons, snorted and went back to sleep. I filed charges the next day.

Gentleman Jim's mom is a real attorney as is my cousin. So we had an opportunity to indulge in legal circumlocution just like real lawyers. The alleged crimes took place at the end of the summer. So, we two surrogate shysters sent legal missives such as interrogatories and discovery requests back and forth all winter long. Jim's mom and Jess soon grew tired of the farce, so the paperwork fell off dramatically. The trial was scheduled for the next June at the lodge.

The judge would be Bob, the bartender from the Whale's Tail bar. Gentleman Jim for the defense and Bad Bob for the prosecution. It would be difficult to find a less qualified cast of characters. The jury was to be composed of six people, picked from the crowd, who were not yet drunk. The scene was set for the biggest trial in the history of Shell Lake. We were all perplexed as to why the national news services hadn't picked up on this extraordinary event.

The big day arrived. Bob, the bar tender stayed the night before the trial with Candace and me at our cabin. This was not considered untoward judge tampering. We had rented him a judge's robe and one of those white wigs' shysters wear in England. I was wearing a three-piece suit, the first one to ever be seen at Shell Lake, and carrying a leather briefcase. Some people commented on the wardrobe choices, both negative and positive. Bob stood up in the bow of my boat in full judge regalia as we motored across the lake to the lodge. Several people said it was an impressive sight. Particularly as the sun was at our backs making us look like superheroes, which we fully believed we were. Candace rode in the middle of the boat looking embarrassed, but she had grown used to being embarrassed while in my company.

There were 50 or 60 people at the lodge looking forward to the trial and drinking heavily, so we arrived at the dock to an enthusiastic reception, maybe with the exception of Junk Food John. My entourage and I adjourned into the lodge where Gentleman Jim and I sorted through the crowd to find six jurors. Our success was dubious at best, but we did end up with a jury. Five were semi-sober, one was drunk, but semi-coherent. Prior to beginning the trial two things happened. First Dave the Torch invited the jury outside to "have a little smoke." No tobacco was involved. Second, I asked that each shyster have a two-minute private talk with the jury to establish the ground rules of jurying. Jim agreed and went first. Don't know what he told them, didn't matter. I had two t-shirts made up earlier. Both said Junk Food John on the front. One said Shell Lake Convict number 00000002 on the back (we had convicted Bill the bear watcher of running a chainsaw before 9: 00 AM the year before) and the other said Deputy Marshal Shell Lake. I explained to the jury that I couldn't give these shirts to Junk food unless he was, in fact, a convict. Then, as insurance, it was mentioned that I would buy their drinks for the rest of the night if I got the conviction. That seemed to seal the deal. Jim's efforts to defend Junk Food John had become quixotic at best. We returned to the lodge. The trial protocol at Shell Lake varies somewhat from the State of Alaska court system as do the pretrial motions.

The jury was seated, and I went first as the prosecution. The room went quiet except for Kenny passing gas and a few beer belches. As my first witness I called Dave the Torch and swore him in on a copy of the Alaska fishing regulations. They were two years out of date, but I am sure still relevant as a swearing in document, at least in the Shell Lake judicial district. My first question was, "When was the first time you got laid and with whom?" Sharon, his wife, perked up with that question. His answer was vague at best. I am sure more detail was solicited by Sharon when they got back to their cabin later that night. There is reason to suspect he had difficulty trying to abjure his testimony. All my witnesses were greeted with a similar highly personal first question, consequently we did have a few reluctant witnesses. The reluctance dealt with by browbeating and booze.

The judge was seated at a table with Gentleman Jim and I buying him drinks. His attention seemed to wander at times as did his consciousness, but in general he was following along. The crowd was having a ball keeping the proceedings very lively. Junk Food John sat in the defendant's chair and nursed a six pack or two of beer.

*Trial at Shell Lake, judge Bob and
Junk Food John with tie*

The trial lasted over two hours. During that time, several people in the crowd lost interest as they had passed out due to overindulgence of various substances including booze. I pointed out that everybody in the room were witnesses to the alleged crimes as they had all been at the party. Due to this and the promised drinks I got a conviction. It was an auspicious win for me. In the spirt of sportsmanship and good taste, I turned to Gentleman Jim and yelled "LOSER." Junk food John was taken aback and just sat there with his mouth ajar with empty beer cans scattered around him. We then went into the sentencing phase.

The judge was shaken awake and advised of the results. He then had me present the t-shirts to Junk Food John. Which I did with considerable bloviating. He was sentenced to wear the shirts at least twice a year at the lake, to continue to be the deputy marshal, without pay, (he never was paid) for three years. Finally, on a warm summer day when there is no wind, to go to the end of the lodge's dock and do a five-minute moon without the benefit of bug dope. This was a big deal as the mosquitoes at Shell Lake are legendary. The party/trial broke up early the next morning. We had run out of booze. My bar bill was staggering, but worth every nickel. The trial was talked about for years thereafter. Junk food John sent me a picture later that summer doing the moon with a picture frame over his posterior. A prime example of Shell Lake etiquette.

Another major event on the lake was Scooter, the ranger, and Champagne Ann's wedding. Once again Bob, the bar tender, was the one officiating the ceremony. He had been designated as a temporary representative of the State of Alaska. He didn't wear the robe or wig. All of us volunteered to fly wedding guests out to the ceremonies as there are no roads to the lake, in fact, it is an hour by air from Anchorage.

There were people from all over the country including a very elderly gentleman from Germany who wasn't in good health. He was a shirttail relative of Ann's. His attendance terminated rather dramatically later in the day.

The wedding went great. The weather was perfect, Champagne Ann had a beautiful wedding dress, Scooter was in a tux and the rest of us had put on our cleanest Pendleton shirts and jeans. The ceremony took place at the end of the lodge's dock. It was one of the best events we had at the lake, other than the trial.

After the wedding there was a reception with lots of food and even more booze. We all planned to spend the night at the lake, so we didn't need a pilot to not drink, turns out that wasn't a good plan. We were only about an hour into the reception when the elderly German collapsed and quit breathing. Per chance there were two nurses in the group who started CPR. All of us pilots stood around with our fourth or fifth beer in our hand wondering who was going to fly him into town. Flying an airplane while drunk is a really bad idea on several levels, but we couldn't just let him croak. It was a, "no good choice", situation.

About that time doctor Jack, an MD, landed in his brand-new Cessna 185 and taxied to the dock fully expecting to join the party. We quickly explained the situation, then helped him take out the back seat and the co-pilot seat and put an air mattress on the floor. His plane was now in ambulance mode sans the siren. I had the victim's shoulders and Kenny, the marshal, had his feet as we lifted him into the airplane. This put his head right next to the pilot seat. As I laid him down the doctor looked at me and said, "We don't need to be in a hurry here." It was obvious this was not going to turn out well for the gentleman. The two nurses piled in, still doing CPR, and they took off.

This whole incident put a damper on the festivities for over 10 minutes. We were soon back in full party mode. The lodge got a phone call two hours later saying he didn't make it. I recall Steve, the Harbor Master, saying, "I can't think of a better way to go than in the back of a new Cessna 185 with two good looking nurses working on me." We all nodded. We then passed the hat and collected money to help the old guy with his final expenses. The party broke up sometime before dawn.

Shell Lake has been a big part of my life. I bought the cabin, we named Old Green, in 1974 in partnership with Gentleman Jim. It was a luxurious eight feet by ten feet with two bunk beds, an oil barrel stove, a small table and an outhouse. Maybe luxurious is not the right word. Sparse might be more accurate. We built a much nicer and larger cabin in 1980 and I bought Jim out in 1984 when he built his own cabin. I got my pilot's license in 1977 and my floatplane (a Cessna 185) in 1978, so we spent most weekends at the lake. It was our get-away place. I proposed to Candace in our inflatable boat in the middle of the lake on a beautiful summer day. She accepted, which made the day even more beautiful.

In 1983 Linda decided to move to California and she took my girls with her. I think that day at Anchorage International Airport saying good-bye to Gretchen and Jennifer was the saddest day of my life. All the happy went away. I got down there to visit them as often as I could, but it was not the same. I really missed my girls.

Candace and my wedding, flight instructor John, presiding August 1985

Candace and I were married in August of 1985 in our house on Campbell Lake by John, our flight instructor. A very Alaskan thing to do. By this time Candace had her pilot's license. All our relatives were there as well as the motley crew from Shell Lake. It was the best day of my life and I like to think of hers also, even though she has never confirmed this while sober. It was interesting that my brothers and sister all said that I had "married up" at different times during the day. I already knew that and still do over 30 years later. Mom withheld comment on this subject. I was her favorite, so she set an impossibly high bar for my spouse. You were well advised to concur with "Ma Bell" regarding most anything.

We planned the "post-reception" at the Captain Cook Hotel. Candace and I rented a room, so we didn't have to drive home in an impaired condition. It was a typical Shell Lake celebration with lots of booze and very little intellectual discourse. The beer belching was in high form. We drank and danced and drank some more. It was a lot of fun. It was well into the evening and all the older folks, such as our moms, had gone home when Candace and I retired to our room. The Shell Lake crowd was still in full party mode.

We had only been in the room for a few minutes when we got a call from the front desk. The clerk said, "There is a bunch of people here who want to know your room number so they can come up." I said, "This is our wedding night, would you want that bunch in your room on your wedding night?" he said, "Have a nice night" and hung up. We weren't disturbed. We did find some of them at our house the next day most of whom were passed out on the floor or the lawn. Our moms, who had gotten up early, weren't impressed. It was a good start for an Alaskan marriage.

Four months later Candace advised me she was pregnant. Now that was a surprise, a very pleasant surprise, but still a surprise. She was 39 and I was 41. That is a little geriatric for being knocked up. At her next birthday, I bought her an apron that said, "I would rather be 40 than pregnant." She was both. Our son Frank Thomas Bell II, AKA FT, came along the next June. He was named after my grandpa Bell. His birthday was on Friday, June 13. My brother John was born on Friday, June 13. When I told mom this, she said "Oh no, look how John turned out!" I noted earlier I was her favorite. John was one of the happiest guys I knew, but his success regarding money and several marriages was dubious. Mom would have preferred a more mainstream life for John, but still she loved him dearly, we all did.

I was in the delivery room for the birth. It was my first time attending the birth of one of my kids. When the girls were born the dads were not allowed in the room. I was a little nervous, she was perfectly calm. It was a C-section operation. The doctor advised us he was going to put Candace out for the procedure. He also told us that once she was under, they needed to get the kid out within a couple of minutes to avoid the drugs getting to him. So, the gas passer puts Candace under, and the doctor makes the incision. It turns out this doctor was a fitness nut. He ran the Hawaii Ironman every year, so he starts in about her "abs." "Look at the abs on this woman!" She was a very loyal gym rat and, in fact, had worked out the day before so I could see his point. Problem was, the "couple of minutes" were flying by and this guy is still going on about her abs. I finally said, "Forget about her abs, get the damn kid out of there." He seemed a little perturbed at my attitude but proceeded with the birthing thing.

This was the first birth I had witnessed so I wasn't prepared for the drama of the procedure. Everyone jokes about the husband passing out during a birth, in fact my brother John actually did do that. Well, I just barely skated past that distinction when they started pushing down on her stomach. Suddenly FT and a bunch of other stuff came out of the slit they had cut in her belly. This is a sight most people shouldn't dwell on. The doctor and nurses were all focused on Candace and the kid, so they didn't notice me staggering around the room. By the time they had him out I had regained my composure, at least superficially.

They checked him out and then another doctor came in to check his arms and legs. He had one of FTs feet in each hand when the kid took his first pee, right on the guys tie. The doc just looked down at his tie and said, "You would think I would learn?" it was a Snap-On tie, so he pulled it off, put it in his pocket, reached in the other pocket and took out a clean tie. He had been there before. Suspect they don't teach that at medical school.

The kid was handed to me and I was told to take him down the hall to the nursery. They would take Candace to her room to wake up. This was very exciting. I had two wonderful daughters and Christopher, but this was my first son from scratch. Ed, a close friend since second grade, was standing in the hallway. I started yelling at him about the size of the kid's gonads and other things. There was a liberal use of profanity in the shouting. He responded in kind. We were two very excited, obscene and loud, hombres. Did I mention this was a Providence Catholic hospital?

We arrived at the nursery to find a very stern looking nurse waiting for us. Her body language was less than welcoming. She told Ed to stay out of the nursery. Then instructed me to put the kid in a warming crib and pointed a gnarled old finger at the door and told me to get out of the room. Her attitude seemed a bit stern. Not sure what to do next, I went out into the hall where Ed was waiting. I was still wearing the hospital scrubs over my clothes I took them off and just stood there looking confused. Ed finally said, "Where is Candace?" Oh yea, Candace, I should go find her.

By the time I got to her room she was wide awake and wanted to see our son. I was summerly dispatched to the nursey to retrieve him. The stern nurse was still in attendance and her attitude hadn't improved. Arriving at the door she inquired as to what I wanted. Advised her I was there to get my kid and take him to his mother.

She said, "What is his number?" Number, what number?

I pointed at FT and said, "That one." She informed me she wouldn't give him to me until I could give her his number and then kicked me out of the nursery again. It was becoming apparent she had some issues with me. I went back to the room where a nice nurse told me the number was on a wrist band on Candace and FT. She was perplexed that the stern nurse was making a big deal out of the number. She was not aware of our brief, but tense, history.

The next day while retrieving FT, with the number, I heard one of the other nurses refer to the stern nurse as "Sister Mary Louise." She was a nun, of course, we were in Providence Hospital, and we had been cussing like sailors the day before. The whole problem became evident. I immediately went over and apologized to her profusely. Advised her I would go to confession that Saturday so if God could forgive me, would she? It worked and she smiled for the first time. Didn't need the number after that exchange. I had become a church diplomat.

Our catholic wedding

This was before cell phones so getting messages to "the bush folks" was difficult. They did receive radio broadcasts and there was a program called the Bush Pipeline where you called the radio station and gave them your message. They would broadcast it at a certain time each day. Everyone in remote places would be listening. The message we sent upon FTs birth was, "To everyone at Shell Lake, Frank Thomas Bell ll would like to announce his birth and let you know he weighs eight pounds and six ounces. His parents are doing well, and he looks forward to meeting all of you as soon as he can work it into his schedule." He made it to Shell Lake for the first time at the ripe old age of two weeks. FT grew up to be a fine young man with a master's degree. He attended Washington State University for a couple of years and then returned to Anchorage to get his degrees from Alaska Pacific University. He now has his own family here in Alaska and has taken over as the CEO of my company and is doing a great job. We could not be prouder of him.

When FT came along Candace decided to begin RCIA studies to become catholic. After her joining the Church, we got married again in a catholic ceremony. Just a little insurance, marriage wise. About this time Jennifer came to live with us and Gretchen stayed with her mom in California. We would have preferred to have both, but Linda would not agree to that.

A couple of years later Candace advised me we had another surprise on the way. There was a pattern developing here that we needed to get ahead of ASAP. First, we need to figure out what was causing them and then how to control it. Elizabeth Rose Bell, AKA Betsy, showed up sometime in July of 1989. (Inside joke)

I was in the delivery room when she arrived. Being a veteran of this procedure there was less staggering around on my part. It was just a matter of averting my eyes at the critical time. She was a beautiful little girl, except when they handed her to me, I noticed her right ear was flat against her head. I turned to Doctor Little and pointed out the ear thing. He looked me in the eye and said, "We don't do exchanges." The ear was fine in a few hours. We now had two teenagers, two little kids, a cat and two dogs in the house. Things were really busy.

Family picture before grandkids, 1989

Regarding Betsy, this girl was meant to be. We were in Mexico on vacation with two of my fraternity brothers and their wives, Rich and Betty and Orlin and Lulu. Candace was seven months pregnant with Betsy and FT was a toddler. We had chartered a boat to go marlin fishing the next morning. Orlin and Lulu were staying at a different hotel. That evening Rich, Betty, Candace and I were lounging at the pool. FT, being a water baby veteran, was playing in the water. The kitchen staff was barbequing chicken on a grill next to the pool. I bought a bunch of chicken to share with all of us. How can you go wrong with BBQ chicken? Candace wasn't hungry so the rest of us chowed down on the dead bird. Looking back on this there is some speculation as to how long that bird had been dead.

We went to bed sometime later and had been asleep about two hours when my stomach went into convulsions. This woke me up and I quickly realized there was big trouble alimentary canal wise. I ran to the bathroom and started shooting stuff out of both ends. This is never a pleasant experience. Bad Bob was one sick puppy. After going through this agony for a couple of hours it was getting more debilitating by the minute. I couldn't imagine how things could get any worse. Then they did.

Candace said, "Something is wrong, I'm bleeding." In my addled mind I searched for a solution to no avail. It is hard to think clearly when your body is trying to kill you. Candace was still capable of thinking, so she called the hotel night clerk, who didn't speak English, and asked for a doctor. He understood the word doctor and the fact that he had a woman screaming at him, that it was an emergency. The local doctor showed up an hour later. He didn't speak English either. We were on a run of bad luck here. He took one look at me and went directly to check on her. He had his priorities. There is reason to suspect he saw me as a retched and pitiful sight with an olfactory downside. So here we are, me totally incapacitated, Candace having some sort of pregnancy issue and a language barrier. No way to put a positive spin on this situation.

He said "*Aborto*" a couple of times which really had us on edge. We found out later he was saying don't worry about the baby aborting, but we didn't know that due to the Spanish/English thing. He checked Candace out and said, "*Manana*," patted me on the shoulder, took his little bag and left. The shoulder pat didn't help with my situation. Candace called Rich and Betty to see if they could help us. Rich said they were both too sick to help and were busy fighting each other for toilet privileges. This pretty much firmed up the culpability of the chicken. We were on our own.

It was now early morning and I wasn't getting better when there was a knock. I staggered out of the bathroom and opened the door. There was Orlin with his fishing pole saying it was time to go catch the boat. I did a couple of dry heaves and slammed the door shut. He got the same reception at Rich and Betty's room. After considering the nature of his experience at both locations he determined that the fishing trip was probably cancelled.

The doctor did return in the morning with his nurse who spoke English. Boy, was that a relief. He explained what a partial placenta previa was and said Candace needed to remain lying down for at least three days and should be OK to travel in four days. This wasn't good news, but better news than losing this baby. I mean we had already named her and everything. It did put a bit of a bummer on the vacation aspects of the trip.

I was a little better, but still quite sick. Neither the doctor nor his nurse seemed to notice or care. As they were leaving the nurse said, "You have food poisoning." That wasn't new news to me. Must be in Mexico they don't treat food poisoning. Seems like if they couldn't help me medically, they could have offered some sympathy. Maybe it's a cultural thing. The doctor and his nurse checked on Candace, and not me, every morning and every evening. They really looked after her and it was greatly appreciated. The day we left for home I asked what we owed him. He thought for some time and then said," $50 US!" I paid him in cash. First and only time I had gotten a good deal on medical expenses.

FT and friend In Mexico prior to our health issues

As noted above, Betsy showed up in fine shape despite all the obstacles she had to overcome just to be born. She has grown up to be an intelligent, beautiful and delightful young woman. She lives in New York with her husband, Harrison. She graduated from the American Academy of Dramatic Arts in Manhattan and has earned her master's degree in education from PACE University in New York. For a kid who was born and raised in Alaska she has adapted to New York quite well. I have actually seen her intimidate a New York City cab driver. That was impressive and a little scary to watch.

Christopher was one of those kids who tended to skip grades. The kid was so smart it was kind of unnerving. He never did get into hunting and only had a mild interest in fishing. This was considered a personality defect in Alaska, but he managed to deal with it. He did enjoy playing chess. There was no way I was going to learn to play chess just to have my head handed to me on a regular basis, so I struggled as to how to connect with this kid. It was best to mostly follow his mom's lead. He was a likable guy and had a circle of friends who were also very smart kids.

Of course, he excelled in school and ended up graduating from high school when he was 16. His SAT scores were off the charts, so our mailbox was full of college brochures every day. He ended up going to Columbia University which is right in the middle of New York City. So here we have a kid who was mostly raised in Alaska being dropped in the center of the biggest metropolitan area in the country. He is six foot three inches and about 200 pounds so that gave us some comfort. We couldn't help but be concerned about his adapting to New York culture, but, as with Betsy, he did just fine. It is hard to be a helicopter parent from 3,000 miles away.

Flying the family to Shell Lake

CHAPTER SEVENTEEN

FAMILY AND BUSINESS ADVENTURES

So now Candace and I had two little kids at home and three kids in college. Alaska went into a major recession about this time. The timing couldn't have been worse. I lost the three office buildings I owned, our house was worth half of what we owed on it and the company was losing money at an accelerating rate. All my UAA business education didn't help a bit.

I put Christopher on one of my survey crews during the summer and his scholarships and loans covered the rest of his college expenses, including medical school at the University of Washington. Jennifer was going to Boston University, so we transferred her to the University of California as her mother lived in that state, so she got in-state tuition. Gretchen went to South Lake Tahoe junior college and we sent her $250/month. She worked various jobs to cover the other expenses. The heyday of making more money than I knew what to do with were a faint memory. So, the kids were covered, sort of, as Candace and I sat in Anchorage staring into a financial abyss. I suppose there are worse abysses to stare into, but this one was still bad.

One additional downside to all of this was the University of Washington thing. As noted above I graduated from Washington State University, a far superior school. The rivalry between these two institutions is intense to the point of ridiculous. I would have to hide the fact that one of my sons was attending the U of Dub from all my

Cougar friends. The family honor was on the line. There were compelling financial reasons for Christopher to attend this medical school, but that wouldn't solicit any sympathy from my classmates. You were either a Cougar and totally despised the Dawgs or you were not. No compromise in that regard. I did get him to promise he would never bring anything purple and gold into my house. He does, however, occasionally ship such items. Christopher married Renata, a young lady we all love who is also a doctor. Unfortunately, over the years, they have been brainwashed into Huskyhood. I am making every effort to save their kids (my grandkids) from this horrible fate. I send them Cougar clothes and toys frequently. The Apple Cup football game between the two schools has considerable family drama every year. FT and I on the Cougar side with Christopher and Renata on the wrong side.

In the meantime, the company wasn't doing so well. Between 1985 and 1988 Alaska was in a deep recession. The company had gone from 200 employees to 16 and was still losing money. All the wealth I had accumulated over the years was depleted in trying to keep the company afloat. I was on the verge of just shutting it down when a friend of mine agreed to bail us out for 50% ownership. I took the deal. The book value of the company was considerably more than he paid, but when you are bargaining with someone who can shut down the firing squad in front of you, you tend to be accommodating. Most of the banks in Alaska were going broke so they had no interest in loaning me anything. I suspect the loan committee had been disbanded and were now wearing cheaper suits.

In order to hold on to some of my engineering staff we sent proposals to various government agencies. We were successful with a proposal regarding renovations on a power plant in Guam. I traveled there to negotiate the contract with the Guam Government. While there Anderson Airforce Base engineers met with me and suggested we open an office on the island. They promised we would get work from them as well as the Navy. When I got home, I suggested to one of my managers and two engineers that they go open this office as it would increase their job security. They readily agreed.

Guam was quite an experience. In Alaska you are always in a hurry to get things done before winter. Guam is the exact opposite. It is always summer, and nobody is in a hurry for anything. "Gov Guam" was the only local government and was managed by the United states Department of the Interior.

I really liked the people of Guam. They were a friendly and carefree people, but it was very frustrating to work with them due to their lack of concern for deadlines. We kept the office for five years and then sold it to the employees and moved on.

The company had two more years of significant struggles but managed to survive. My net worth didn't. I bought the partner out two years later, for more than we had agreed to, but again he was there when I needed him, and we were off and running again. By 1990 we were making a good profit and were back up to 80 people.

During the recession I had lost my ownership in three office buildings at a considerable loss. Now that things were going better, I bought the building we had originally moved into in 1976. In the intervening years I had moved the office three times so this was kind of a home coming.

We had moved out of this building in 1980 to a newer and bigger space. At the time I had installed venetian blinds in the window of our office. I informed the owner, Charlie, that I intended to take the blinds with me. He advised me that because the blinds were attached to the windowsills by screws, they were part of the building therefore his property. We exchanged a couple of tersely worded letters, but in the end, I left the blinds behind. The building had changed hands a couple of times before I bought it in 1990. The first thing I noticed was the blinds were still there. I quickly sent Charlie a letter telling him I had got my blinds back. We went out for a beer and had a good laugh. The mid-eighties had been just as brutal for him.

It was in 1991 that I fell into the black hole of politics. Anchorage municipal government is composed of a mayor and an assembly. The assembly has 11 members elected from six districts. There are two assembly members from each district. It took me two tries to get elected to the South Anchorage assembly district. I represented about 30,000 of the wealthiest people in the city.

I was then working a 70 to 80-hour week with community council meetings four nights a week, Assembly meetings on Tuesday nights and a company to run, in addition to being part of my family.

This was a ridiculous schedule and a very stressful life. Therefore, when my three-year term was up, instead of a dignified exit, I ran for reelection and won. Didn't do this because I wanted to, it was because a whole lot of civic leaders, including the mayor, brow beat me into it. I should have been stronger.

I recall a person asking me what the term was for the assembly. When advised it was three years he exclaimed "Three years! Felons don't get three years." I identified with his sentiment.

I was six months into the second term. It was 11:00 PM and I was listening to a guy testifying against putting fluoride in the city water system. He was wearing a tin foil hat to keep the government satellites from reading his mind. I thought, "What did you do to yourself? Two and a half years of this to go."

The next day I announced that there was no possibility that I would run for another term. Two years later I ran for mayor, continuing a record of being stupid. Lucky for me and, most probably, for Anchorage I was unsuccessful. I then swore off politics. Twelve years later I was again brow beaten into running against a 10-year incumbent for the state senate. Between him and the unions they outspent me four to one. They burned through over $500,000 on that race. Out of 15,200 votes I lost by 59 votes. I then went through the 12-step program and was finally cured of politics. I went back to being reputable.

Running for state senate 2014

The company has continued to prosper. Since 1989 we have turned a profit every year, some years over a million dollars. In 2007 I concluded that I had accumulated far more money than Candace and I would ever need. Over the years many of my employees had worked for me 20 or 30 years and left with nothing but social security. I was determined to fix that. This was accomplished by converting the company into an ESOP (employee owned) so now all the profits go to their retirement accounts. In 2018 I stepped down as CEO after 44 years at the helm. FT has taken over and is doing a remarkable job, even if I am a little prejudiced in that regard. I still come into the office, but mainly to just kibitz. I can feel that 18-year-old kid, from so many years ago, slapping me on the back and saying, "Good job."

Another big part of my life is hunting, fishing, flying and writing books. The responsibilities of running a business and raising a family occupied most of my time, fortune and energy, but I still found time to indulge in my avocations. Sometimes at great risk to myself and occasionally to my family and friends, particularly the flying part. The outdoors is what drew me to Alaska in the first place. It is difficult to explain to someone who hasn't lived here what Alaska life is like. This is a unique place with unique people. I could go on about the special things regarding our state such as having more licensed pilots per capita than any other state or more caribou than people. Suffice it to say we are very different than the lower 48 in many ways.

During my first few years in Alaska I did my hunting and fishing on the very limited road system. There were plenty of things to hunt and lots of fish, so I was content. I heard all the tales about fly in trips and was jealous. Les, one of my co-workers at Tryck, Nyman and Hayse, was born and raised here. When hunting season rolled around in my first year, he suggested we go moose hunting, I quickly agreed.

The plan was to take his canoe, load it on his pick-up and drive up to the Denali Highway and float down the Maclaren River to its intersection with the Susitna River. Then we would motor up the Susitna River back to the highway. This involved a road trip of a few hundred miles and a river trip of 30 or 40 miles all in total wilderness. An ambitious undertaking to say the least.

It was a four-day holiday weekend so there was lots of time. We left Anchorage Thursday night and headed north. The hunting season opened about the time we left town. Upon passing through the town of Sutton I noted that the sun was coming up and it was a nice clear day. Things were going great. The first 50 miles of our trip was behind us. We had four days, lots of food, good weather and even some booze. An ideal hunting trip was before us.

About that time a bull moose ran across the road right in front of the truck. We hadn't anticipated this situation. I kind of froze up and just stared at the critter. Les slammed on the breaks and yelled "Shoot that moose!" I unfroze, grabbed my rifle, jumped out of the truck and looked through the scope. Unfortunately, the scope was turned up to full power and the moose was so close all I saw was moose hair. Figured, well, got to hit him somewhere and pulled the trigger. Some people refer to this as a "hope shot." Hit him right in the back of the head and he was done before he hit the ground. I later explained to Les I had planned to head shoot the moose. He didn't buy it. There we were, the truck partially in the ditch, me standing in the middle of the road, which is a totally illegal place to shoot from, and the moose piled up 50 feet off the shoulder. About this time a pick-up with a family drove by. The dad gave up a thumbs up and continued on his way, typical Alaskans, nothing to see here just some guys who shot a moose.

This was the first bull moose I had ever seen. As we walked up to him, he just kept getting bigger and bigger. I turned to Les and said, "Now what?" He chuckled and told me to roll him over on his back so we could start dressing him out. There is reason to suspect there may have been some sarcasm in this comment. I grabbed a leg and heaved as hard as I could and only moved it about 10 inches.

This brought a full-throated laugh from Les, "You're not dealing with one of those little lower 48 deer here. This thing weighs 1,500 pounds," a bit condescending, but quite true. He went back, got the truck and backed up as close to the moose as he could, tied two legs to the truck and pulled him over on his back, problem solved.

It took us a couple of hours to quarter him out, put the meat in game bags and load it in the truck. When we finished Les turned to me and said "Well, you ruined our moose hunting trip. It's too hot, so we need to get him back to town and out of the sun." Floating down one river and motoring up another was out the window. The big adventure had turned into a short drive and a quick shot. Most Alaskans would consider this as good luck. I got back to the house at noon. We had been gone 12 hours. The moose was hung in Les's meat house where it could cool off and age a bit. Linda and I were about to be introduced to the Alaska hunting culture in spades.

Les with moose

Two days later Les called and told me to go rent a meat grinder, pick up 100 pounds of beef suet and meet him at his place. It was an interesting shopping list. I was sure it would all make sense at some point. Did find it odd that when I asked the guy at the butcher shop for the beef suet he said, "Man you got your moose already?" More Alaskan culture. We then drove over to Les's house.

Unbeknownst to us the plan was to butcher this moose into steaks, roasts and hamburger in the garage. We always took our deer to the butcher who did that sort of thing. Well, not this time. This was Alaska not Ephrata. Les and his wife had butchered many moose over the years and had all the knives and stuff. We had squat. The meat was laid out on a long table. I had skinned a lot of cattle, but not butchered them, this just seemed much more imposing. We stood there looking at them like, "Are you kidding?"

Les handed me a knife fand a roll of butcher paper and tape to Linda and said, "Let's get to it." To say it was a learning experience would be an understatement. Under Les's careful supervision we cut that critter into as many steaks and roasts as possible. Then we cut the odd pieces of meat into stew meat. The rest went through the grinder with the beef suet. Finally, it all had to be wrapped and taped. It was kind of fun when we started. It wasn't fun at all within a few hours. We started at 10:00 AM and finished at 3:00 AM the next day, with a short break for dinner. Linda and I drove home with our 1966 Mustangs trunk clear full of moose meat. I had to be at work at 8:00AM which made for a rough day at the office. Didn't seem to bother Les. Had to rent a locker for most of the meat as about 10% of it fit in our refrigerator freezer compartment. I now fully understood the old Alaskan saying, "The fun part of the moose hunt is over when you pull the trigger."

This was just the beginning of my outdoor endeavors in Alaska. In fact, after 40 years of these adventures, I decided to write a book about said adventures or misadventures, depending on how you look at it. I have described these stories as the kind of adventures that were not funny when they happened but were funny when you got home and nobody was dead.

A friend of mine is a journalist who also writes books. He is a very prolific author and enjoys considerable literary success in Alaska. Tom Brennan approached me one day at a Rotary meeting and asked if I had any funny Alaskan adventure stories. I replied in the affirmative. This resulted in two of my stories being published in his book "Moose Droppings and Other Crimes Against Nature." I was quite pleased to have my stories published.

This inspired me to start chronicling my various exploits in the wilds of Alaska. Every time I was weathered in at moose camp or on a long flight, I would write a story. The stories began piling up on the corner of my desk. One day Billie, our marketing manager, asked me what the ever-increasing pile of paper was. Told her I was writing my outdoor stories. She asked if she could look at them and I said, "Sure, knock yourself out." It was a couple of months later when she marched into my office with the pile of paper which she now referred to as a "manuscript." She announced that she had converted it to proper English and that it should be sent to a publisher. I was dumbstruck! Me, an engineer and a marginally literate individual, publish a book? No way.

After considerable cajoling, she convinced me to send it to two publishers, one of which was Safari Press in California. I figured I had blown $5.50, the price of a good pike plug, on postage for nothing. You can imagine my surprise when Safari Press responded within a week.

They stated that they were really entertained by my stories, but a lot of work was needed for them to be published. I needed to develop my characters better and to describe the scenes in more detail. I was willing to do these things if I had some idea as to what they were talking about. Develop characters, describe scenes? I recognized the words but had no idea what they meant when used in this context.

It was at this point that I played my Washington State University card and contacted Pat McManus, a very successful outdoor writer and a fellow Cougar. He mentored me at length, I am sure many times through clenched teeth. His book "Deer On a Bicycle, which is a "how to" book on writing humor was very helpful. At his suggestion I also read a couple of Russell Annabel's books, which have detailed descriptions of scenes. This started what turned out to be a extremely laborious process, of editing and refining the stories. I would edit a story and send it to Safari Press. They would send it back with more suggestions resulting in going through the process again. Then do it once more with Pat. My respect for Tom increased several fold, as he did this for a living. Two years later I had a completed manuscript of "Oh No We're Gonna Die" and had a tenuous relationship with the folks in California. I was going to be a published author, hooya. Not as big of a deal as passing the professional engineer's exam, but still a significant accomplishment.

I remember it was Christmas Eve when I got the letter from Safari Press. It stated that book sales were dropping off and that they were declining to publish my book. I was devastated. All that work for nothing. I am not good at failing so I try to avoid it at all costs. Wasn't sure how to solve this one.

A few weeks later I was at a Rotary meeting lamenting on the demise of my publishing career. One of the guys at the table, named

Flip, was a book distributor, he suggested I meet with him and bring my manuscript. We got together the next day.

We talked about self-publishing and how to go about doing that. His company had 2,500 outlets in Alaska so they could give the book good exposure in the state, not so much in the "Lower 48." He agreed to read the manuscript and give me an opinion. Just maybe I was a bit premature on the failure thing.

We were at Rotary a few weeks later when he approached me and said he thought the book would do well in Alaska, but there were no guarantees. Book sales were down worldwide including our state. It would be a long shot, but not really that long, maybe a medium shot. Candace encouraged me to move ahead. A few weeks later we negotiated an agreement to produce and distribute the book.

The agreement entailed me paying to have the book printed and shipped to Alaska. Flip would then distribute it throughout the state. This was my introduction into the trials and tribulations of the publishing business, of which there are many. Most authors lose money or make very little with a few spectacular exceptions. How anybody makes money publishing and distributing books is beyond me. It is a very low margin business. I had a better profit machine with Bell's killing service.

The first decision was how many books to purchase. If you order 1,000 books, they are $4 each if you order 5,000, they are $2.50 each. So, do I risk $4,000 and have less profit or risk $12,500 and have more profit if I sell all of them. I decided to order 5,000 books including 500 hard covers which were $5 each but sold for $10 more. Go big, win big. Flip commented that if they didn't sell, he hoped I had lots of room under my bed. Not a lot of encouragement there. Safari Press also agreed to sell books throughout their system.

The first 5,000 books sold in six months. Flip was astounded. I wasn't, but then I had no idea as to what was normal. He had over 2,000 other books in his system and mine was his best seller. I was on the verge of breaking even on this deal. To date the book is in its ninth printing and we have sold about 50,000. That means one in every twelve Alaskans has one. People were stopping me in the street to tell me how much they enjoyed the book. I was a minor celebratory. Well, at least, in Alaska and in my own mind.

Those people who were stopping me in the street often started the conversation with "The third story in your book, well the same thing happened to me." My reply would be, "Tell me the story." I then embellished the story, inserted lots of humor and emailed it to them. They were advised I was doing a second book and would like to include their story. So, if there was anything in the story they didn't like let me know. All but one agreed, so we published "Oh No We're Gonna Die Too" which is also selling quite well. I was not competing with Pat McManus or Stephen King, but I was now making some money.

My third book "Outdoor Stupid From Around The World "recently hit the bookstores. I have high hopes for this one. I am also writing a memoir which should be on book shelves in early 2023, contrary to normal expectations, I had become a reasonably successful author. Who would have thunk?

Oh No! We're Gonna Die

HUMOROUS TALES OF CLOSE CALLS IN THE ALASKA WILDERNESS

by Bob Bell

Oh No were Gonna Die

CHAPTER EIGHTEEN

ALASKAN ADVENTURES

As noted earlier one of the main incentives I had to move to Alaska was the outdoor adventures that were available. As it turned out a big part of my life has been hunting, fishing, and flying in Alaska. These were mostly pleasant and exciting activities. Although there were several exceptions to the pleasant part. These exceptions are detailed in my books. Some of my favorite stories from my first book are as follows:

TOUGH GOING ON TUSTUMENA

Tustumena Lake is a large body of fresh water on the Kenai Peninsula in Southcentral Alaska. It has a well-deserved reputation for sudden changes in weather and big waves. From all the stories I have heard about this lake, I am sure the bottom of the lake is covered with the bones of unlucky and careless Alaskans. One of the problems with this 26-mile-long aquatic wonder is that the road only goes to one end of the lake; therefore, the only access to the rest of the lake is by boat, floatplane or shank's mare.

I planned to hunt moose at a place called Bear Creek, which is near the end of Tustumena farthest from the road. Jittery John, a draftsman who worked with me and was a cheechako, reluctantly agreed to come along. He was not well versed in the outdoors and he was very skittish about bears. Being a long-time Alaskan (almost two years) I assured him there were no bear problems where we were going. The dummy actually believed I knew what I was talking about.

Relaxing at the campfire

I owned a flat-bottomed Smokercraft riverboat with a very old 55 HP Mercury outboard that ran on occasion. Jittery and I towed the boat to the end of the road where we loaded up the camping gear and headed out on the lake. It took us about three hours to get to Bear Creek due to the motor quitting several times, but it was nice weather, so no big deal. Even though to most people it would have been a warning, to us it was just an inconvenience. As they say, ignorance is bliss, so we were quite happy. Tustumena was being nice. Of course, she was just setting us up.

We made camp at the mouth of Bear Creek that evening and caught some salmon for dinner. Again a warning. If it is easy for you to catch salmon where you are camped, it is also easy for bears to catch salmon there. In other words, not a good place to camp. Also the name of the creek should have been a clue. So we weren't clueless, we just didn't know how to recognize a clue. We neglected to heed this warning or even know that it was a warning.

That night we had several very large visitors who not only kept us awake and alert but also helped themselves to our food, bit a hole in our gas can and tipped over our boat. We were left with some freeze-dried food, half a can of gas, permanent finger imprints in the pistol grips of our guns and a new appreciation for the science of picking campsites. This was an unfortunate turn of events, but in retrospect, it was to be a minor bump in this trip's odyssey.

Undeterred and still relatively stupid, we rose at first light and promptly went moose hunting. The easiest walking was to just follow along the creek bank as it meandered up into the mountains. The problem was that the creek bank was mostly grass, which was shoulder to head high. We considered this a problem because it was difficult to see very far, so it would be hard to spot the moose. We also wondered about all the salmon carcasses that were strewn along the bank--how did those fish get so far from the water? There was a nice, well-worn trail through the grass, so we pushed on occasionally wondering what made this nice trail. We were still in the ignorant and blissful mode.

The fish and trail questions were suddenly and dramatically answered when two grizzly bears stood up just 20 feet in front of us, causing all bliss to immediately disperse. With the high grass we could see them when they stood on their hind feet, but could not see them when they were on all fours. We were playing a high stakes game of hide-and-seek in the tall grass with us having much higher stakes than the bears. In fact, the bears may have considered us steaks. As I saw it, the bears could win or we could not lose. There was no way we could win.

Each time the bears stood up, we would duck and when they were on all fours we would retreat further down the creek. Problem was they were going the same way we were going, so we were not getting the separation we wanted. In fact, they were gaining on us. The bears also seemed to be getting more and more agitated with the game and with us. Grizzlies are not known for their tolerance. We finally came to a large birch tree and set a new world record in tree-climbing. By the time the top of the tree was achieved, there was a smoldering pile of birch bark shavings at the bottom, near where we had left our guns.

The bears arrived shortly thereafter, and in a perfunctory manner tore our backpacks all to hell and moved on. Our situation had now improved to being up a tree with the bears between us and camp, somewhere in the tall grass. Not a big improvement, but a temporary respite from playing hide and seek for keeps. Logic suggested we not follow down the creek but go up the hillside and make our way back to camp with a much better view. Never having tried logic, we figured, why not? Jittery seemed a little distracted but still responded when spoken to.

This meant fighting our way through 200 yards of alder and devil's club, which was no fun but better than bear wrestling. Once we got through the brush it opened up into a birch forest with good visibility, so we began side-hilling our way back to camp. Other than bears tearing up our camp and chasing us up a tree, things seemed to be going well so far!!

Partway back we spotted a bull moose on the other side of the creek. Our situation now having improved from very precarious to just risky, we opted to go back to very precarious. We immediately charged down the hill, back through the alders and devil's club, across the creek and promptly shot the moose. We now had 1,000 pounds of bear bait on our hands. We skinned and butchered the bull and took turns packing meat to the boat and guarding the kill. The packing was relatively easy due to the ample supply of adrenaline. The bears didn't make an appearance. I am sure they were just waiting for darkness. They also needed time to digest all of our food.

Now we were at our campsite, with salmon flopping all over the place, 600 pounds of moose meat stacked in the boat, and at least two grizzlies in the grass nearby biding their time. Everything we had, except our sleeping bags and the tent had been torn up by the bears and we were out of food, the last of which was in the backpacks. Jittery kept looking at me like a bomb disposal technician wondering if he should cut the red wire or the blue wire. He knew something bad was probably going to happen. He just didn't know what it would be or what to do about it.

We reflected on our situation for a while (30 seconds) and figured it was time to go home. Now this is where the story gets exciting. Our trials and tribulations to date were about to be relegated to humorous footnotes to the truly perilous part of this story.

We loaded all the torn-up camping gear into the boat. With the moose meat, the gear and us, we had about six or eight inches of freeboard. No sweat! It was a nice day with very little wind. If the motor kept quitting, we could just paddle to shore, fix it, and move on. Anything was better than having to duke it out with the bears. Jittery was beginning to fidget a little and seemed more distracted. I am sure Tustumena was rubbing her hands together. "I got em' now," she muttered.

Once we got going, it dawned on us that we probably didn't have enough gas to travel around the shoreline due to the bear bite in the gas can. It was much shorter to just run across the middle of the lake. Tustumena is five miles wide at this point, but the lake was almost dead calm, so why not? We had already survived hide-and-seek with the bears. What could be worse than that? With the total confidence that comes with complete ignorance, we changed course and set sail across the lake.

The bliss was back as we neared the middle of the lake. Then the motor quit. I tried to start it for some time to no avail. I pulled off the cowling and began to tinker with stuff. Jittery was starting to make small high-pitched noises. Other than that, he seemed to be taking it all quite well. I noticed a hole in the fuel line and, in true Alaska tradition, duct-taped it. The engine started right up. Got it made now!

Jittery pointed to a rainsquall that was coming down the lake toward us. Well, bummer. We might get rained on. No big deal. See what I mean about complete ignorance?

We were probably between one and two miles off shore when the wind and rain slammed into us. The lake went from calm to three-foot waves in less than a minute. We had no choice but to turn into the wind and head to shore. We were in a flat-bottomed boat with six inches of freeboard and an unreliable motor, slamming into three-foot waves two miles offshore. Suddenly, we were back to very precarious on a whole different plane. Once again, the bliss evaporated. The bear wrestling was beginning to look like a safer activity. Jittery was now the color of new snow and was sweating profusely. I was beginning to be concerned for his mental state.

I was trying to keep control of the boat; Jittery was bailing like crazy because some of the waves were breaking over the bow and the rain was coming down in buckets. With the flat bottom, each wave we hit felt like we had been dropped from 10 feet on to concrete. Jittery was losing the battle with the water and was starting to hyperventilate. I pulled the plug in the back of the boat and water was going out as long as I could keep the speed up. Of course, that increased the shock of each wave. I also noticed a piece of duct tape fall out of the engine. On the "concern for your well-being scale" with crossing the street being at one and having Hannibal Lector as your roommate at 10 we were definitely at 9 or more!

Jittery was losing the bailing battle, so he opted to throw out all the camping gear and the moose horns. The camping gear had little value in its bear-eaten state, but that was a nice set of horns.

I was also trying to figure out what we would do when the motor quit, as it most assuredly would. We spent the next year or two (seemed like) in this state of frenzied activity, with the threat of motor failure looming over us the whole time. That piece of duct tape kept swirling around in the little whirlpool behind the motor shaft, almost as if reminding me that it was no longer on the fuel line. I noticed that Jittery had gone from nervous to just short of total panic. I was calm but had to yell a lot to reassure Jittery.

For some reason the motor gods were asleep and the old Mercury kept running. As we approached the shore, the boat had about a foot of water in it, the freeboard was down to half, and Jittery was about used up physically and emotionally, but it appeared we were going to make it. Nice try Tustumena!

That is when the motor god woke up. Just as we reached where the waves were breaking, the motor quit. The boat immediately turned sideways to the waves and the next wave flipped us over. I landed in about two feet of water and was rolled up in a ball by the next wave and deposited on the beach.

Jittery's experience was just as delightful. He did some sort of inverted body surf thing. It was quite impressive. Once we reoriented ourselves, we managed to get the boat turned right side up, but the waves breaking over the stern soon filled it with water. We were already soaked, so we just waded in to retrieve the guns and the moose meat. We were not dead, so things were looking up! We were a wet, sorry looking mess sitting on the beach in the rain.

The day had gone from scary to a real pain in the butt. The storm blew over in an hour and the lake calmed back down, its work having been completed. Even with new duct tape we could not get the motor restarted, probably due to its being under water for so long. So we bailed out the boat and loaded up the wet, sand-covered meat and pushed the boat along the shoreline the three or four miles back to the road. We arrived in the dark, soaking wet and exhausted. Moose hunting in Alaska can sure be an adventure. I could tell by Jittery's body language that he probably would not accept another invitation to go hunting for anything in the near future. In fact, I found him to be somewhat uncommunicative on the ride back to Anchorage.

That moose meat was the toughest eating of any moose I've ever had. Seems appropriate.

I KILLED 80124-OR DID I?

In 1976 I bought my first Cessna 185. This is a four-seat, high-wing, single-engine airplane with a 300-horsepower engine. It is one of the more popular airplanes in Alaska. Her number was N80124.

I came across her while doing a survey job just east of Nome. It was a federal Bureau of Land Management (BLM) survey, noted earlier, where we were setting section corners over several hundred square miles in very remote country. Most of the work was accomplished using helicopters, but we also needed a fixed-wing aircraft to move people and supplies between the various base camps.

I was told there was a Cessna 185 for sale in Kotzebue, so I flew over there to investigate. 80124 was parked on the landing strip with a "For Sale" sign in her window. It was love at first sight. I located the owner, reviewed the log books, and after a prolonged and intense negotiation of just over two minutes, purchased my new buddy. In the course of the next four months 80124 completely paid for herself on that job.

That fall I flew back to Anchorage in my new plane, feeling like I had Alaska by the tail. I had some exciting times in this plane, including learning to fly a high-performance tail dragger and earning a float rating. I recall one time when a friend of mine named Merrill, who was an airline pilot, was giving me a lesson in 80124. We had gone up to Birchwood strip to do some touch and goes.

Everything went well until we were headed back to Anchorage. We were at 2500 feet when the engine quit. Merrill simply said, "Go through the emergency procedure," so I did, and the engine started right back up. (It is common practice when giving instruction to pull the gas and kill the engine as a training procedure, so I was not all that concerned, and I was pleased that I had passed the re-start test.)

When we arrived back at Merrill Field in Anchorage (my friend Merrill is named after the same guy as the airfield) and got the plane tied down, Merrill said we should pull the cowling and see if we could figure out why the engine quit!!! It had been a real emergency, but I hadn't panicked in the " training exercise." This experience would help me in the future when we had emergencies because I had learned to stay calm when things happened.

80124 did this to me a couple of more times until I figured out that when the tip tanks were empty and the tip tank pump was on, it pumped air into the main tanks. When a bubble of air got sucked into the fuel line it would kill the engine. I duct-taped the tip tank switch closed - problem solved.

80124 was not ideal for a floatplane. She didn't have a short-takeoff-and-landing (STOL) kit or a longer bladed float prop. She also had some floats I had bought at an auction that were not the best performers available. They were Aqua floats and were built in such a way as to increase the drag much more than most other brands of floats. Because I had learned to fly floats in 80124, I didn't realize just how poor a performer she really was. I would go to places that my pilot friends would say were "no sweat" for most 185s and end up scraping treetops on takeoff. I just assumed it was my piloting skills and not the airplane.

After 200 or 300 hours of flying time, I had pretty much figured out what 80124 and I could or could not do. Over the next 1,000 flight hours we became close friends. We traveled throughout Alaska, picking our landing spots with care. We did have a few close calls, but 80124 always came through when I needed her. I think it was because she had more horsepower than I had IQ.

The one time I really let her down was on a cold November day. I was flying my family out to Shell Lake for Thanksgiving. I had delivered JJ and Christopher to the lake and was returning to get Candace and Gretchen. I was on straight skis and landing on Campbell Lake. The lake was glare ice with no snow. (When landing a plane on ice, you pull the nose up at the last minute to stall the plane just before it touches down. It is called flaring the plane.)

As I was approaching the lake I observed three kids playing along the shoreline. I was determined to keep an eye on them as I landed. Just as I flared, two of the kids decided to run across the lake right in front of the airplane. I hit the throttle and popped the plane back up into the air and went over the kids.

Then I made a mistake. Instead of going around and doing the landing over I just set her back down on the ice. Now I was sliding down the lake on very slick ice without enough lake remaining to stop before I hit the bank.

I was headed right at residential property that sloped up from the lake, so I assumed I would just end up in John's back yard. No harm there. Unfortunately, John had a one-foot-high brick wall at the edge of the lake. I hit that; broke both of the skis and both gearboxes, and the nose of the plane hit the ground, bending the prop. It took more than $23,000 to fix the damage. I also had to charter an air taxi to get the rest of us to Shell Lake and back. 80124 forgave me for that screw-up and performed just fine after she got out of surgery five months later.

In the fall of 1985, I was caribou hunting south of King Salmon with several friends, including Fritz, who had his 185 along as the second plane. Fritz's plane had all the good stuff. He had a STOL kit, EDO floats and a float prop.

I had forgotten my caribou tags, so I made a side trip to get them. I landed in the river at King Salmon to visit the state fish and game office to pick up the tags. This involved docking on the beach. We grounded on the gravel beach, tied the plane up and took care of my tag business. Then we returned to the plane, spun her around and loaded up.

As I taxied out into the river I noted that the right wing seemed to be lower than the left wing. After a minute, it was very much lower than the left. We quickly realized that the right float was sinking. This would cause the plane to turn over, which would ruin our whole day. I immediately turned back for shore and hit the throttle. We barely made it back. Upon examining the float, we discovered that a rock had punched a hole in the right front float compartment. 80124 had thrown a shoe. We now had a repair problem in a small remote town.

We needed to get the plane out of the water to patch the bottom of the float. After inquiring around town, we located a contractor who had a wheel-mounted crane and agreed to lift the plane for a couple hundred dollars. He drove the unit to the beach, deployed his outriggers and picked her right up. He then said he had some business to take care of and would be back later. We paid him the $200 and off he went. We completed repairs in two hours, but then could not find the contractor to lower us back down. After several hours, we finally found him in a local bar. He had been there with our $200 since he left us hours earlier. Even in his impaired condition we got the plane back in the water. I think 80124 was trying to hint that she didn't want to be on this trip.

When we got back to the caribou camp, the other guys pointed out that I was supposed to have picked up some beer. I had forgotten due to all the other problems. My popularity in the camp dropped considerably. "It's too bad you poked a hole in your float, it's good you didn't sink the plane in the river, and we're sorry it cost you $200 to get it fixed, but you forgot the beer! How could you be that insensitive?" I resolved to revise my friend-choosing program as soon as I got home.

After two days we hadn't seen any caribou, so Fritz and I took the planes up to look for the herd. We flew for three hours before finally locating the animals. By this time we were low on fuel, so we headed for Naknek to fuel up. At that time the gas dock was located on a lake at the airport. It is down in a hole so there are 30 to 50-foot banks around most of the lake, which coincidentally had a bad reputation for turning airplanes into wrinkled balls of aluminum along its shores. When I landed, the plane seemed to kind of drop out of the air the last few feet, giving me a long bounce upon landing. 80124 was hinting again. She didn't like this place or this air.

Fritz had a similar landing. I commented to Ken, my passenger, that the air seemed a little strange. He just shrugged. He was not a pilot, so it didn't mean anything to him. He was soon to find out just how important air characteristics really are. As we fueled I just kept watching the light wind on the water. Everything seemed normal but I had a bad feeling. Fritz also commented that the air felt funny when he landed. The warnings were there, but we didn't have the mental capacity to process them.

The plane was empty except for Ken and he only weighted about 150 pounds. There was plenty of lake, even for 80124, so it should be no sweat as far as taking off was concerned. Fritz was still fueling, so I opted to take off first. Everything went fine until we were about 50 feet in the air. All of a sudden 80124 just quit flying. The airspeed was over 50 knots and the nose was at the right attitude, but for some reason we were dropping right out of the air. There was nothing I could do but keep full throttle and hope the ground effect would catch us before we hit the water. Ground effect occurs when the air deflected down from the airplane hits the surface; the updraft sort of cushions the plane and helps it fly. But not this time.

We hit the water about 50 feet from the end of the lake and bounced big-time! It was obvious that we were going to crash into the alders at the end of the lake. It seemed like everything slowed down considerably at that point. I swear it seemed like I had an hour to decide what to do next, but the problem with all this perceived extra time was that I still had no good options. We were going to crash; it was just a matter of picking the spot.

I opted for full power to keep the nose as high as possible and try to hit the alders floats first and then cut power. As we slid through the alders I thought we would be stopped by the branches and that maybe we could save the airplane, too. That hope was dashed when the right float hit a rock and the plane went over on its back. This also seemed to happen in slow motion. When we hit on our back, we broke off both wings, drove the left flap through the back seat, and bent the fuselage. The only part of the airplane that was not smashed was the front half of the cockpit. 80124 and I were not having a good day. One fuel tank was cracked and gas was running all over the place. Ken and I were left hanging from our seatbelts in the upside-down plane.

I have been bummed out on many occasions, but this had to be one of the top three. Ken advised me that he was not hurt, but suggested we get the hell out of there. I agreed and we let our seatbelts go. This is where we incurred the only injury of the incident. Ken forgot to brace himself and was almost knocked out when landed on his head. I got out my door and turned to see how Ken was doing. He started yelling he could not get his door open. I suggested he come out my door, which he did with much enthusiasm.

80124 in her final resting place, almost

We then left the fatally wounded 80124 and walked back to the shore. Fritz was already taxiing down the lake to check on us. Boy did

I feel bad, but also damned lucky that no one was hurt. I sat on a rock on the shoreline with my head in my hands mourning my good friend 80124 as we waited for Fritz. We rode back to the gas station with him.

The local cop was waiting to take our statements. As we discussed the event with him a woman ran up yelling that a plane had crashed. The cop said, "Yes, it's at the end of the lake."

She said, "No it was at the end of the airstrip." Sure enough, a Cherokee 6 had the same experience. They took off, got 50 feet in the air and then just fell to the ground. There were four people on board, but no injuries. Both planes were totaled. Naknek Airport was two for two on airplanes for the day. The other pilots decided to wait a few hours before taking off. It was a wise choice; I was not sure the lake had its 24-hour bag limit of airplanes.

Ken and I got a ride to King Salmon with the cop to get a flight home. On arrival, I called my wife and asked her to pick us up at the airport. She asked why we were flying home commercially. I replied, "I killed 80124." We both commiserated about the demise of 80124. She also had a good relationship with the plane after many hours of passenger time. Later that day Fritz went back to the caribou camp. He had to ferry my passengers back to King Salmon to catch a commercial flight.

80124 taking off from shell lake

The National Transportation Safety Board investigated both incidents and determined that a "microburst" had caused the accidents. This occurs when the wind is blowing straight down and literally shoves the airplane right into the ground. Neither crash was pilot error. But, I still felt really bad about good ol' 80124. She had been a good friend and it was not a good way for her to go, even if it was not my fault.

The only good thing was that I did have hull insurance. With that money I bought N4448R and have been flying her for over 30 years now. She is a 185 complete with all the good stuff like a float prop, STOL kit and EDO floats.

It was about three years later as Triple 4-8-Romeo and I were flying into the Cordova airport when the tower got a call asking for landing instructions from Cessna 80124! I followed her in and went right over to the plane and introduced myself to the owner. It turns out my insurance company had sold 80124 "as is, where is," and this guy had bought her. He'd had a fire that burned up the cockpit in his old 185, but he'd saved the rest of the plane. He just put the wings, etc. on 80124's cockpit and was good to go. Because the cockpit carries the aircraft's registered number with it, 80124 was resurrected in Cordova.

He let me hug her once more before we parted company.

FISH MUSHING AT THE KING HOLE

We once had a secret fishing spot we called the King Hole. It has since been discovered by some "guides" and is pretty well fished out. The King Hole had a small run of fish and just could not take the pressure of a professional operation. We seldom took more than 25 or 30 fish out of the hole each year. The guides took that many in a week. It was a good spot, in its prime, to catch king salmon without the crowds.

One of the reasons there were so few people at the King Hole was that it was a real challenge to land and take off in that small stream. The landing channel was about 500 feet long and then went around a 90-degree turn. It was also only 75 feet wide with brush and trees on both sides. That was enough room to land if you were skillful, but too short to take off.

The takeoff trick is to go around the 90-degree bend, get the plane on the step, and then make a step turn around the bend and take off in the 500-foot channel, all the while keeping your wings out of the trees and your passengers from having a heart attack. It is quite a sight to see a floatplane careening around that corner on one float with the trees whizzing by 5 feet off the wing tips. It was an exciting landing and takeoff that most pilots preferred to forego. It's amazing there aren't large piles of twisted aluminum all around the King Hole, but I do not recall even one accident there. We were very tight mouthed about the King Hole, so very few people even knew about it to begin with.

The King Hole is really a small, slow-moving stream that runs into a very large fast-moving river. The kings come up the river and into the stream to spawn. It is located about 70 miles north of Anchorage in a low-lying area in the Yentna River valley, 60 miles from the nearest road. It is surrounded mostly by tundra with trees and brush along the banks of the stream. The water is somewhat colored, but much clearer than the water in the river, which is glacial-fed and full of rock flour. The kings run in June, so the whole area is bright green with very lush flora.

One of the best fishing spots was a small spit right at the mouth of the stream. The trick with this spot was to keep the fish from running into the fast-moving river and breaking your line. Once you got a fish on, you would walk upstream and try to keep the fish in the slow water. My wife Candace, *aka* Ma Bell, and I were there with several of our friends from the Shell Lake crowd. The group included Scooter, the Shell Lake 'ranger." Scooter was a very outgoing fellow who had a way of enjoying himself under any circumstance. Scooter's wife, Champagne Ann, was also in attendance, another person who fully appreciated humor. The rest of the party was Kenny, the Shell Lake "marshal," and Dave the Torch, the Shell Lake "fire marshal." Both of these guys were what I would describe as lovable oddballs.

We were fishing with eggs at the mouth and were getting some nice kings. I wandered back into the woods to take care of nature calling. In doing so, I discovered a small canoe about five feet long and 18 inches wide. It was made out of canvas and small- diameter branches. It had obviously been there for several years, and its structural integrity was thus somewhat suspect. I carried it back to the group and announced that I would be taking the canoe out in the stream to catch a king. We should have realized this was a formula for disaster, but it seemed like a good idea if you didn't give it much thought.

Landing a king at the king hole

I got my paddle and anchor out of the plane, picked up my fishing rod and launched. I was surprised that the canoe didn't leak, turn over or create any other disaster that normally should have happened. Everyone was getting a kick out of me paddling around in this miniature boat. I was "the man." I stopped near the mouth and started fishing.

It was not long before I hooked a good-sized king. I was using 40-pound test line, so when the king took off up the stream, I just held on and off we went, with the king pulling me like a dog team pulls a sled.

I was yelling, "Mush fish, mush!" I had this guy right where I wanted him. Everyone was laughing so hard they could barely stand up. The way things were going the king would soon tire and I would have him. Things did not look good for Mr. King. I anticipated he would tow me a mile or so upstream and then tire out. I would paddle back downstream with my catch to the applause and admiration of my friends. This was not really a plan, it was just reacting to an uncontrolled series of events.

The king then made a strategic decision. He switched ends and started running downstream toward the river, with me in tow. Being at least as smart as the fish, I just threw out the anchor to stop the canoe; the problem was that I forgot to tie the rope to the canoe (which brings into question my comment about being as smart as the fish).

As the last of the rope disappeared over the side of the canoe my options narrowed: cut the line and let the fish go (which I believe is against the law in Alaska), or be dragged into the fast-moving river.

I reasoned that the first option would result in considerable ridicule from my friends. The second would result in an exciting ride part way down the river, ending with me pinned against a logjam with the other debris. With the speed at which the water was moving in the river, the odds of survival unscathed were akin to a P.E.T.A. member at an NRA convention.

In the meantime, the fish was accelerating and, consequently, so was I. As we approached the mouth of the stream and my group of friends, I began giving them instructions on how to save me. I do not think they could hear me over the laughter. I noted that no one was making preparations for my arrival or rescue. This was not the glorious return I had envisioned.

I had resigned myself to cutting the line as I sailed past the group. At the last minute, Candace waded into the stream over the top of her hip boots and grabbed the canoe with a gaff hook and pulled me to shore.

She told me later that it suddenly dawned on her that if I went into the river I would probably lose the 40-pound fish, so she had to do something; besides, she needed me to fly the plane. I appreciated the fact that she had come up with two good reasons to save me. She did reflect on the fact that I was well insured and she would have become a wealthy widow, but concluded that the widow status was only a matter of time considering my exploits to date. My friends, on the other hand, were perfectly content to watch me go down the river in a very small boat.

Just wait until one of them is in a tight spot....

SKINNY DIPPING FOR BLACK BEARS

As I grow longer in the tooth I find myself going to more and more funerals. I have to admit in a couple of instances I just went to make sure they were dead, but mostly they are sad affairs where you are celebrating a life and saying good-bye to a friend. We recently had a funeral for my good friend "The Bear". There were hundreds of people there as he was quite popular in Alaska and a really good guy. The Bear was one of those bigger than life kind of guys. He even went out with a bang with papers throughout the Northwest reporting on his demise. He was a true Alaskan. As I got up to speak at his service I reflected on how lucky I was to have been friends with him for so many years. I told some funny stories of our adventures, polled the audience as to how many fish and game people were present (none), and said good-bye to my friend. The Bear was prominently featured in several stories in my first book.

This story is about the last hunting/fishing trip The Bear and I took together. If I were to script a final trip I would have planned something just like this one. We had some unplanned adventures, we caught fish, we stalked a black bear or two, we told some stories, even some true ones, and we relaxed from our hectic lives, and just spent some quality time as old friends. We had about as much fun as two old farts can have in a weekend.

It was early May when we pulled out of the quaint Alaskan village of Whittier in my 28 foot boat, the Watermark, for a couple of days in Prince William Sound. The weather was perfect and we cruised along on calm seas taking in the spectacular scenery. The Sound in spring is just fantastic, the snow on the higher slopes, the green along the shore, and the critters with their newborn offspring. May is also known for its good weather. Our plan was to head down to Bainbridge Passage to look for black bears and then out to Elrington Point to nail a halibut or two. As usual we had gone through an extensive planning process. I called him up on Thursday and said the weather looked good in Prince William and let's go kill something this weekend. He said "okay" and the plan was done. The Bear brought the food and I brought the booze. I do not know how many trips we planned this way, but most of them turned out to be more adventurous than we wanted. I think mostly due to the planning process. Seems most of our plans do not work out as planned. I do not know if that is because we are poor planners or just stupid, probably both.

It took us about two hours to get to Bainbridge Passage. In route we went through Dangerous Passage and glassed for bears with no luck. We looked at where the old village of Chenega had been located. It was completely wiped out in the 1964 earthquake and tidal wave, killing 26 of about 120 people in the village. The village was relocated about 15 miles south of Evans Island. We stopped at Icy Bay and picked up a small iceberg for the cooler. There were lots of them in the area.

It is interesting that this 10,000 year old ice seems to take much longer to melt due to its being under pressure for so long. Things were really going well which is unusual for one of our trips. When we came around Countess Point to head into the passage, we discovered it was blocked by icebergs. There was a wall of ice completely blocking the passage. As we sat there wondering what to do, we noticed a commercial fishing boat on the other side of the ice that seemed to be working its way through. It took him a half an hour, but he steamed clear and went on his way. Of course, our reaction was if he can do it so can we and we promptly began picking our way between the chunks of ice. The fact that the other boat was a very stout 65 foot steel hulled commercial fishing vessel and we were a 28 foot, fiberglass hulled, fragile, recreational boat never entered our thought process. Once again casting doubt on our planning abilities.

The Bear was on the bow pushing ice away from the boat with a pole and I was driving. At first it went okay, but as we got closer to the middle, the ice chunks got bigger and more compact. Now we were pushing ice with the hull of the boat and the pole. Thoughts of the Titanic and her relationship with icebergs popped into my mind several times. I am not sure how that fiberglass hull stayed intact, but it did and we made it to the other side. Several times I had visions of The Bear and me sitting on an iceberg, surrounded by pieces of the Watermark, waving to passing boats hoping for rescue.

Now that we were in the passage, we began a slow cruise down one side glassing for bears. Both sides of the passage are steep terrain going up several thousand feet. It is mostly covered in alder and other brush with a few trees. We stopped now and then and fished with limited success. We saw some sows with cubs, but nothing to shoot. This was very frustrating because I have always had good luck in Bainbridge Passage. I took a six foot eight inch boar there just a few years earlier.

After a few hours we decided to go on to Elrington Point to see if we could improve our luck. It took another hour to get there. Now, when you are at Elrington Point, you are no longer in Prince William Sound, you are in the North Pacific Ocean. The waves that hit you there are coming from Hawaii.

It was still a nice day, but we had a two foot swell and a little wind, nothing to write home about. We went around to the south side of the point and started fishing for halibut. We were catching a few little ones, but it was a nice sunny day so we were content to catch "chicken" halibut and watch the sea lions basking in the sun on the nearby rocks.

All of a sudden something on the beach caught my eye. I grabbed the binoculars and there was a real nice boar black bear walking along the beach. I handed the glasses to The Bear and he studied him for a few seconds and then said lets go get him. I said, "okay, let's drop the anchor, get the skiff and the outboard and head for shore," another well thought out plan.

We were at the entrance to South Twin Bay which is about a mile long. The shoreline at this point is very rocky, but there was a 10 foot wide gap in the rocks with a gravel beach near the bear. The plan was to take the skiff to the beach, pull it up out of the water, stalk and shoot the bear, put the bear in the skiff and return to the boat. With a plan that simple, what could possibly go wrong? Well, as it turned out, several things. We put the skiff in the water. I told The Bear to put the paddle in the skiff while I went to get my gun. When I got back The Bear was in the skiff with all his gear so I just jumped in and we were on our way, full of confidence, anticipation and ignorance.

As we approached the beach, I noticed that the bear had moved off the beach and was a couple of hundred feet up the hill. He still had not taken notice of us. We got to the beach, pulled the skiff up out of the water and headed up the hill after the bear. I had a nagging feeling that I had forgotten to do something, but in the heat of the moment I brushed it aside.

We had only gone a short distance when I spotted the bear lying under a tree, but I could only see a patch of black fur. Time for plan B. I told The Bear to get a good rest and cover the bear. If he stood up let him have it. In the meantime, I would climb higher on the hill so I could see him better and get a clear shot. I got another 100 feet farther up the hill and had a good view of the bear as he snoozed. That is when I noticed our skiff floating out into the bay! Our plan had failed to consider the tide coming in. Maybe that was what was nagging at me.

I immediately lost all interest in the bear and began scrambling down the hill. I shot by The Bear like my hair was on fire. He just stood there wondering what the hell was going on. By the time I got to the beach the skiff was 100 feet offshore. If we lost that skiff we were in some serious trouble. We were on an uninhabited island 30 miles from the nearest village. At this point, we had very limited options and a somewhat flawed planning process. As I walked across the rocks taking off my clothes I just kept thinking to myself "do not think about it, just do it" and I did! I dove off the rocks into 35 degree water.

After the initial shock my first thought was, "Boy, you have really screwed up this time," but there was no turning back now. I started swimming for all I was worth. I was still 25 or 30 feet from the boat when I started losing control of my arms and legs. I tried a backstroke for a while, but it was starting to get a little scary. It felt like I was swimming in molasses. Somehow, I got to the skiff. I was hanging onto a rope and wondering if I had enough strength to pull myself aboard.

All of a sudden a 300+ pound sea lion came out from under the skiff and brushed me back about a foot. The next thing I knew I was flat on my back in the bottom of the skiff. I guess I found the energy. I still do not recall how I got in that boat. I suppose adrenalin may also have been involved. The sea lion hung out for a few minutes, barked at me and left. I have often heard the saying "I love it when a plan comes together." I, personally, have never had that happen.

I lay there for several minutes letting the sun warm me up and reflected on the fact that at 64 years old I needed to quit getting into these kinds of situations. I, then, attempted to start the motor. It would not start. That is when I discovered that The Bear had not put the paddle in the skiff like I asked him to. So I was now up the bay without a paddle (sorry for the pun). I was a couple of hundred feet from the boat so I took the cowling off the motor and used it as a paddle to get back to the boat. You have to wonder what would have gone through someone's mind if they had cruised into the bay at that moment and found a naked old fart paddling a skiff with a motor cowling.

In the meantime, The Bear had picked up my clothes and gun and was walking away from me and toward the head of the bay. He could not hear me screaming at him to go back to the beach we had landed on in the first place. The roar of the surf breaking on the rocks was too loud. We now had a four or five-foot swell. The Bear was a dear friend, but sometimes he could make Forest Gump look like a genius.

I got to the boat and put on my last set of clothes and got back in the skiff, with the paddle, and began the mile trip to the head of the bay to get The Bear. I was not having good thoughts about him at this point. The head of the bay was a gravel beach, so the surf was breaking on this beach big time. With no motor I was not sure how I would get The Bear onboard without flipping the skiff.

When I got close enough so he could hear me I told him I would ride a wave in stern first. He was to jump in and I would paddle us out on the next wave. This was another well thought out plan. We had had several so far, none of which had worked. I rode the wave in and The Bear just stood there, I went out on the same wave. I then berated him in words I had learned in third grade. On the next wave when the water went out The Bear followed it out so that when I came in on the next wave the water went right up to his waist. I shot right past him on the incoming wave. I grabbed him by the belt on the way out and pulled him in the skiff. Did I mention this was a ten foot inflatable skiff? Not a lot of room in a boat of this size and The Bear is a big guy. When I pulled The Bear into the skiff he ended up face down on the floor with all of our gear under him and with me kneeling on his back paddling like crazy trying to keep the next wave from putting us back on the beach. He was yelling for me to get off of him. I was screaming at him to get out of my way, and I am sure the black bear was up on the hill laughing his butt off.

Somehow, I managed to paddle us away from the surf. I then began the long paddle back to the boat berating The Bear for not coming back to the original beach. He spent the trip working on the motor in a very sullen mood. By the time we got back to the boat we were friends again, but just barely. Problem was I now had no dry clothes. I spent the next two hours in a towel waiting for the sun to dry my clothes. The Bear spent that time complaining how hard it was to walk to the end of the bay on the rocks. This once again put a strain on our friendship. We drank a few beers and a couple of shots of whiskey and things seemed okay again.

We decided not to hunt bears anymore and went back to halibut fishing. We moved out of the bay and tried some deeper water. At one point we were both into large halibut which is a problem as to how you shoot or gaff a large fish when you both have one on. Luckily, The Bear lost his so we could get mine. It was a nice 150 pound fish. The Bear didn't seem to be as happy as I was about landing the fish.

We decided to spend the night in Fox Farm Bay. The Bear cooked dinner and I gutted the fish. The new rule in Prince William sound is you can not fillet the fish until you get back to the harbor so the state fish and feathers guy can look at them. It was a nice evening so we sat on the back deck, ate dinner, had a few drinks and told lies to each other. We called it a night when we ran out of beer.

The next day we were up at the crack of noon. It was another calm, sunny day. The weather gods were smiling on us. We fired up the boat and headed for Bainbridge Passage. As we came out of the passage, which was now clear of ice, into Prince William Sound we were greeted by a sea as flat as a lake. Not a ripple on the water and no swell. I had never seen the sound this calm. We stopped at the Pleiades Islands so The Bear could lose another big halibut. We did pick up some yellow eye and black cod.

We spent the rest of the trip just cruising around the sound in perfect weather, calm seas, bright sun and good company. We saw another black bear on the beach, but declined to try for him. Not enough time to put together a good plan. The Bear was a good guy, an excellent outdoorsman, and a dear friend. I miss him.

BEAR ON

Tourism is a big industry in Alaska. We all appreciate the economic benefits it brings to our state and do what we can to help the industry. Unfortunately, sometimes tourism conflicts with our fishing, and then we have to make a difficult choice. We usually go with our fishing having the priority. This is a story about making that choice.

So we go back to Big River Lake which is about 100 miles southwest of Anchorage on the west side of Cook Inlet. It is a pleasant one hour flight in my Cessna 185. The mountains on both sides of Cook Inlet are spectacular and there are lots of critters to observe to include white beluga whales, moose, bears, etc. Wolverine Creek is a small, clear water stream that flows into Big River Lake. It is a large lake about two miles wide by one mile long with low tundra to the west and steep mountains, forested in spruce, birch and alder, on the three other sides. You land on the lake then taxi through the weeds to the creek. This is a remote area; the nearest road is 50 miles away across Cook Inlet. The lake is very glacial and the water is full of rock flour so you can only see about half an inch below the surface. The creek water flowing into the lake forms a strip of clean, clear water about one to two feet deep, 20 feet wide and up to 75 feet long depending on the lake water level. After traveling up Big River and then through the lake, you arrive at where the red salmon school up to clean out their gills before trying to get up the creek to spawn.

Wolverine Creek flows out of a lake several hundred feet higher on the mountain and then down a very steep canyon. The salmon have a rough trip to get to their spawning grounds so they rest up here before heading upstream. The creek being quite shallow makes the salmon easy pickings for the bears and their human counterparts. The state has designated this a fly fishing only area. Reds do not tend to bite so the technique to catch them is to lay your fly line in among the fish and watch for it to start moving. This usually means the line is running through a fish's mouth as he moves upstream. You then just jerk and the fly is embedded in the side of the fish's mouth. The rule is the fish has to be caught in the mouth in order for you to keep it. This rule does not apply to the bears. As a matter of fact, I do not think there are any rules that apply to bears. Reds are very high energy fish so when you hook one he will go crazy with lots of aerobatics and long high speed runs. They are a lot of fun to catch and are also excellent table fare. With all the jumping, splashing and carrying on they are also an excellent bear attractant.

When I first started coming to Wolverine Creek over 30 years ago it was not well known as a fishing destination. The only access is by float plane and the red salmon were not very big in comparison to other runs in the area. So there was not a lot of interest by other pilots who could go to other places and catch bigger fish. I was willing to catch smaller fish in trade for the exclusive fishing. It was also easy pickings because the fish were so concentrated. Generally, I had the place to myself other than the bears, and we had an understanding, if they didn't try to kill me I wouldn't shoot them. A win-win deal. They got their limit of fish as I did and then we went our separate ways. About 10 years ago the air taxi guys found it and started hauling in out of state clients. At first it was just a few people. The problem was these "outsiders" didn't know squat about bears. They left fish or fish parts lying around for the bears to scarf up. In some cases, they even threw fish to the bears. The bears quickly became habituated to getting free food from the pilgrims and learned they had nothing to fear from people. In fact, they learned the people were afraid of them. As this bear training was going on, the number of air taxi outfits increased as did the number of naive fisherpersons. It appeared to me as the number of rubes went up the cumulative I.Q. went down. This included the mostly out of state-based guides. As things stand now during the red salmon season there is a large concentration of 25 to 50 nimrods, standing in small boats, (most with little or no bear experience or knowledge) and two to five brown or black bears jammed into the area around the clear water at the mouth of the creek trying to catch salmon. Just to make it a little more interesting, the lodge on Big River Lake and some of the air taxis decided to start a bear viewing industry at the same place. So now we have fisherpersons standing shoulder to shoulder in their boats, trying to catch fish in a very confined area while the bears are diving into the water right in front of them and tourists are trying to take pictures of the bears. The only ones who seemed to know what they were doing were the bears. I have never seen an actual recipe for disaster, but I bet this situation contains all the necessary ingredients.

Needless to say, my quiet, pristine and exclusive fishing hole was now total chaos with fishing lines going in every direction, bears darting between boats and nimrods, photographers yelling at people to get out of the way and air taxis unloading and loading tourists. After being snagged by nimrod hooks, chased around by bears and irate tourists a few times I decided to just quit going there. It was not worth the trouble and I didn't really want to watch some rube getting eaten by a bear. Besides rube is just not good bear food.

Big River Lake is right at the entrance to Lake Clark Pass, so I flew past the lake several times each year on my way to and from the Iliamna area. I was on my way home from fishing in the Kvichak River, which is 100 miles farther from Anchorage, but, there are no crowds, the fish are bigger, and the bears are generally afraid of you. When I flew past Big River Lake on that Sunday evening in June, I noticed there were no tourists fishing at the creek. I landed and had the place to myself. Just like in the old days. I caught a limit of reds and headed home. It turns out the air taxis pull all their pilgrims out of there about 5:00 PM on Sunday and quit for the day. From that day on we would head down there on Sunday evening and enjoy unencumbered fishing. The bears were still a problem, but we were well armed and we maintained a safe separation when possible. Besides there were enough fish for us and the bears. Life was good again. Then a new problem arose. The bear viewers would show up in their fancy little boats and complain that we were in the way of their bear pictures. We would explain that we were just some Alaskans catching some fish for our families. Diplomacy is not considered a virtue in Alaska. Some Alaskans even consider it a weakness. The conversation generally went downhill from there.

On this particular trip to Wolverine Creek I had Delusional Dave with me and Raunchy Rick. Delusional Dave is an engineer with my firm. He has been on several adventures with me and just doesn't seem to learn, so he keeps coming back for more life-threatening escapades.

Raunchy is a short squat guy in his 40's. He is a local conservative talk show host and a quasicompetent outdoorsman. He used to be a fishing guide for the rubes at Wolverine Creek, but eventually found a real job and left. Raunchy can't even pronounce diplomacy. All of us are long term or lifelong Alaskans.

When we arrived at the creek, the air taxi guys were just finishing up, so we anchored the plane 100 feet from the creek and watched the last of the pilgrim and bear show. I have never understood why someone would travel all the way to Alaska, fly out to a remote site, and then fish shoulder to shoulder with a bunch of strangers while worrying about being bit by a bear. For a few more bucks you can go to an un-crowded fishing spot where the fish bite and the bears do not. I guess if you are from Podunk, Idaho you just do not know any better.

Once they left, we pulled the plane up to the mouth of the creek and started fishing. Because of the bear problem it is recommended that you fish off a boat or the floats of the airplane. It is also suggested you do not get in the water to avoid conflicts with the bears. We were fishing off the floats and things were going well. The brown bears that had been playing with the tourists had filled up on reds and left so we didn't have any worries.

We had only been there 30 minutes when three black bears showed up. I guess it was their shift. These particular bears showed no fear of us which was a little unnerving. Black bears and brown bears normally do not mix. The brown bears tend to invite the black bears to lunch with the black bears being the main course. Another big difference between brown bears and black bears is that brown bears will bite you, throw you around and then bury you in sticks and leaves, but they seldom kill you. Black bears, on the other hand, do not play with their food. They will kill you and eat you. Therefore, their proximity caused us to be alert. Every time we would hook a fish, they would try to get it before we could pull it in. So, two guys would fish while one held the gun in case they got too aggressive. It was a little tense, but we were doing okay. Everybody was being somewhat tolerant.

Then the bear viewing boat showed up. They were in a square barge-like boat with a sunroof and lawn chairs. They had a little table to hold their wine and cheese. It was a calm sunny day so they could have been floating on a lake in Georgia with an antebellum mansion in the background. The contrast between them and three Alaskans on a beat-up floatplane, in blue jeans and well-used Pendleton shirts with very old fishing equipment and eyeball to eyeball with the bears, was significant. They pulled up to within 60 feet of us and anchored the boat. We nodded at them and continued fishing. Within a few minutes the guide (and I use this word loosely) stated that we were not following the rules and we should not be where we were with the plane. We were located exactly where the boats had been earlier, so we were somewhat perplexed by this comment. We also noted the conversation had started off on a low note. No "How are you, catching Any fish" or other normal pleasantries. Usually, the bear viewers were friendly or at least willing to share the space with us. This group was different. We inquired as to what rules he was referring to and he replied the rules set out for the area. We inquired as to who made up the rules and he didn't have an answer. We then stated our rules which were that we were going to catch three more fish to fill our limits and then leave. The conversation took a nosedive at that point. I recall Raunchy telling the "guide" if he didn't like it he could go back to Oregon early. That shut him up. One of the tourists stated she had our airplane's tail number and was going to turn us into "the authorities". I informed her that would be me as I was a board of game member. One of the other viewers stated he was videotaping us. Delusional inquired if he gave him our address would he send a copy to us?

While this exchange of information was taking place, I snagged my fly on a rock about 30 feet from the plane. The water was only two feet deep, so I politely excused myself from the conversation, stepped off the float, walked over and unhooked the fly. As I walked back to the plane, I had my five weight fly rod in my right hand and was holding the fly between the fingers of that hand. I was about 10 feet from the plane when Raunchy yelled that a bear was chasing me. I turned around to find a medium sized black bear less than 20 feet away and closing fast. My first instinct was to swat at him with my fly rod which I did without even thinking. When I flipped the rod at him the fly came loose from my fingers and the line shot out at the bear. The fly hooked him in the fur on the side of his head. This caused him to reconsider his plan to jump me and he took off for the shoreline. My reel was now screaming as the line was ripped off. The only thing I could think to do was yell "BEAR ON". The bear took off for the brush and I could not turn him because I only had a ten-pound tippet on a five-weight rod so he broke off.

Later Raunchy, Delusional and I pondered whether you net or gaff a bear? As it was not bear season, we surmised you would net and release. That would be exciting to say the least. The release part could be subjective. Would you release the bear or vice versa? Anyway, I turned back to the plane and observed Delusional with the gun pointed at where the bear had been and Raunchy on his knees laughing so hard, I was afraid he would pass out. The bear viewers had gone ballistic. They were hyperventilating, screaming obscenities and threats and generally having a real bad day. They even spilled their wine. I got back to the plane and tied on a new fly and continued fishing. It took us another 15 minutes to catch the rest of our limits, the whole time putting up with a constant barrage of invectives from the boat. It is a good thing bears do not understand English, they would have been appalled. We didn't hear any words we hadn't learned in the 3rd grade, so we were okay with the whole thing. Alaska tourism probably took a hit, but we got a limit of reds, so it pretty much evened out. We loaded up the plane and taxied past the boat. When I had the boat right behind the plane, I poured the coal to the engine. The prop blast blew anything not tied down out of the boat, we lifted off the water and we were on our way home. Never did hear from the authorities.

Last but not least is a story from book three.

MY FRIEND WARDELL

I have been hanging around Alaska for over 50-years hunting, fishing and piloting airplanes and boats. In this time I have assembled a circle of friends and associates with whom I participate in these activities.

This cast of characters runs the gauntlet from highly intelligent to IQ-challenged, physically superior to puny, young and personable to grouchy old farts and a few more in between. These attributes make each and every outing involving any of them a unique and often terrifying adventure. Included in this group of misfits is my good friend Wardell, who is also a pilot and has been doing his thing in Alaska for a comparable amount of time as I. He is a real estate company executive and a very intelligent and intuitive individual although he can ignore these last two traits with uncanny ease when making decisions in the wilderness. He also tends to overreact to stressful situations. Although I try not to make mention of them often. Another of Wardell's positive traits is that he is an excellent mechanic and can fix most anything in the field and is called upon to do so with great frequency when in the company of our group.

One example of Wardell's suspect outdoor decision-making concerns long distance snowmobile trips. He will consistently average 80-mph on the lengthy trip to his cabin on a wilderness lake. The fact that he hasn't killed himself on one of these forays is pure luck. He has, however, killed a few coyotes that didn't get out of the way fast enough in deep snow. They ended up pressed into the snow with snowmachine tracks across their backs. Interestingly, Wardell's shortcomings are not restricted entirely to him, as his gear is equally deficient. To our group's great relief, Wardell just got a new gun. His old gun was some octagon-barreled semi-automatic .30-06 that was surely much older than him. I have little doubt that it sold for a bargain price when it was new several decades ago. It did shoot on occasion but seldom put the bullets where Wardell was aiming and, as a result, many moose have lived to a ripe old age. After dealing with this for several years, he finally retired the poor old gun. The fancy new one is equipped with a composite stock, stainless steel barrel and a 3 x 9 power scope. He even found it in a left-handed bolt action. Being left handed is another item on the long list of odd attributes involving Wardell.

This was his first year with the new gun and its first outing was at "moose camp," a uniquely beautiful site in a very remote area north of Anchorage. The camp is a special place with spectacular views of Mts.

McKinley and Foraker, their snow-covered peaks framed by the blue sky and the horizon on clear days. The area is covered in alders, birch, spruce and willows, and in the season we frequent it, all are in fall colors of brilliant yellows, reds and greens. The sounds of Lake Creek can be heard in the distance and when gentle fall winds blow through with a hint of winter, it is as pristine and peaceful a place there is to be found, until we arrive in the company of Wardell.

There are several very large clearings throughout the area making it ideal moose habitat. On this trip Wardell, Bixby, another of our challenged associates, and I had been hunting for a few days with no luck, mostly due to lack of effort and over consumption of beer after dinner, pretty much our usual routine. There are certain nuances to the moose camp, such as not allowing the fact that an over consumption of beer at night might impact hunting ability the next morning.

Bixby is a retired cop and has been hunting and fishing buddy of both Wardell's and mine for many years. Just like Wardell, Bixby also has the ability to ignore good sense. One day, we had just completed our morning hunt and were back at our 4-wheelers unloading the guns for the trip back to camp. Wardell went to unload his new gun by working the bolt to eject the bullets, when he threw the bolt the first time; the gun went off without his finger on the trigger. We already call him 'Wacky Wardell" due to his aforementioned tendency to over-react to most situations but in this case, he simply stood still, looking like a skunk caught in headlights. Bixby and I were looking for our hats that had flown off when we jumped several feet in the air at the sound of the blast. Wardell's newly acquired high tech. firearm was defective! We discussed this fact with Wardell in straightforward and simple words we had learned in the third grade from foul mouthed friends. Wardell was sufficiently contrite so we didn't continue to berate him on the issue for much longer. However, for the rest of the hunt, Wardell and his new gun hunted alone and well out of range of Bixby and me. On this hunt, the bull moose population was not further reduced by us

Another fairly recent trip on which Wardell's typical behavior made a significant impact involved Kerry, a good friend of mine from

New Zealand who came up to hunt with us at moose camp. A personable and hard working hunting guide and taxidermist back home, Kerry wanted to get a moose in Alaska and some pictures of grizzly bears. There were five of us on this trip including Wardell, Bixby, Kerry known instantly as "The Kiwi" and Dave, known as "Delusional Dave," because he keeps thinking our next trip won't be as life threatening as the last. To compare and contrast the dispositions of the group, four of us were generally calm and reasonable in personality reflecting the calm and pristine setting and then there was Wardell. Kerry was the new guy in this group on several levels: first time hunting with us, first time in the area, first time being involved with a bunch of crazy Alaskans and their form of interaction with wildlife and first time on any kind of outdoor adventure with Wardell. Kerry spent much of his time just looking on in what was sometimes amazement and other times shear terror as the various adventures unfolded. He did get his moose and some pictures of grizzly bears, only much more up close and personal than he had anticipated. This involved some serious high-speed tree-climbing as a result of an ownership misunderstanding over some moose guts with a huge grizzly sow and a large second year cub. The camp was a little more bear sensitive than normal due to this event.

One night, after a gourmet dinner of hot dogs and beans, we sat around the stove and imbibed in a few beers. "Few" being a relative term. It had been raining and the sky was still covered in thick dark clouds so it got very dark very quickly and as our beer supply was becoming challenged, we opted to retire early so we would have adequate libations for the next night. Our main camp amenity was a sturdy 10 x 20ft canvas Quonset hut-shaped tent. We sleep on cots placed on the wooden floor about three feet off the ground. Our bear protection consisted of a thin layer of tent canvas and our rifles, usually located under our cots. For some reason that particular night I put my gun in a corner of the tent, which was to cause some problems later. With five cots, a cooking area and equipment storage, it is quite cramped inside the tent resembling a room in a fraternity house only more disheveled. Moving about in this environment was difficult at best when you could see what you were doing. Our bear emergency action plan was left to the impromptu or, in other words, non-existent.

At about 2:00 a.m. when all of us were sound asleep, a grizzly bear decided it wanted to join us in the tent. This was not a good decision on the bear's part for several reasons but primarily due to the fact that Wardell was in the tent. The first thing I remember is Wardell screaming at the top of his lungs, *"BEAR ATTACK!"* This activated the impromptu emergency action plan resulting in total chaos breaking out in the tent. People were running into each other in the dark, trying to get out of their sleeping bags, knocking over cots and all the while Wardell continued screaming at a deafening pitch and had now become incoherent babble. Otherwise, by our standards, our emergency plan was working as expected. Even at this late hour there is often at least a bit of light to see by this time of year, but the sky was still completely shrouded in heavy clouds and as a result it was pitch black outside and even more so inside the tent. You could not see your hand in front of your face. In fact, you wouldn't be able to see a full grown grizzly bear in front of your face which has considerably more serious consequences and was more relevant to the current situation. I staggered out of my sleeping bag and began frantically searching for my gun under my cot, which of course I could not find because it was in the corner. I was yelling for someone to get a flashlight but there was far too much noise coming from Wardell for anyone to hear me. I finally acquired my gun and stumbled over gear and bodies to the door where I was greeted by the ominous sounds of a bear rummaging around nearby in the all encompassing darkness.

Things were getting a little precarious, made more evident by the alarming sound of gun bolts slamming home behind me, somehow audible above the accompanying high-pitched shrieking from Wardell. I had options; I could step out of the tent, hopefully not on the bear, or stay put and risk being shot in the back by one of my panicked friends. It was obvious that neither of these two choices were ideal. I chose the bear, stepped out of the tent and walked about 10-feet toward the nearest clearing. Wardell's screaming had stopped and in the sudden silence, I finally located the bear by the subtle, but heavy-sounding noise of his trend as he approached me. Upon squinting just right, I could see a fuzzy looking patch of the darkness moving nearby and gave it a round from my .300 Winchester Magnum. A bear-sized patch of darkness ran off into the woods across the clearing from camp. About this time, 'The Kiwi' showed up with a light and we scanned the area for a while but found no sign of the bear. Other than the sound of labored breathing from Wardell, it suddenly seemed very quiet and peaceful again. We opted not to pursue the bear in the dark; discretion dictated we instead wait until daylight to reassess the situation—the first logical decision of the night.

While the rest of us went back to bed, Wardell stayed up whimpering and clutching, still on this occasion, his old decrepit rifle to his chest. As a side note, being a great source of help during the whole ordeal, Bixby, who snores like crazy, never got out of his sleeping bag. I berated him that I am up half the night because of his snoring and the other half shooting grizzly bears. The least he could do is participate in the latter. The next morning, we had breakfast and devised a plan, a plan we hoped would set a new pattern and actually work for us. You could argue that our emergency plan had worked as expected, but that would be unearned praise. The bear had run into what was about a two-acre island of trees across from camp containing considerable underbrush. The plan was 'Delusional Dave' and I would stalk into the trees and see if we could pick up a blood trail. Wardell, Bixby and 'The Kiwi' would go around and cover the back of the patch of woods in case the bear attempted to exit that way. Delusional and I gave the others sufficient time to get to their assigned positions and then we slowly and cautiously started into the brush.

It is generally accepted knowledge that having approximately 800-pounds of grizzly bear jumping on your chest is not something to strive for, particularly a more irritable, wounded one. We hadn't gone but a few steps when several shots rang out on the other side of the trees. Wardell began screaming again, this time exclaiming that he had shot the bear. We all rushed to the area where the shots came from and discovered Wardell jumping around with his old thunder stick smoking like a flintlock and several spent rounds on the ground around him. "I got him! I got him!" he yelled. We located the bear a short distance into the trees where even an amateur woodsman could easily tell it had been dead in the spot for several hours. It was also noted by the group that there were considerably fewer new holes in the bear than the number of spent cartridges at Wardell's feet. The bear incident was over and, other than the bruin, everyone was alive. Wardell's high-pitched, labored breathing went back to normal a few days later.

Now I do not want to give the impression that Wardell is always hyperventilating. He can in fact be quite deliberate, calm and cunning like on a fishing trip a few years ago. West of Anchorage there is a fishing hole called the "Silver Hole", a very short piece of water requiring unique piloting skills not only to land on but, even more importantly, to take off again. Wardell's Super Cub has a much shorter take off and landing requirement than my Cessna 185 so as a consequence we traveled to the Silver Hole in Wardell's plane. This particular trip was in pursuit of King Salmon a few summers ago and, coincidentally, my first trip to fish the Silver Hole. We flew in his Cub and landed without incident. After fishing for some time without much luck, we noticed two individuals on the opposite bank doing quite well. They limited out very quickly and went into catch and release mode. There was only enough room to beach one plane on that side of the water, so we waited until they departed and then taxied across.

Excited to try our luck in the "hot hole," we inspected the area and found it was necessary to crawl through 100-yards of alders and brush to get to a15-foot long stretch of clear bank where we could fish. There was a 5-foot high vertical wall down to the water and my first thought was, considering we didn't have a net, "How were we going to get a 30- or 40-pound King from the water to the top of the bank?" My second thought was, "Hey, we're here to fish and we'll worry about the bank if we catch one." Of course, neither of these thoughts included solutions or common sense, we went with the second thought. Wardell immediately began pummeling the water to a foamy froth with his fishing line to no avail. On my second smooth cast I hooked a nice, bright 35-pound hen and the fight was on. After about 15-minutes, I had the fish subdued and floating on her side at the bottom of the bank. I asked Wardell to grasp on to a root protruding from the bank and lower himself down to grab the fish. He declined this invitation. We then started to evaluate our options further. We could just break off the fish—unacceptable; we could try to procure a long, forked stick and try to thread it through the gills of the fish—not really possible, or we could try to pull a 35-pound fish up the bank on 20-pound test line, another success challenged option. I considered throwing Wardell into the river to retrieve the fish, but it was his airplane and I didn't want to walk home through 70-miles of Alaska wilderness.

I looked for other options and noted 30 feet down river a small tree that had fallen into the water. It looked possible to climb down the tree to the river using the brush on the bank as hand holds. Then the fish could be allowed to slowly drift down stream to the person on the small tree sticking their hand through the thick brush and into the icy water to retrieve the fish. Once again I invited Wardell to do the honors and again he declined. This was one of Wardell's rare good decisions and when this happens, I immediately take it upon myself to fill in with a bad one. I handed him the fishing rod and made my way to the tree and down its 2-inch trunk to the water. In another rare moment for him, Wardell rather skillfully guided the fish down to me where I could procure it. Now, while I am precariously balanced on the 2-inch trunk, the fish decides to make one last attempt at freedom and begins to thrash about wildly. I'm holding on to a branch with one hand, clinging to the fish with the other and trying to balance on the very thin tree trunk with both feet. I knew there was no way this was going to work out for me and it didn't. I lost my balance and dropped down on the tree with considerable force. It didn't break the tree, but did considerable damage to my pride and posterior. I did not, however, release the fish.

Wardell dropped the rod and ran down the bank as close as he could to where I was now hanging from a thin wisp of the tree. I handed him the fish and he started back to the fishing spot. After a few steps, I reminded him I was still at the bottom of the bank. Even a fleeting glance in my direction would reveal that I was now partially submerged and tangled in the brush and could use a little help. Seeing my condition, Wardell hesitated. From years of familiarity with him, I could tell he was contemplating that with me stranded; he would have no competition and could easily catch his limit from the hot fishing spot. He could rescue me later. With sincere and direct threats of physical violence I convinced him to come help me out of my predicament. We calmly returned to fishing and managed to catch our limits. We continued using the tree as a hauling-out point and Wardell took his turn without incident.

One last recollection illustrating Wardell's shortcomings and long-comings, he and I were again ensconced at the moose camp. We had been hunting for several days and it was time to get back to work, we needed to get to Anchorage. Upon review the weather was marginal at best with only a few hundred feet of ceiling and maybe two miles of visibility. Wardell's Super Cub is, in reality, a paper airplane and flies much slower than my Cessna 185, a real airplane made of metal. He plods along at about 90 mph and I scream along at 150 mph. These facts would soon come into play for us. The hatching of this plan involved Wardell going up to have a look around and see if we could make it out and if so, I would follow. I got on the radio so I could talk to him while he was investigating the possibilities along the Kahiltna River valley where the camp is located.

He said he could see the Kahiltna through a glory hole and that I should take off and follow him so we could fly down the river to Anchorage. This is a situation known among Alaskan pilots as the "get home syndrome," and is a combination of peer pressure, business or job pressure, wanting a shower and clean clothes pressure and down-ward pressure on your IQ. The latter being the most significant. Here we were with a comfortable camp, plenty of food, warm sleeping bags and still we feel it is necessary to risk our lives to get home. The risk/reward ratio is suspect on this and I am sure Darwin would have had a comment or two on the plan.

Without further thought I threw my gear in the plane and took off and after several minutes of circling around under the clouds I found Wardell. He indicated he had spotted another "glory hole" and contin-ued to pursue a clear view of the river. In pilot-speak, a 'glory hole' is simply a hole in the clouds you can fly through to get to the other side of the clouds. You have no idea what you might encounter on the other side and I think it is called a glory hole because many pilots have gone to their glory in heaven shortly after flying through one. With none of this in mind, Wardell flew through the glory hole with me close behind. At this point, you could have added our IQs together, doubled it and still had a single digit. On the other side of the clouds we encountered more very marginal conditions. Did I mention glory holes are generally one way? If you look back through the glory hole, the clouds on the other side make it invisible. Now our predicament was we were flying with less than 200-feet of ceiling and less than ½-mile of visibility and no place to land our float planes for miles in any direction. It should be noted that landing float planes on anything but water almost always results in a substantial crash. This results in a reduction in the value of the plane and also the life expectancy of the occupants.

To add to the drama, Wardell is flying at 90-mph, requiring me to throttle back so my nose is high and the plane is considerably less maneuverable. I am hanging in the air trying to keep him in sight and the old adage of the blind leading the blind sprang up in my mind, only at 90-mph. Next, fog gathered around us so we had to navigate down the river by looking down and following the bank as there was no forward visibility. Wardell's radio updates began to come through in a very shrill, agitated voice. Of course, I remained calm and collected as I contemplated my imminent demise in a pile of twisted aluminum. I kept telling myself the situation could be worse, but it was hard to comprehend how. Somehow we finally arrived at a body of water known as Shulin Lake which was plenty big enough to land on and wait out the weather. Wardell announced he was at the lake, but the weather was much better and he was continuing on. When I got to the lake I saw we had over two miles of visibility, but still very low ceilings. We had begun this flight by making a few bad decisions and kept the pattern going by making one more as we continued down the river with the IQ calculation unimproved. The conditions again deteriorated to as poor as before and the clouds closed in behind us so turning back was not an option. Recounting, we had gone from very bad conditions to extremely bad conditions to bad conditions and back to extremely bad conditions in about 10 minutes.

With our hearts in our throats and attention hyper-focused on the bank below us, we continued our stress filled pilgrimage down the river. At this point I was sure the big guy upstairs was saying "I'm going to have to bail these idiots out again," and he allowed us to make it to the Susitna Valley and the Yetna River where the ceiling was almost 300-feet with visibility at two-miles. These are conditions I would normally avoid, but now they seemed wonderful. About this time a helicopter pilot came on the air and announced the visibility as about the same all the way to Anchorage. We were saved! Or so we thought, but again the conditions deteriorated as we continued and we were thrust right back into the soup. Wardell's voice was up several octaves and I was again making peace with my maker.

A bit of pilot protocol: when you are flying along a river it is proper to fly on the right side; this way you can avoid ruining each others' day with a head-on collision with someone coming the other way. Suddenly while I was very focused on the riverbank 200-feet below me, a Cessna 206 shot by me going up river. He missed my wing by less than 50-feet. Another part of the accepted and generally practiced protocol is to be on the air-to-air radio frequency 122.9, so I pressed my talk button and proceeded to berate the other pilot with words that would have embarrassed a commercial crab fisherman. To my utter disbelief, he was not on frequency. Wardell later said he appreciated the language lesson which he has used to great effect several times since. Shortly thereafter we broke out into good flying weather and proceeded to Anchorage without further complications. We stowed our planes after landing and adjourned to a local bar where, after a few beers, we swore a pact that we would never fly in such weather again. Proudly, with only a few minor exceptions, we have stuck to the pact.

In conclusion, I am happy to report that to date; Wardell still hasn't caused either of our demises and is continuing to tempt the fates in the great land of Alaska. I am sure he will continue to careen up the Yetna River at ridiculous speeds on his snowmachine en route to his cabin in winter and he'll be back at the moose camp each fall with his "new gun" hopefully repaired. Wardell will continue to crawl through the air in his Super Cub to the Silver Hole and for some unknown reason, I will continue to accompany him at my peril, but I wouldn't have it any other way.

Alaska has been everything I dreamed about as a kid and much more. The size, remoteness, weather and unique culture has presented challenges in both business and recreation. Providing professional services in environments as diverse as urban Anchorage to a remote tent camp above the Arctic Circle is challenging at best. Managing employees who are strictly in-town office people to folks who need to take a month off to hunt whales near their village requires some free thinking. Just getting people and material to some job sites is very difficult. Doing business in Alaska is challenging and exciting.

My recreational experiences speak for themselves regarding danger and rewards of participating in outdoor adventures. I wouldn't trade my experiences for anything. Alaska has been both good and challenging for me. I feel privileged to be part of it.

So, how would I define my life to date? Well, I started out as a small-town kid. My life was mostly just going along to get along. I only had short term goals such as getting enough money to buy beer for the weekend, getting my driver's license and a car, making it through college, finding a girl and a good job. No long-term life plans. The only exception was to move to Alaska and start an engineering firm. No specifics in that regard.

Then I found myself in a very frightening situation in Vietnam. I was convinced my life was over. I survived that day against the odds. That experience caused me to reflect on what life was really all about. I felt like I had been given a second chance and I should make it count for something, rather than just living life. I felt like it was important to try to make a difference. We can't all be president or cure a disease, so what could I do? The answer to that question had to evolve over time.

I found I could make a difference in providing jobs for over 1,000 Alaskans, help build Alaska and America with engineering services, serve in public office, serve on public and private boards and commissions and raise a family of productive and caring people. In the process of doing these things I also made a good life for me and my family. We all define success differently. I feel I have succeeded in making my life count as best as I could. There is comfort in that.

So here I am starting my eighth decade harking back to Ephrata, WSU, Vietnam, Alaska and family. As I round the final turn in the track of life and enter the home stretch it is all good. Some better than others, but still good. There is an old saying, "Live a good life so in your old age you can look back and enjoy it again." Well, I will defiantly be in that mode when I get to old age. I don't consider myself old, as much as chronology gifted. There is still lots to look forward to, such as more grandkids, new Alaska adventures and trips around the world. If I had my life to live over again, I don't think I would change much, well maybe that day in Vietnam. I have a fantastic partner in Candace, wonderful and successful kids, eight grandkids and I am sure more to come, as well as enough money for a very comfortable retirement.

That 18-year-old kid working on a Washington State survey crew wanted to have his own engineering firm, did it, and live in Alaska, doing it. I am one lucky Regular American Guy.

Before there was *A Regular American Guy*, there was *Oh No We're Gonna Die, Oh No We're Gonna Die Too*, and *Outdoor Stupid From Around the World*.

Alaska fisherman, hunter, and bush pilot Bob Bell has been writing about his adventures and misadventures in the outdoors for more than a decade. His three previous books allow you to see where he left off before releasing his fourth book, which you now hold in your hands. A long-time Anchorage engineer and surveyor, Bob shares a few of the best stories he has heard around the campfires and other friendly gatherings.

This book is different as it is a memoir but is written with the same humor as his other books.

Available at your local bookstore or from the following distributors:
Publication Consultants at www.publicationconsultants.com
Todd Communications at sales@toddcom.com
Safari Press at safaripress.com
And directly from Bob Bell at bbell@frbcmh.com